THEY CAME TO
DESTROY AMERICA

THE FBI GOES TO WAR AGAINST NAZI SPIES & SABOTEURS BEFORE AND DURING WORLD WAR II

The landing site at Ponte Vedra Beach, 1942.

BY STAN COHEN AND DON DeNEVI
WITH RICHARD GAY

PICTORIAL HISTORIES PUBLISHING COMPANY, INC.
Missoula, Montana

LIBRARY OF CONGRESS
CONTROL NUMBER: 2003-103429

ISBN 1-57510-101-7

First Printing: May 2003

PRINTED IN WINNIPEG, MANITOBA, CANADA

Cover Graphics: Egeler Designs, Missoula, Montana
Cover Photo: Hancock Point looking west across Frenchman Bay to Lamoine. RG

Typography: Leslie Maricelli
Layout: Stan Cohen

Pictorial Histories Publishing Co., Inc.
713 South Third West, Missoula, Montana 59801
Phone (406) 549-8488 Fax (406) 728-9280
website: pictorialhistoriespublishing.com

PREFACE

WHILE THE GREATER PART of this book deals with the German landings on the east coast of the United States–*Operation Pastorius,* June 1942 and *Operation Magpie,* November 1944–it also delves into some pre-war Nazi spy operations, the subversive organizations in the United States and several other operations planned but not executed such as *Operation Pelican.* Other stories and photographs pertinent to the subject are also included.

The stories of *Pastorius* and *Magpie* have been well-documented through the years and are important today as a predecessor of future military tribunals proposed for accused terrorists. This, however, is the first time that a thorough photographic search of these operations and other Nazi incursions within and on American shores has been attempted, with the stories and photo evidence put together in one volume.

The authors have searched FBI files, dozens of books and documents, and personal interviews to piece together the stories included in this book. Even with this search, some facts could not be found; but work will continue to update the stories in future printings.

It was amazing to learn of the hundreds of German and German-American sympathizers and spies that were in this country in the 1930s and early 1940s. The German-American Bund itself had thousands of dedicated Nazi sympathizers. It is a credit to the FBI, the prime government agency for protecting the country from Axis spies and saboteurs, that no actual incidents of sabotage occurred in the country either before or during the war years. There are, however, a few incidents that have been explained as possible sabotage, i.e. *The Normandie;* but no positive conclusions have ever been reached.

Although a great quantity of defense related information was relayed to Germany prior to the Pearl Harbor attack, the FBI also turned several spy operations to their advantage sending much false information to Germany. Only three landings of Nazi spies or saboteurs on American shores occurred during the war. All were quickly rounded up, due in large part to traitorous actions by the saboteurs themselves.

For a more detailed account of the many spy organizations and landings on our shores the authors direct the reader to the bibliography in this book including the two books written by the perpetrators themselves.

These stories should be a reminder to every reader that the same dangers that existed in 1941-45 are with us today and Americans should not let their guard down.

Stan Cohen, Don DeNevi and Richard Gay

J. Edgar Hoover at his desk in the Justice Department in 1935. He was born in Washington, D.C., in 1895. After finishing high school, he worked in the Library of Congress and went to the Department of Justice in 1917. He became director of the Federal Bureau of Investigation in 1924, and reorganized and improved its methods for fighting crime. The bureau and Hoover became famous as G-Men for tracking down criminals in the 1930s. Before and during World War II, Hoover and the FBI broke many German spy rings in the United States. He directed the organization until his death in 1972, almost 50 years.

INTRODUCTION
THE FBI GOES TO WAR AGAINST NAZI SPIES & SABOTEURS
BY DON DENEVI

BY EARLY SEPTEMBER OF 1939, America had shrugged off the last lingering effects of the Great Depression and was turning to face a new and deadlier peril.

Europe was officially at war, although only Poland had thus far felt the thrust of the powerful German blitzkreig. There was little doubt that Nazism in Adolph Hitler's Germany, Fascism in Benito Mussolini's Italy and Communism in Joseph Stalin's Soviet Union threatened European, and, sooner or later, American democratic principles.

In the Far East, meanwhile, Japan's warlords were not attempting to conceal their eager designs for embracing China, the Dutch East Indies, Malaya, and the Philippines in a "Greater East Asia Co-Prosperity Sphere." With Tojo and his generals casting their eyes deep into the eastern Pacific, and with war now raging on every horizon in the world, a new set of challenges faced the Federal Bureau of Investigations.

As America began mobilizing its resources for "any emergency," President Franklin D. Roosevelt, on Sept. 6, 1939, publicly disclosed that he was charging the Division of Investigation, as it was referred to then, to investigate all espionage, counterespionage, and sabotage matters, along with the intelligence divisions of the War Department and the U.S. Navy.

At that point, the Division of Investigation had field offices in 42 cities, and employed 658 Special Agents, along with 1,141 support personnel. J. Edgar Hoover, the Director of the FBI since 1924, knew it would not be long before a matching column would be needed to list the results of its new responsibility against the more popular American enemies such as "Pretty Boy" Floyd, Charles "Machine Gun" Kelly, John Herbert Dillinger, "Baby Face" Nelson, and Kate "Ma" Barker and her son, Fred. One by one, these infamous public enemies, among hundreds of others, had fallen to Hoover's "G-Men" during recent years, drawing public acclaim throughout the country and forging a reputation based upon fidelity, bravery and integrity.

As the decade of the 1930s came to a close, Hoover's staff and teams of special agents had already been busy ferreting out potential spies and saboteurs infiltrating the shores of the United States. Between 1933 and 1937, an average of 35 espionage cases a year had been investigated. In 1938, the number jumped to 250.

Hoover, of course, knew that during the late 1920s and early 1930s, pro-Nazi and pro-Fascist activities had been confined largely to propaganda. But as peace steadily deteriorated in Asia and Europe, the foreign propagandists were quietly being infiltrated by special agents trained in espionage and sabotage dispatched from Rome, Berlin and Hamburg.

The most serious espionage case that the Bureau was involved with prior to the President's "any emergency" fiat occurred in early 1938 and involved Ignaz T. Griebl, a mild-mannered, bespectacled physician who was a popular leader, and womanizer, in Manhattan's German colony of Yorkville, and Guenther Gustav Rumrich, who had deserted from the U.S. Army in 1936 and volunteered for German military intelligence, the Abwehr, in Hamburg.

Apparently, in 1934, soon after Hitler assume power, Griebl, whose brother was a personal friend of Goebbels, wrote a letter to the Propaganda Minis-

Dr. Ignaz Theodor Griebl

ter volunteering his services as a spy. He claimed that in 1922, when he was a medical student in Munich, he served the fledgling Abwehr by posing as an art student on a secret mission to Paris. He explained that he had been a lieutenant in the medical reserve of the U.S. Army and could probably gather some useful information for the Third Reich. His offer was promptly accepted. Soon, a rather large spy ring developed in and around New York with Griebl in charge. He reported directly to Hamburg's 1M, or the

Chief of Naval Intelligence, Dr. Erich Pfeiffer.

For more than three years, the spy ring flourished under Griebl's leadership. He and his team gathered such valuable information as the specifications of army pursuit planes designed and constructed at the Seversky plant in Farmingdale, Long Island, and blueprints of various navy destroyers under development, as well as those of a navy scout bomber.

In 1936, 26-year-old Guenther Gustav Rumrich, deeply impressed with the autobiography of Col. Walther Nicolai, the head of the German spy network during World War I, that he read in the New York Public Library, wrote directly to Nicolai via the Nazi party's propaganda organ, the *Volkischer Beobachter*, asking if he could be of service to the Fatherland. If so, Nicolai could insert a commercial notice in the "Public Notices" section of the *New York Times*. In early April 1936, Rumrich was pleased to find the following advertisement in the classified section: "Theodore Koerner—Letter received, please send reply and address to Sanders, Hamburg 1, Postbox 629, Germany." Theodore Koerner, of course, was Rumrich's code name.

Meanwhile, an American attaché in London got wind of the fledgling spy and informed the U.S. War Department which promptly notified J. Edgar Hoover. The Director then sent his staff the following memo: "It has come to my attention that an effort is being made to steal the United States' secret East Coast defense plans. The identity of the foreign agent is currently unknown to us and the military."

But it was Rumrich who did himself in!

Anxious to collect a $1,000 bounty that Hamburg had offered its agents for some blank American passport applications, Rumrich impulsively telephoned the chief of the State Department passport division in Washington, D.C. He identified himself as "Edward Weston, Undersecretary of State," and ordered 50 passport application blanks be sent to him at a hotel he had just registered himself in. The chief immediately notified the FBI and within an hour Hoover had several special agent tails on Rumrich. Angry that the State Department hadn't delivered the applications, Rumrich took the train back to New York where he was arrested. With the entire spy ring now collapsing, Griebl fled to Germany.

When Rumrich was searched by the FBI, a penciled note was found in his pocket identifying him as an agent who would attempt to steal American east coast defense plans. He confessed that his orders from Hamburg included obtaining information on America's military strength, its defense plans, and the blueprints for the new aircraft carrier, *Enterprise*,

under construction. Unfortunately, one of the agents inadvertently mentioned the arrest to a reporter from the *New York Times*. When a front-page headline appeared the next day about the capture of a leading figure among top Nazis in the U.S., Rumrich's confederates scattered. Eighteen German and German-Americans were indicted, although only four were convicted. The others were listed as fugitives from the American legal system. Those who were caught received between two- and four-year sentences. Rumrich, himself, was sentenced to only two.

As Germany, Italy and Japan continued to embark on an unchecked series of invasions during the late 1930s, European Fascists and Nazis had their counterparts and supporters in the United States in the German-American Bund, the Silver Shirts, and various other groups. Although Hoover and most of America feared the groups would serve as launching pads for subversion, sabotage and espionage, investigations were forbidden by the U.S. Department of Justice because Bund, Silver Shirts and other Fascist group activities were entirely legal. Yes, their teachings had a tendency to be subversive, but they did not violate any law of the United States.

In June 1940, Mr. Hoover informed the graduating 14th session of the National Police Academy that "international gangsters" were being dispatched to our shores in order to weaken America's "internal security." Therefore, local and federal law enforcement agencies were to become the "first line of defense" in the nation's fight to preserve its integrity and security against the likes of Hitler, Mussolini and Stalin. A little more than a year later, at the 18th session's graduation exercises on Oct. 11, 1941, the Director announced that the Law Enforcement Officers' Mobilization Plan for National Defense was a success, and he called for continued assistance from the graduates in the fight for national internal security.

Meanwhile, the FBI was busy tripling its workforce. When the forerunner of the FBI National Academy was established on July 29, 1935, it had a class of 23 police officers. By the 19th session, when the FBI was given authority to gather intelligence on subversive activities in the Western Hemisphere, where the Bureau established the Special Intelligence Service, the class was over 80. In fact, between the years 1935 and 1945, the FBI's work force would jump to over 13,000 from the 600+ it saw when the Academy opened its doors.

Hoover, in his quick, decisive style, was preparing the FBI for a wartime emergency, "just in case." He constantly admonished his staff about the mistakes made by the Bureau and the government in World War I. For example, he deplored the fact that when, on July 30, 1916, Germany began sabotage efforts in the U.S., the Bureau had only 400 special agents to monitor more than one million enemy aliens. He recalled the stupidities that resulted in a vigilante system organized for combating subversion, in the lack of preparedness for dealing with spies and saboteurs, in violations of civil rights during the mass "slacker raids" and the roundup of aliens. Hoover, therefore, ordered analyses made with recommendations which would correct the errors of the past—as far as possible. He recalled that at the request of the Army and Navy, the FBI surveyed more than 2,200 key industrial plants in the U.S. in addition to Army and Navy arsenals and aircraft factories. The FBI, under the leadership of A. Bruce Bielaski, prepared ways and means of tightening security. Methods of sabotage were analysed and preventive measures outlined. Suggestions were made on fire prevention and tightening of anti-sabotage guards at vital points of production, and for fingerprinting employees as a means of weeding out those such as criminals and potential saboteurs.

Meanwhile, two events marked new and changing roles for the FBI. The first dealt with the establishment of the Bureau's "Disaster Squad" to identify a number of Bureau employees who were killed on a flight that crashed near Lovettsville, Va. The second was the dispatching of a team of FBI special agents to England to study British civil defense work and the security lessons learned by the British in the Battle of Britain. Upon their return to Headquarters, the Director ordered the agents to instruct local cops on the problems they might expect from spies, saboteurs, parachutists and Fifth Columnists in the event of enemy air attacks and how to best deal with them in light of the British experience.

Then, in January 1941, at the request of the State Department, the FBI quietly began observing the activities of German, Italian and Japanese consular officials, as well as personnel from the Soviet Union. Few people know this chapter in the Bureau's history, but Secretary of State Cordell Hull wrote about the results of the top secret surveillances in his memoirs:

"The Federal Bureau of Investigation had communicated to us in May 1941, that they had uncovered espionage activities by Lieutenant Commander Tachibana, a language officer of the Japanese Government, and asked our attitude toward his arrest. We agreed on May 27, and Tachibana was arrested in Los Angeles. Ambassador Nomura besought us

on June 14, in the interest of promoting friendly relations between our two Governments, to permit Tachibana to be deported immediately without trial. I went carefully into this case and decided to grant Nomura's request."

Of course, the FBI was involved in numerous other such cases. Hull consented to the prosecution of four Japanese officers in Hawaii who had not registered with the State Department as foreign agents. In addition, the Bureau gave the State Department documents and photographs illustrating that German and Italian consular offices throughout the United States were being used as centers of espionage and propaganda. So, in June 1941, Hull ordered these consular offices closed.

Earlier that year, under Mr. Hoover's personal supervision, special agents staged one of the most unusual espionage and counterespionage dramas in American history. The result was the arrest by the FBI on June 28 of Frederick Duquesne and 32 other Nazi spies.

The story actually began in January 1940 when William Sebold, a naturalized American, returned from a vacation to his native Germany and headed for the New York field office of the FBI. He described how the Gestapo had threatened to place all his relatives in German concentration camps, since there was Jewish blood in every member of the family, if he didn't become a spy for the Fatherland. Sebold agreed without hesitation. Nazi intelligence officers instructed him in the use of the short-wave radio, taught him a secret code, and provided him with microphotographic techniques, as well as instructions, to be passed on to German spies already in America.

With Sebold's full support, and amazing acting performances, Hoover and his team set an elaborate trap.

First, FBI agents had Sebold wire a coded message to Berlin indicating that he had arrived safely and on schedule. Then Bureau laboratory engineers constructed a short-wave radio station at Centerpoint, Long Island. FBI agents were careful to register the station as an approved amateur station in case any radio "hams" around the nation became suspicious. Messages began to flow back and forth between Long Island and Berlin. So well-supervised was Sebold, and so well-crafted were his messages, that German intelligence had the greatest confidence in their naturalized American. Meanwhile, Sebold's family went into hiding. Each of Sebold's messages had just enough authentic information in it to be thoroughly convincing, although none of the information was sent without first being cleared for security by the U.S. Army and Navy.

In his superlative book, *The FBI Story*, a nation-wide best-seller that was made into a movie starring James Stewart and Vera Miles, author Don White-head wrote of the Sebold drama:

"The FBI had established Sebold in a mid-Man-hattan office after all the 'props' had been installed. A mirror on the wall reflected the image of anyone looking into the glass—but in the adjoining room this mirror became a window through which agents took movies of everything that went on in Sebold's office. Hidden microphones carried each word spoken to a recording device. On Sebold's desk was a clock (and behind it a wall calendar) which showed the precise time of the day when Sebold had visitors, who always sat in a chair facing the mirror.

"Sebold contacted the German agents in New York and gave them the microphotographic instructions brought from Germany. Visitors drifted in and out of Sebold's office to receive instructions and to turn over to Sebold messages to be relayed to Germany. Among the callers was Frederick ''Fritz'' Duquesne, a long-time adventurer and German espionage agent whose spy career went back to the early 1900s. Duquesne was the ringleader. He and his confederates were particularly interested in sending information to Germany on production of war materials, ship movements to and from England, military aircraft production, the training of Army Air Corps personnel and the delivery of aircraft to Britain. The radio station on Long Island sent and received approximately 500 messages."

Once Hoover was certain he knew absolutely every spy in the ring, he decided to close in. Thirty-three people were arrested in an eight hour period. All were convicted, including the suave, nonchalent "Fritz" Duquesne.

On Dec. 5, 1941, Hoover instructed his agents across the country to be on alert for "the immediate apprehension of Japanese aliens in your district who have been recommended for custodial detention." Little did he, or anyone else in American government and military circles, realize the attack on Pearl Harbor was less than 48 hours away.

On the morning of Dec. 7, 1941, between 7:55 a.m. and 9:45 a.m., a total of 110 minutes, Japanese torpedo planes and dive bombers blasted the American fleet anchored at Pearl Harbor and strafed the neat rows of Army, Navy and Marine planes parked on the aprons of airfields nearby.

The bombs were still crashing down when the Honolulu Special Agent in Charge, Robert L. Shiv-

Frederick ''Fritz'' Duquesne PHPC

ers, called the FBI Headquarters in Washington, D.C. Local time was 2:30 p.m. as the young operator switched the urgent call to the FBI's private line in New York where the Director had gone for the weekend. Through his connection across the 5,000 miles of ocean and land, Shivers shouted, "The Japs are bombing Pearl Harbor. There is no doubt about it. Those planes are Japanese. It's war! You may be able to hear the explosions yourself. Listen!" Shivers held the telephone to an open window and Hoover could actually hear the muffled sounds of bombs and explosions hitting the American warships. The Honolulu Special Agent then provided the Director with the few items of information he had of the deaths and destruction. After a brief pause, Hoover then ordered Shivers to put into effect immediately the war plans which had been worked out months before.

Due to the edict of two days earlier, each field office knew precisely what to do when the order arrived for the general roundup. Since early Spring, the FBI had quietly been assembling lists of aliens who were "anti-American," or who "would likely prove to be most dangerous in the event of war." Such careful advance enemy alien preparations made it possible to take into custody 3,846 people of Japanese, German and Italian descent. The roundup was a remarkable performance in speed, coordination, and cooperation between squads of local police and FBI agents. But unlike the roundups of World War I, the machinery was in place for each arrested alien to have a hearing before a civilian board and to be represented by counsel.

Nonetheless, the government's later decision to evacuate Japanese Nationals and American citizens of Japanese descent from the West Coast and send them to internment camps was the most serious discrimination during World War II. Because the FBI had arrested the individuals whom it considered security threats, Hoover took the position that confining others was unnecessary. The President and his advisors, however, chose to support the military assessment that evacuation and internment were imperative. With the enactment of the necessary orders, arresting curfews and evacuation violators became a responsibility of the FBI.

While most FBI personnel during the war worked traditional war-related or criminal cases, one contingent of Agents was unique. Separated from Bureau rolls, these Agents, with the help of non-covert Legal Attachés, composed the Special Intelligence Service (SIS) in Latin America. Established by President Roosevelt in 1940, the SIS was to provide information on Axis activities in South America and to destroy its intelligence and propaganda networks. Several hundred thousand Germans or German descendants and numerous Japanese lived in South America. They provided pro-Axis pressure and cover for Axis communication facilities. Nevertheless, in every South American country, the SIS was instrumental in bringing about a situation in which, by 1944, continued support for the Nazis became intolerable or impractical.

Meanwhile, back on the East Coast during the early months of 1942, FBI agents were busy. On Feb. 20, Hoover ordered a German double agent, under FBI supervision, to establish on Long Island a radio contact with Hamburg. The ruse was so successful that he supplied the Abwehr with false information right up to the very day British forces captured Hamburg on May 2, 1945.

Less than three weeks later, on March 10, 1942, Brazilian police arrested Josef Jacob Johannes Starziczny, a German spy whose radio message to Hamburg concerning the sailing of the *Queen Mary* was intercepted by the FBI special agents attached to the SIS. The *Queen Mary*, with 10,000 American troops on board was thus saved from attack by German U-boats.

The cases that follow, by far the most serious the FBI engaged in during the war years, are what this book is all about. Challenged by more cunning, intelligent and experienced saboteurs, Hoover and his special agents were in for the fight of their lives. That their training and professionalism ultimately defeated "those who would come to destroy America" is self-evident and this book provides the reader with a clear picture of the FBI's activities, as well as the deep personal committment of the men and women behind the organization.

Briefly, the original, hitherto unpublished, case summaries prepared by FBI special agents, often within moments of arrests, deal with Nazi saboteurs who were landed on the beaches of Long Island and Florida during mid-1942. On June 12, four well-trained German agents, led by George John Dasch, were paddled from a U-boat to an isolated beach near Amagansett, Long Island, New York. A second team of four German saboteurs, led by Edward Kerling, landed at Ponte Vedra Beach in Florida. On June 19, Dasch, leader of the first group, gave himself and the entire group up to the FBI, and within days of the initial landing, all eight saboteurs had been arrested by the FBI. After a brief trial, the eight saboteurs were turned over to a military commission by Presidential order on Aug. 8, 1942. Six were sentenced to death, one to life imprisonment, and one to 30 years. Because Dasch cooperated with the FBI, and since he had received the minimum sentence of 30 years, Hoover urged President Truman, in 1948, to commute his sentence and deport him back to Germany along with the other imprisoned saboteur, Ernst Burger.

There were certainly other battles to be fought by the FBI against Nazi spies and saboteurs in the three years that followed prior to the end of the war with Germany in 1945. For example, FBI agents tracked and arrested Bernard Julius Otto Kuehn, the agent whose house in Hawaii sent signals to Japanese pilots attacking Pearl Harbor. On Feb. 21, 1943, Kuehn was found guilty of espionage. On Jan. 1, 1945, Erich Gimpel and William Curtis Colepaugh, two Nazi spies, were captured by special agents after having landed from a U-boat at Hancock Point, Maine, on the night of Nov. 29, 1944. Colepaugh turned himself in to the FBI on Dec. 26, 1944, and told them where to find Gimpel. On Jan. 1, 1945, the FBI called a news conference in New York and announced the spies were "captured." The Maine landings could have had disastrous consequences on the outcome of the war if the spies could have sabotaged the Manhattan Project.

The world the FBI faced on Dec. 7, 1941, was very different from the world J. Edgar Hoover was in when

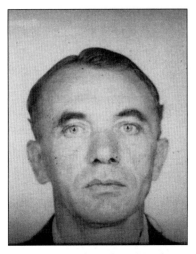

Bernard Julius Otto Kuehn

Friedel Augusta Berta Kuehn

he assumed leadership of the Bureau in December 1924. And, the world he faced in September 1945, was a far cry from the one he had to do combat in on December 7, four years earlier. But of all the thousands upon thousands that his special agents were challenged by and successfully brought to conclusion, none was more potentially dangerous to the safety and security of America than *Operations Pastorius* and *Elster*. What follows is a completely thrilling account of how the FBI operated during the most frightful days of World War II. There is enough material in the case summaries to keep "who-done-it" readers busy for months. Readers can determine for themselves the sort of organization the FBI was in those days, along with its growth, trials, tribulations, failures and triumphs.

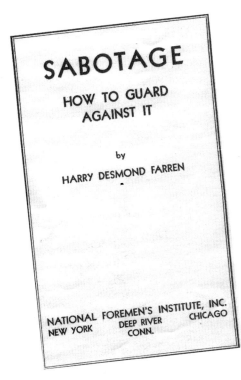

Although the United States was still at peace in 1940 when this pamphlet was issued, the thoughts of war were on the minds of many Americans.

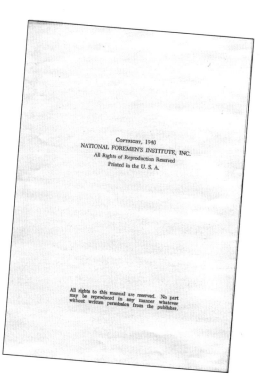

Acknowledgments

MANY PEOPLE THROUGHOUT THE United States helped the authors with this book. Thank you to Robert McGonigal of *Classic Trains* Magazine, who provided photos of the potential sabotage sites; the staff and members of the National Archives and Records Administration in College Park, Maryland; and especially Mr. Fred Romanski who provided files of *Operation Pastorius* and the German-American Bund; Harry Cooper of Sharkhunters Inc. who provided information on the three submarines which carried the Germans to America; Peter Hansen of Lenexa, Kansas; Diana Dayton of the East Hampton Library; Carleton Kelsey of Amagansett, New York; Dennis Wrynn of the Suffolk County Community College on Long Island; Camille Ruggiero of AP/Wide World Photos; Charlie Campo of the *Bangor Daily News*; Ms. Lois Johnson of Hancock, Maine; David Hardy of the FBI, Washington, D.C.; Bill Levy of Newark, New Jersey; Gary Skoloff, West Orange, New Jersey; Dr. Marty Davis, Huntington, New York; Charlie Hopkins, Green Cove Springs, Florida; John Woy, San Rafael, California; George Reith, Pebble Beach, California; *Newsday* in Melville, Long Island; Ebbie LeMaster of Ponte Vedra Beach, Florida; Martina Caspers of the Bundesarchiv in Koblenz, Germany; Kristine Krueger of the Academy Foundation, Margaret Herrick Library, Beverly Hills, California; Craig Dixon, John Hughes, Marcia Porter and Jan Taylor of Missoula, Montana, and Frances Taber of Fernandina Beach, Florida, who took the photos at Ponte Vedra Beach Inn.

A special thanks to John Cullen of Chesapeake, Virginia, who consented to several telephone interviews, and, especially to Richard Gay of Blue Hill, Maine, who came on board this project late in the production stage and provided a great amount of photos and written material on *Operation Magpie*.

Leslie Maricelli and John Cohen, staff members of Pictorial Histories Publishing Company, provided typing, editing and layout services.

PHOTO IDENTIFICATION

NA – National Archives and Records Administration, College Park, Maryland
FDR – Franklin Delano Roosevelt Presidential Library, Hyde Park, New York
AP/World Wide Photos – New York, New York
Kalmbach Publishing Co./*Classic Trains* Magazine, Waukesha, Wisconsin
PHPC – Pictorial Histories Publishing Co., Missoula, Montana
RG–Richard Gay, Blue Hill, Maine
Other photos are credited to their source.

THIS BOOK IS DEDICATED TO ALL THE GOVERNMENT AGENTS AND MILITARY PERSONNEL WHO PROTECTED OUR COUNTRY DURING WORLD WAR II AND TO ALL THE MEN AND WOMEN WHO ARE DEDICATED TO THIS TASK TODAY.

GERMAN SPIES AND SABOTEURS DURING WORLD WAR I

ON THE NIGHT OF July 29-30, 1916, an explosion ripped through the Black Tom Island munitions supply terminal on the New Jersey side of New York Harbor. This was the greatest explosion to occur in a military installation in the United States.

America was not at war at this time and was officially neutral, but the country had become "the arsenal of democracy" for the Allied powers and their chief supplier of armaments.

German spies and saboteurs and German sympathizers in the United States had been waging war against the country since World War I began in August 1914.

Black Tom was the most devastating sabotage effort during the period, but five months later a large shell manufacturing plant at Kingsland, New Jersey, only eight miles northwest of Black Tom was also destroyed by sabotage. There were other suspected acts of German sabotage in the United States during the country's neutrality, most notably, at several steel mills, a train loaded with dynamite in California and fire on ships at sea.

Diplomatic relations with Germany were broken off on Feb. 3, 1917, and war was declared on the Central Powers on April 6, 1917.

Destruction on Black Tom Island after the explosion on July 29-30, 1916. PHPC

The Canadian Car & Foundry plant at Kingsland, New Jersey, after the Jan. 17, 1917, explosion. PHPC

"MISGUIDED LADY" PUTTING UP POSTER.

Neutrality issues were a problem in World War I as in World War II. LIBRARY OF CONGRESS

Paul Koening was a sometime detective in the U.S. for the Hamburg-American line who recruited and directed spies and saboteurs in the U.S. until he was arrested in 1915.
PHPC

The greatest service you can render your country is to write at once to your Senators, your congressman, the President of the United States and your local newspaper protesting against any further steps to involve the United States in the European war.

Also send in your name as a member of the America First Committee, which is working to save America from this war. National Headquarters, 141 West Jackson Boulevard, Chicago, Ill.

309

Can Hitler Invade America?

★

The facts in this pamphlet were compiled for the America First Committee by John T. Flynn from information gathered from military authorities and writers on military affairs.

This article by John T. Flynn appeared in the April, 1941 issue of Reader's Digest.

By permission of the Reader's Digest, it is reprinted with additional notes.

PLEASE PASS IT ON TO OTHERS TO READ

Additional copies may be obtained from:

NEW YORK CHAPTER
AMERICA FIRST COMMITTEE
515 Madison Avenue, New York City
TELEPHONE: PLAZA 3-5425

194

Notice some of the prominent names listed here: Alice Roosevelt Longworth, daughter of Theodore Roosevelt; Capt. Edward Rickenbacker, famous WWI aviator; Mrs. Burton K. Wheeler, wife of Montana's senator and Catholic Bishop Hammaker.

QUOTATIONS OF
LEADING MILITARY AUTHORITIES

"No foreign power or group of powers can operate across the ocean and stand in combat with the American Navy and planes operating from home bases."—Admiral William S. Sims, shortly before his death.

"Of course there is no possibility ever of any hostile attack on either of our coasts."—Rear Admiral W. W. Phelps, Nov. 18, 1935.

"I do not think that any fleet could ever make a landing an effective force on our coast, whether we had a navy or not, provided there are enough shore-based aircraft available. . .I do not think that any thinking person ever feels that any nation can successfully invade our country leaving out the aircraft or anything else."—Rear Admiral Cook, 1938.

"Considered from the defensive standpoint America is the strongest military nation on the earth—that is, it is the easiest nation to prepare for defensive warfare. It would not take much to make it invulnerable against any nation or combination of nations that might be brought to bear against it."

—Major General Hagood, 1937.

"Our fleet IS LARGE ENOUGH TO HANDLE SIMULTANEOUSLY A COMBINATION OF ENEMIES, being about as large as Britain's scattered fleet, considerably superior to Japan's, three times as large as Italy's, four times stronger than Germany's, only slightly inferior to the combined navies of all three totalitarian nations, and far stronger in naval aviation than any navy in the world."

—Hanson W. Baldwin, July, 1939.

"Continental United States, even without the extraordinary defense measures adopted by Congress, is well-nigh impregnable. So are its outlying possessions, except the Philippines, Wake and Guam. Such impregnability can be brought to a point of completeness with relatively small additional effort."

—Hanson W. Baldwin, July, 1939.

CAN HITLER INVADE AMERICA?

THIS little pamphlet is intended to answer the question—Can Hitler Invade America?

This is a very important question. It is important because Americans are told that this terrible war in Europe is our war.

It is called our war because, we are told, if Hitler defeats England the United States is next on the list. Having crushed England and taken the English navy, it is said, he will then INVADE AMERICA. And because so many people believe this to be true they are willing to go to any lengths to aid Britain to defeat Hitler.

This whole argument turns on one point—that Hitler, after he defeats England, CAN INVADE AMERICA. And so the great question is — CAN HE?

Now then, let us begin at the beginning.

There is no doubt that Hitler and his great Nazi army is a powerful military machine. There is also no doubt that Hitler will stop at nothing to gain his objectives—to take any country that he wants.

He overran Czechoslovakia and Poland swiftly. Then he turned to overrun Norway, Denmark, Holland, Belgium, France in startling quick succession.

Because he could do this we are warned that he can do the same thing to the United States and that the only thing that protects us from Hitler is the British navy.

Let us see therefore just what Hitler would require in order to invade the United States.

First of all, we start out with the fact that all these countries put together — Poland, Czechoslovakia, Norway, Denmark, Holland, Belgium, France —are much smaller than the United States.

Their total populations equal 110,000,000. Our total population is 130,000,000.

They were divided into seven different countries. Each one was small compared with Germany. They were scattered around Germany's rim. Hitler could attack each one separately. And each one —save France—was just a small morsel for him. But the United States is a unified country—a single nation—and the attack would be against the whole United States.

In the next place, all these countries were right on Germany's land frontiers. In each case all he had to do was to roll across their land borders and he was inside their gates. They had fortresses, barricades. But these were nothing against his vast mechanical equipment. When he had defeated France he turned to fight England. Germany has 80 million population and a gigantic army and an air force three times the size of Britain's. England has only 50 million people. But when Hitler turned on England there was the English Channel —only 23 miles wide at its narrowest point. This is only about half the distance from Washington to Baltimore. But when he faced that problem of crossing that narrow strip of water—he has not yet, after fifteen months of war and seven months since France fell, even attempted to cross it with soldiers or tanks.

When he attempts to invade the United States —or Canada—he would have to face the problem of crossing with his armies THREE THOUSAND MILES of the Atlantic Ocean and facing not 50

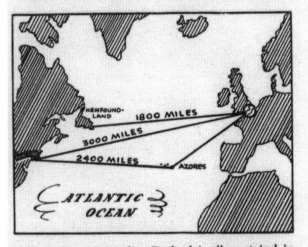

The problem of invading England is all comprised in the small circle. There is a narrow strip of sea—less than 26 miles at its narrow point—which Germany must cross to invade England either with an army or with planes. Sending planes over, of course, is a simple matter as far as distance is concerned. But invading the United States or Canada means traversing the immense mileage of ocean either to New York or Newfoundland or from the Azores or other equally distant ports.

million people on a small island with but small natural resources, but a vast nation with 130 million people and resources far exceeding his own.

Now let us look at this problem as realistically as possible. Just what would be the job that Hitler would have on his hands?

We have spoken of the "might" of Hitler's armies. In what does that might consist? His armies are mighty because they are equipped with an endless supply of tanks, armored trucks, machine guns and great cannon and mortars, anti-aircraft guns and anti-tank guns and great motorcycle squadrons and planes. His army was no longer an army on foot. It was an army in trucks and in tanks plunging against its adversaries and mowing them down and rolling over them.

Of course if Hitler ever attempted to invade America he would have to bring not only his soldiers but all this equipment. Without it he would be helpless.

Let us see then what he would have to bring across the 3,000 miles of ocean to invade America.

First, we have to decide how many men he would use to invade America and defeat us. Now right here the reader must understand that the German army leaders have shown immense intelli-

gence. We know that they are not coming to America with a handful of men—they are not going to attempt to conquer us without bringing enough men here to do the job. How many men would that be?

When Hitler invaded little Norway he sent 60,000 men.

When Mussolini attacked Ethiopia he used half a million men—When Hitler went into Poland— just across his borders and with only 36 million population—he marched with 1,000,000 men.

When he moved against Holland, Belgium and France he used not less than TWO MILLION MEN. Estimates place the number far higher.

Now is it not a fair assumption that to defeat the United States here he would have to have at least as many men as he took into France? Does anyone suppose that Hitler could conquer this country with anything less than three or four million men? He would have to have an army that size and all the equipment necessary to make it irresistible.

But let us suppose, however, that Hitler was crazy enough to try to beat the United States with a mere million men. Just how much equipment would he have to bring along with the men to make them effective? The mass of war instruments that such an army requires staggers the imagination.

The following figures are based on the equipment carried by American army units and are, therefore, very much under what the German army units carry.

This army would require:

19,320 machine guns	2,520 75mm. field guns
7,770 automatic rifles	1,120 155m. howitzers
2,590 anti-tank guns	6,930 mortars

Vehicles:

65,590 trucks	1,610 tractors
19,820 trailers	1,756 ambulances
4,500 tanks	1,120 passenger cars
7,910 motorcycles	450 air-compressors
70 electric lighting sets	

Planes:

1,820 light bombers	5,880 reconnaisance planes
1,650 pursuit planes	350 transport planes
(a total of 9,800 planes)	

Anti-aircraft guns:

840 3mm. AA guns	1,680 37mm. AA guns
1,680 .50 calibre AA guns	

Of course such an army must have food, fuel and ammunition. This vast armada, with its modern weapons, would have to bring its food, its oil, its ammunition until the country is conquered.

It would require:

9,000,000 lbs. of rations and supplies a day
1,500,000 gallons of gasoline a day
150,000 gallons of oil.

What quantities of shot and shell would be required it is difficult to say, but the amount would be staggering. After Hitler's army got here, it would have to keep open behind a line of supply from its main supply base capable of keeping a continuous flow of provisions, fuel, ammunition and replacements of arms and equipment.

The problem of transporting this vast army and the mountains of equipment and continuous supplies it would require is utterly beyond the power of any country.

First, the men must be sent over in ships. And these ships must be convoyed. They cannot be sent across the ocean in little vessels. Ships of less than 2,000 tons would, of course, be completely useless.

Of course to send a million men over at one time would be out of the question.

Mr. Hanson Baldwin, the military expert of the New York Times, says:

"The world's tonnage facilities are such that no power or combination of powers could possibly transport more than 300,000 men in a month. An initial expeditionary force of about 50,000 would be the maximum practical number that could be brought against us, if the size of convoy, number of ships and planes needed for protection and the like are considered."

In the World War we sent two million men to France. But we had, according to Col. Leonard Ayres, who wrote the official report on this great enterprise, the ships of twelve different countries—American, British, French, Italian, etc.—and the convoys of the American and British and French navies. The Germans were without a fleet. We landed these men on a friendly shore where they were received with open arms. And we sent an army of engineers and mechanics ahead of them to build ports and docks to unload the equipment.

Let us suppose that Germany has defeated England and taken the British navy. She now decides to send her army to America. Major George Fielding Eliot, military expert of the pro-war New York Herald-Tribune, says:

"Troops cannot be transported overseas in any number save when naval command of the waters over which they pass has been previously assured, since a troop convoy is a large, slow and vulnerable target and will surely suffer heavily if its escort be attacked by anything like an equal force."

In the circumstances we have assumed that Germany, even with the British fleet, would not have complete command of the seas. For there would remain the American navy. And that navy would have to be wiped out before the German navy would command the seas on this side of the ocean. Two things must be remembered. First, at the end of this war the American navy would be larger than the German navy and the British navy combined. Second, the German government would have to do its naval fighting on this side of the ocean. It is an axiom of sea warfare that a naval vessel loses a fixed percentage of its effectiveness every 100 miles it gets from its own base. Great battleships have to fuel up frequently and must be accompanied by immense auxiliary ships.

Three thousand miles away from their own coasts this navy would be utterly helpless against a navy which is merely its equal in numbers, but which would be three times its strength in effective fighting power. There is not a naval authority who believes that the German government would attempt a mass naval battle in our waters against our naval strength.

If a flotilla of 30 or 40 ships with 50,000 men, convoyed by a larger number of warships and all their equipment attempted to land here, it could not sneak in on some dark night. Plane scouts would herald its approach days in advance. When it got here it could not empty its cargo on an open beach. Which means the flotilla would have to come into one of our harbors, all of which are protected by artillery and would be sown with mines. Major Eliot makes this clear. He says:

"Large armies, accompanied as modern armies must be by artillery of various calibres, tanks and other heavy equipment, as well as vast quantities of munitions and supplies, cannot usually be landed on an open beach; but must first obtain possession of a secure harbor with the necessary piers, cranes, and other accessories for getting ashore their accessories."

Even the planes used by this invading force must be transported to this country by ships. Mr. Baldwin says:

"Today planes must be transported by sea to the Western Hemisphere; the air armies of Europe and Asia are not yet able to bridge the Atlantic and Pacific under their own power. Isolated planes can do it but not mass bombing formations."

There are planes that have flown across the Atlantic, but they must find a friendly landing here. They cannot come here as hostile craft and be welcomed on hospitable landing fields. It is possible to build bombers that could come here and land a few bombs but this would have no military effect at all.

For every man transported here there must be at least seven and a half tons of shipping. An attacking force of 100,000 would require 750,000 tons. An average of 5,000 tons would require 150 vessels convoyed by a flotilla of naval vessels made up of seven battleships, several aircraft carriers, seven light cruisers, a couple of mine-layers and at least seventy destroyers. Imagine this immense armada, moving slowly over the seas and approaching our coasts—3,000 miles from their own base and at the mercy of our navy and our air force, and compelled to make a landing at a port protected by heavy guns and mine-sown seas.

By the time a million men were landed, if that is conceivable, the attacking government would require 13,000,000 tons of shipping plying back and forth from the other side of the Atlantic to ports here to keep this great army supplied with provisions, fuel and ammunition. This would mean the arrival and departure of at least eighty ships a day and all at hostile ports and through hostile seas. The whole idea is so fantastic that no serious mind will entertain it for a moment. And, as a matter of fact, there is no military authority in this country who believes that an invasion of America by Germany with or without the British fleet is possible.

Hanson Baldwin, in Harper's Magazine for August, 1940, said, referring to an invasion of this hemisphere: "The problem seems impossible; not even Britain or a combination of Britain and Germany has sufficient shipping to divert such an enormous amount of it from their ordinary and vital trade routes to military purposes. We do not, therefore, have to fear the employment of mass armies in this hemisphere; the most we have to guard against is the possible transportation of a *small expeditionary force.*"

To come here, after defeating England, Hitler would have to set out for America upon a vast

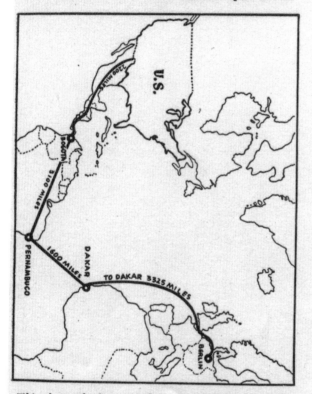

This shows the immense distances which Hitler would have to travel with his great army of a million men to attack the United States by way of South America.

military adventure, using up all the military resources he has. He would leave behind him on his rear Russia, which would welcome his plight, and 200,000,000 sullen people in Europe who, we may be sure, would be watching the moment to cause him trouble. That moment would come when he was compelled to strip himself in Europe to fight here. And he would fight here a battle that he would be sure to lose. Dictators cannot afford to take on such battles. They must win.

The President said in his last Message to Congress, January 6, 1941, "Even if there were no British navy it is not probable any enemy would be stupid enough to attack us by landing troops in the United States from across thousands of miles of ocean, until it had acquired strategic bases from which to operate."

Here is a complete admission by the man who has done more than anyone else to frighten the American people with the fear of invasion that a direct invasion is not possible. Yet hardly were these words cold on the President's lips when Mr. Hull went before a Congressional Committee and said if the British navy were eliminated to cross the Atlantic by Hitler would be a comparatively easy matter.

The President saves his point by insisting that Hitler would first have to acquire bases in this hemisphere. Now just look at this with a little common sense. Hitler will not come across thousands of miles of ocean to invade us directly because of the great distance he would have to transport his armies and equipment. Therefore if he attempted an invasion from bases those bases would have to be much closer to the United States than is Germany. Otherwise there would be no sense in bases.

The bases in this hemisphere which would answer this description from which Hitler could attack us are Brazil, various points in the West Indies, Bermuda, Newfoundland, Greenland and similar points.

Brazil is the favorite South American base to which the President is fond of referring. This is because Hitler can take over West Africa and concentrate his forces at Dakar there.

Africa bulges out on its west coast toward South America and South America bulges out toward Africa in Brazil. Dakar in Africa is only 1,600 miles from Pernambuco in Brazil. Hitler will be able to cross over the Atlantic at this narrow stretch to Brazil and, as Senator Claude Pepper has described it, roll on into Venezuela, into Colombia, up through Central America into Mexico and on to the Rio Grande.

This amazing proposal is so grotesque that it hardly calls for an answer. It overlooks the fact that Hitler must take his vast force to Western Africa by sea—which is 3,200 miles from Germany—and then 1,600 miles across the Atlantic to Brazil. He will have travelled near 5,000 miles. Before he started from Germany he would be 3,300 miles from the United States. After travelling 5,000 miles to Brazil he would be 5,300 MILES FROM THE UNITED STATES. He would be further away than before he started.

He would have to have of course at least a million men—which would be a ridiculously small number. He would have to bring along all that immense accumulation of trucks, and trailers and motorcycles and tanks and guns and supplies. He would have to conquer Brazil, Venezuela and Colombia. He would have to move his men up through the narrow Isthmus of Panama and on through the mountainous regions, the swamps, the trackless plains of Guatemala, Nicaragua, Panama, Salvador and Honduras, dragging along his thousand-mile train of trucks and tanks and guns and trailers and supplies into Mexico and up over the wide plateaus, the pathless jungles, over the mountain gorges and the fever-infested plains of Mexico—his million men, his 65,000 trucks, his 20,000 trailers, his 10,000 tanks and incredible supplies of food, fuel, oil and ammunition—conquering all these countries as he goes and leaving behind great numbers of troops to hold them in subjection until he came at last to the Texas border—after a journey of nearly 10,000 miles over land and oceans. And he would still not be in the United States.

This, of course, is a bedtime story to frighten children and is based upon the assumption that American citizens are morons and will believe anything. Yet this is the basis of the argument that "we are next on Hitler's list."

Others tell us he will go to Greenland. Greenland is a vast tract of artic wilderness, its coasts rimmed by immense mountains, its interior covered with ice in places a thousand feet deep. Military and aviation experts know it is impossible to build these bases there to accommodate either naval or airplane units large enough for attack here. Even if it were possible Hitler could not do this unless he had command of the seas. And if he had command of the seas he wouldn't go to Greenland.

There are, however, other bases from which attacks might be launched. The map (Map 4)

This map shows the various bases from which an enemy might attempt to attack the United States. All those belonging to Britain, Holland, France are within a few days of our waters, some in our waters. They could be taken without firing a shot or losing a life if England were defeated. Germany would then have to take them from us which would be as difficult as landing in the United States.

will show these. You will see very quickly how little we have to fear on this score.

These bases are Newfoundland, Bermuda, the West Indies or any British or Dutch or French possessions in the general neighborhood of the Northern coast of South America.

Germany, it is feared, might, with the British fleet, capture these bases, if Hitler defeated England. If England were to be defeated the American fleet could seize any one of these bases within two days, three at the most. American warships kept within a day or two run from these places—mostly islands—could almost the very day that England fell take possession of these places without firing a shot, spending a dollar or losing a man. There is no need of going into a war—perhaps a ten-year war—to keep the Germans out of bases which we could capture in a few days and at no cost if Britain is defeated.

As for Newfoundland, there we would pursue the policy we would adopt for all of Canada and the country to the North of us in this hemisphere. We would announce that we would resist with force any attack upon that country. It would take Germany years to prepare for such an expedition and when prepared, even if she were stupid enough to attempt it, the same arguments which reveal the folly and impossibility of a frontal attack on the United States apply to Canada backed by the United States.

Why, then, do men talk about Hitler coming here? Because this is the cornerstone of the propaganda to get us into the war. Propagandists have pointed out that to get America in the war, "Americans must be frightened by some threat." And this threat has been manufactured by British and American interventionist propagandists and industriously circulated by them to get us into this war.

Americans are willing to aid Britain because they hate fascism, they are against Hitler, they look upon the English government, despite its aristocratic character, and its empire, as a more civilized form of government than Hitler's dictatorship. They are willing to help through a generous sympathy and not because they think this is our war.

Any airplane attempting to bomb us from Europe or from the Azores would have to face the certain fate of being destroyed. There is not in existence any fleet of planes that could menace us from Europe or from any base such as Greenland or the Azores. And of course everyone knows by now that you do not conquer a country like America merely by dropping bombs on it. It must be occupied. We are not vulnerable as Britain is, which depends for the very food she eats as well as for almost everything else, on shipments from abroad. She can be blockaded. We cannot.

All this does not mean that our country is not menaced by dangers. The most serious dangers are interior. It does not mean that we must be unarmed. It means that we must provide this country with whatever defenses are essential to make an invasion by any force, however great, impossible. And that is easily possible to us. What is impossible to us is to create inside of many years an aggressive force capable of invading Europe or Asia and carrying on an aggressive war there. And few Americans want to do that.

TABLE OF CONTENTS

PREFACE III

INTRODUCTION IV

ACKNOWLEDGMENTS X

GERMAN SPIES AND SABOTEURS DURING WORLD WAR I XI

THE GERMAN-AMERICAN BUND: A NAZI ORGANIZATION IN AMERICA, 1933-1941 1

SPIES AND SABOTEURS IN THE UNITED STATES 19

AMERICA'S DEFENSES 37

THE WORLD WAR II BEACH PATROL 44

OPERATION PASTORIUS 47

    THE EIGHT SABOTEURS 50

    THE LANDINGS 60

    THE BETRAYAL 70

    THE ARRESTS 74

    THE OTHER CONSPIRATORS 79

    THE TRIAL 81

    THE TRIBUNAL JUDGES 97

OPERATION PELICAN 131

UNTERNEHMEN ELSTER (OPERATION MAGPIE) 133

SPIES, SABOTEURS AND HOLLYWOOD 157

BIBLIOGRAPHY 164

ORGANIZATIONS WHICH HAVE INFORMATION PERTAINING TO THE SUBJECTS OF THIS BOOK 165

ABOUT THE AUTHORS 166

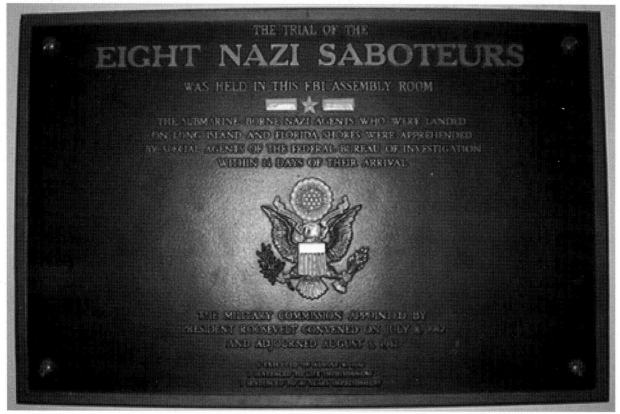

Until 1977 the above historical marker had been mounted inside an FBI classroom. The marker was re-mounted in its' present location on the fifth floor of the Justice Department Building in Washington, D.C., in 1979.

THE GERMAN-AMERICAN BUND:
A NAZI ORGANIZATION IN AMERICA, 1933-1941

THE GERMAN-AMERICAN BUND, an organization espousing National Socialist ideology, was in existence in the United States from 1933 to December 1941, when the national officers disbanded the group and placed all its assets in trusteeship. The Bund enjoyed its period of greatest growth under the leadership of Bundesführer Fritz Kuhn from 1936, when the Bund changed its name from The Friends of the New Germany, to 1939, when 22,000 people attended a Bund-sponsored George Washington's birthday rally in New York's Madison Square Garden. The members of the Bund were all supposedly American citizens, although the organization had a "sympathizer" class of membership for resident aliens. The overwhelming majority of Bund members were of German extraction; most were recent immigrants and naturalized citizens.

The leadership of the Bund attempted to meld Nazi racial theories with native American patriotic values but met with little success, even in the German-American community. Although racism and anti-semitism were present in America in the 1930s, the volkish values of Nazism proselytized by Bund leaders never took root in a society where pluralistic tradition and tolerance were strongly ingrained. Most German-Americans who joined the Bund were not attracted by Nazi ideology but by the spirit of German community and "gemütlichkeit" the group offered.

As Nazi persecution of German Jews increased, hostility toward American Nazis also increased. The Bund was the subject of several Congressional investigations headed by Martin Dies and Samuel Dickstein. The New Jersey legislature passed the Anti-Hate Statutes directed specifically at the Bund. Fritz Kuhn was prosecuted and imprisoned for misappropriating Bund funds. Pacifist and isolationist sentiments waned after war broke out in Europe and American public and official attitudes became even more anti-German. In 1941 the Treasury Department froze Bund bank accounts and denaturalization proceedings were begun against several Bund leaders.

There were also many anti-Nazi groups opposed to the Bund and Germany. Some of these were the American Committee for Anti-Nazi Literature, American League for Peace and Democracy, American League Against War and Fascism, Labor Conference to Combat Hitlerism, and the Non-Sectarian Anti-Nazi League to Champion Human Rights.

The Bund had contact with isolationist and nativist groups including the American Patriots, the Silver Shirts, the Ku Klux Klan, and the No Foreign War Committee, and maintained relations with other German groups such as the Steuben Society of America and Der Stahlhelm.

The Bund saw its future in the children of its members. Youth programs were available for all age groups, utilizing educational materials imported from Germany.

Controversy surrounded the Bund and disputes concerning the organization were often settled in court. In 1935 a power struggle among the national leaders of the Bund was settled in the Supreme Court of the State of New York. The case, **Henry Woisin as Treasurer of The Friends of New Germany vs. Anton Haegele, et al.**, determined which Faction of the Bund leadership owned the printing press of the Bund newspaper, thereby gaining control of all propaganda issued by the group. In 1939 the Court of General Sessions of the County of New York was the scene for **The People of the State of New York vs. Fritz Kuhn**, in which the Bundesführer was accused and convicted of embezzlement of Bund funds and forgery involving alteration of the account books of the Bund. In 1940 the case of **The State vs. August Klapprott, et al.** was heard in New Jersey courts. The case involved the arrest at the Bund summer resort, Camp Nordland, of several Bund members for violating the New Jersey Anti-Hate Statutes. The American Civil Liberties Union filed briefs for the Bund in several court cases.

In January 1939, Fritz Kuhn invited several conservative politicians to speak at the Bund's George Washington Birthday Rally and Pro-Americanism rally to be held the next month at Madison Square Garden. None would speak although several professed patriotic principles similar to those of Bundesführer Kuhn. "Free America" from international Jewish communism was the theme of the rally. Columnist Dorothy Parker found the Bund members also wanted to be free of her. While seated at a press table she laughed out loud at one of the Nazi speakers. She was promptly ejected from the arena. "Free America" meant freedom from Jews, communists, and everyone who disagreed with the Bund. Speakers at the rally praised Hitler and attacked President Roosevelt. The crowd of 22,000 booed the name of Mayor LaGuardia although the New York City police were protecting them from an estimated 50,000 anti-Nazi demonstrators outside the Garden.

The Bund was all rhetoric but no action because they never attained a broad-based support. But by concentrating on rhetoric the Bund did get headlines. With their rabble-rousing, anti-semitic tactics though, the Bund alienated the thoughtful individuals they needed to attract to make an impact in America. The Bund leaders were left with their meaningless words, their anti-semitic books and pamphlets, and no voice in a society which they did not understand.

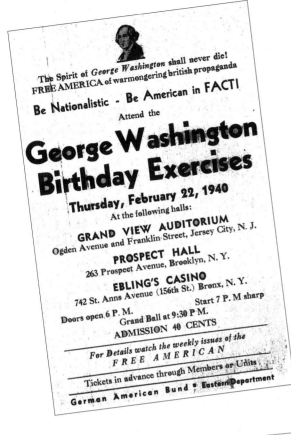

The Spirit of *George Washington* shall never die!
FREE AMERICA of warmongering british propaganda

Be Nationalistic - Be American in FACT!

Attend the

George Washington Birthday Exercises

Thursday, February 22, 1940

At the following halls:

GRAND VIEW AUDITORIUM
Ogden Avenue and Franklin Street, Jersey City, N. J.

PROSPECT HALL
263 Prospect Avenue, Brooklyn, N. Y.

EBLING'S CASINO
742 St. Anns Avenue (156th St.) Bronx, N. Y.

Doors open 6 P. M.   Start 7 P. M sharp

Grand Ball at 9:30 P. M.

ADMISSION 40 CENTS

For Details watch the weekly issues of the
FREE AMERICAN

Tickets in advance through Members or Units

German American Bund ▪ Eastern Department

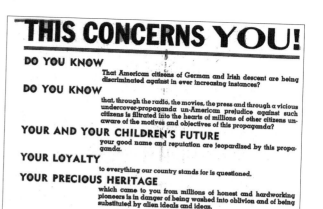

THIS CONCERNS YOU!

DO YOU KNOW
That American citizens of German and Irish descent are being discriminated against in ever increasing instances?

DO YOU KNOW
that, through the radio, the movies, the press and through a vicious undercover-propaganda un-American prejudice against such citizens is filtrated into the hearts of millions of other citizens unaware of the motives and objectives of this propaganda?

YOUR AND YOUR CHILDREN'S FUTURE
your good name and reputation are jeopardized by this propaganda.

YOUR LOYALTY
to everything our country stands for is questioned.

YOUR PRECIOUS HERITAGE
which came to you from millions of honest and hardworking pioneers is in danger of being washed into oblivion and of being substituted by alien ideals and ideas.

YOU MUST OPPOSE THIS PROPAGANDA!

HOW?
PROMINENT SPEAKERS WILL ANSWER THIS SUPER-VITAL QUESTION AT A

MASS MEETING
on
TUESDAY, SEPTEMBER 12th
8.30 p.m.

NEW YORK TURN HALL, 85th Street and Lexington Avenue
(Admission Free)

It is your duty to come with your relatives and friends! This fight is forced upon us and we should take it up like true Americans.

WE WILL TAKE IT UP ON SEPTEMBER 12th.

ANTI DISCRIMINATION COMMITTEE
(A. D. C.)
of the German-American organizations
and societies of Greater New York.

There were dozens of other organizations similar to the German-American Bund which were anti-communist, anti-semitic and advocated staying out of the European war.

PATRONIZE GENTILE Stores ONLY!

The "Citizens Anti-Nazi Committee", a subdivision of the "American League Against War and Fascism", a purely communistic organization, has appealed to the citizens of Philadelphia not to buy from certain stores listed on a leaflet, because these merchants are advertising in a German-American newspaper.

The stores listed as Nazi stores are German American stores, owned and operated by gentile American citizens. They have nothing to do with either a Nazi organization or a Nazi newspaper.

We emphatically protest against this Boycott!

The "Deutscher Weckruf und Beobachter" is an American newspaper, printed in the German and English language and stands for true Americanism, for the genuine truth and nothing but the truth. It is fighting for the interest of American patriotism, labor and religion.

If you believe in these ideals, do not be misguided and

Patronize Gentile Stores Only!

German-American Businessmen's Committee

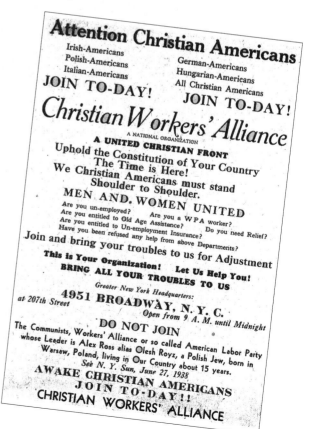

Attention Christian Americans

Irish-Americans
Polish-Americans
Italian-Americans

German-Americans
Hungarian-Americans
All Christian Americans

JOIN TO-DAY!
JOIN TO-DAY!

Christian Workers' Alliance
A NATIONAL ORGANIZATION

A UNITED CHRISTIAN FRONT

Uphold the Constitution of Your Country
The Time is Here!
We Christian Americans must stand
Shoulder to Shoulder.

MEN AND WOMEN UNITED

Are you un-employed?   Are you a WPA worker?
Are you entitled to Old Age Assistance?   Do you need Relief?
Are you entitled to Un-employment Insurance?
Have you been refused any help from above Departments?

Join and bring your troubles to us for Adjustment

This is Your Organization!   Let Us Help You!
BRING ALL YOUR TROUBLES TO US

Greater New York Headquarters:
4951 BROADWAY, N. Y. C.
at 207th Street
Open from 9 A. M. until Midnight

DO NOT JOIN

The Communists, Workers' Alliance or so called American Labor Party whose Leader is Alex Ross alias Olesh Royz, a Polish Jew, born in Warsaw, Poland, living in Our Country about 15 years.
See N. Y. Sun, June 27, 1938

AWAKE CHRISTIAN AMERICANS
JOIN TO-DAY!!
CHRISTIAN WORKERS' ALLIANCE

STATEMENT OF NATIONAL LEADER FRITZ KUHN

OF THE

GERMAN AMERICAN BUND

New York, June 1st, 1939.

The relentless campaign of public enlightenment, which the German American Bund has been carrying on since its inception, and which has been continued with undiminished force since I became its National Leader in 1936, has been so successful in unmasking the true enemies of the U. S. A. and in stimulating effective anti-Marxist activity on the part of other American Groups, as to move our enemies to go to unheard of lengths in their desperate attempts to cripple us.

Despite a long sequence of federal, state and municipal investigations and sundry trumped-up court cases, NOTHING dishonorable, treasonable or in any way disloyal has been shown against the Bund, its subdivisions, related organizations or myself.

In the search for material which could possibly be used against me, UNLAWFUL methods were employed to seize books and records by District Attorney Thomas E. Dewey's office. On May 2nd, during my absence in Los Angeles, his men **broke into my private office without a search warrant** and took whatever they could lay their hands on! No one other than myself had a key to my office. The sum of thirteen hundred and eighty ($1380.00) dollars disappeared from my desk. No one seems to know what became of it.

This breaking and entering was entirely unlawful, undertaken in the face of outraged protests by several officers of the Bund who were present. Not content with this, agents of Mr. Dewey went so far as to similarly violate the homes of two Bund Officers and my own home. One of the residences thus raided was not even in New York County!

Now this **illegally** confiscated material is being studied in hopes that a "case" against me may be constructed.

For weeks previous to my apprehension the daily press had been prophecying my imminently impending arrest. Was this in the hope that I by any chance would flee and thus give the impression of guilt?

I have been constantly available to the District Attorney's office and awaited arrest in my office for days. My trip to Chicago on May 25th was undertaken with the express consent and knowledge of the District Attorney's office, which had been informed as to when and where I and the Bund Officers accompanying me were going.

The reports indicating an attempted get-away on my part are therefore obviously inspired untruths, affording the reader an excellent insight into the workings of the smearing campaign in progress against me. A telephone call from the authorities would have sufficed to keep me in New York and the "exciting motor chase into Pennsylvania" would not have been necessary.

As regards the charges: I declare on my word of honor that I am innocent! Does this action against me represent a persecution, the explanation of which must be looked for in the field of politics?

1. All monies collected and which were turned over to me will be duly accounted for.
2. I have not spent a single cent of the Bund's money in any manner other than as authorized by the National Convention of the Bund.
3. The absurd statements of some of the newspapers, to the effect that I have been planning a divorce or even a separation from my family are so ridiculous as not to require any denial or explanation from me.
4. Contrary to public statements, I have never in my life undertaken any unlawful activity and have never, in this Country, in Germany or elsewhere, been in conflict with the authorities.

It is perfectly clear to me that no means will be eschewed by our opponents to "eliminate" me, and that not being possible in a lawful manner, the press is beginning to make use of the basest weapons conceivable to morally destroy me, to blacken my good name!

I also am aware, however, that all upright and honest Citizens of every race or creed, realize that I am being persecuted and defamed because I am the Leader of the German American Bund, and that it will not be long before the growing number of similarly outspoken and courageous, patriotic Organizations will be treated in the same manner!

The hundreds of encouraging letters reaching me, are proof of a rapidly growing appreciation of the meaning of the vicious attacks to which I am being subjected.

I am not dreaming of running away. On the contrary; I shall fight for my rights and shall carry the struggle against all subversive elements forward as never before, until a truly FREE AMERICA is again achieved!

Signed, FRITZ KUHN.

OUR FIGHT IS YOUR FIGHT!

SUPPORT THE GERMAN AMERICAN BUND

Information: P. O. Box 1, Station K, New York, N. Y. or:..

Appeal to Friends . . . .
of
FRITZ KUHN
and others who want to have a
Great Wrong Righted
by contributing to the
APPEAL FUND
now being raised to secure his release from prison.
To give him back to his wife and children.

● You may know the cost of an appeal will be $1500.00. Your contributions will be confidential and most gratefully received.

All the money over the amount needed will be given to some Worthy Charity, designated by the Committee or Fritz Kuhn.   THANKS A LOT.

Contributions may be forwarded to the Secretary-Treasurer or Mrs. E. Kuhn, by check, money-order or cash.

Argument for Appeal is coming up in September, 1940
t
Fritz Kuhn Appeal Fund   MRS. E. KUHN, Pres.
3303 Third Avenue   FRED. W. YOCKEL, Sec'y-Treas.
Bronx, N. Y.   CHIEF NEW MOON, Solicitor.

Fritz Kuhn, left, and August Klapprott, right, July 30, 1939, Camp Nordland.

FRITZ JULIUS KUHN

Heinz Spanknoebel was the leader of the Hitler Movement in the United States in 1930. In 1933 a new group was formed called Friends of the New Germany after Hitler became Chancellor. Spanknoebel was indicted for being a German agent and Fritz Julius Kuhn was handpicked by the German government to take over as the Bundesführer, or leader. Kuhn was a short, paunchy man with a thick German accent and little patience. He was born in Munich, Germany in 1896 and served in a Bavarian Army unit in World War I. He became a chemist after the war and moved to Mexico in 1934 where he married his wife, Elsa, who he knew from Munich. They later moved to the United States, settling in Detroit where Kuhn became an American citizen. Kuhn worked at Ford's River Rouge automobile plant but took a leave of absence to work full-time for the Friends of New Germany. The name was changed to The German-American League and, in 1936, to The German-American Bund. It was thought Henry Ford might have helped the Bund financially as he was a known anti-Semite. Kuhn soon built the Bund into a national organization with locals in many large cities and a membership, (estimates vary) of up to several hundred thousand. In 1937 Kuhn ousted Walter Kappe, the organizer of Operation Pastorius in 1942, from the editor's post at the official Bund newspaper, *The Deutscher Weokrus and Beobachter*. On May 2, 1939, Kuhn's office was raided by police officers under a warrant issued by District Attorney Thomas Dewey. Kuhn was charged with the embezzlement of Bund funds and on December 6, he was convicted and sentenced to two-and-a-half to five years in prison. The Bund's second-in-command, Gerhard Wilhelm Kunze, took over. Kuhn would mount a campaign to try and prove his innocence after his arrest and conviction and he appealed to his friends from the Bund, but to no avail. He was sent to the Kenedy Alien Detention Camp in Kenedy, Texas. He, along with 12 German sailors from the *Graff Spee,* executed an escape from the camp, but were soon caught.

After the war, Kuhn's citizenship was revoked and he was sent back to Germany where he died in Munich in December 1951.

Fritz Kuhn, right, and Herman Schwinn, left, review Bund members at Camp Siegfried in 1937. Scenes like this could have been taken in Hitler's Germany, or Mussolini's Italy or Franco's Spain in the 1930s. NA

Bund members came from all walks of life, from the very young to senior citizens, as can be seen from these three photographs and the one at the top of the next page. The young were sent to various summer camps for Nazi indoctrination, and this was here in the United States! The Bund was by far the largest and most visible subversive organization in the country before America entered World War II. Remnants of the organization lasted into 1942 and many of the German spies and saboteurs who came to the U.S. in the 1930s and early '40s were past members. NA

Sports at the summer youth camps was a major activity.

A German Day celebration in 1936.

A German-American Bund youth rally. Notice the Nazi flag was usually exhibited with the U.S. flag to portray the supposed solidarity between the two nations. Youth groups were a major function of the Bund. NA

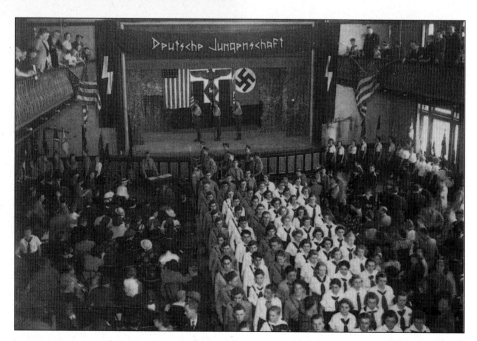

MADISON SQUARE GARDEN RALLY – FEBRUARY 20, 1939

OUTCRY EVEN BEFORE THE rally was strong. Numerous people wrote to Mayor LaGuardia or signed petitions asking that the City revoke the permit or license to hold the event. Protests also came from German social clubs. The Friends of German Democracy–most members were WWI veterans of the German Army and Navy–asked that the rally be cancelled, and claimed that the rally organizers were fronts for a "regime of horror and persecution, of murder, and extortion." The German-American League for

Culture–Eastern District protested that "the Bund tends to identify millions of loyal citizens with its un-American principles of race-hatred and dictatorship" and wanted the mass meeting stopped.

Because the rally was to be held in a privately owned hall, no special permits were needed, so the mayor couldn't withhold a permit to stop the event. Chicago and San Francisco were scheduled to host similar rallies but did manage to prevent them.

The Socialist Workers Party and others complained afterward about police brutality against the protestors, while Nazi-sympathizers enjoyed police protection. Although Mayor LaGuardia later claimed that "reports of improper action by [the police] are entirely unfounded," the Socialists noted that dozens of picketers were brutally assaulted and a number of them were clubbed.

JOIN IN
A Mass Demonstration
For True Americanism!
Monday, February 20th, 1939
at
MADISON SQUARE GARDEN
Tickets Sold in Advance Only – Order Yours Now!
GERMAN AMERICAN BUND   New York, N. Y.
178 East 85th St., Room 6

Bundesführer Fritz Kuhn spoke before 22,000 people at the Bund's largest rally in Madison Square Garden, New York City, on Feb. 20, 1939. A huge figure of George Washington dominated the stage as 1,200 Bund Storm Troopers marched into the hall to the sound of drums and *Sieg Heils*.

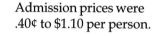

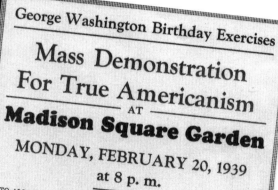

Admission prices were
.40¢ to $1.10 per person.

PRO - AMERICAN RALLY

MASS-DEMONSTRATION FOR TRUE AMERICANISM

FEB. 20TH 1939 MADISON SQUARE GARDEN GERMAN AMERICAN

George Washington Birthday Exercises

Mass Demonstration
For True Americanism
— AT —
Madison Square Garden

MONDAY, FEBRUARY 20, 1939
at 8 p. m.

TO ALL AMERICAN PATRIOTS:

The increasingly violent, malicious and poisonous attempts to silence and cripple the German American Bund by lying press and radio propaganda, by attempted riots and coercion of hall-owners, by strikes to force dismissal of Bund-Members from their employment and by fraudulent indictments and convictions, (remember the "Camp Siegfried" Case at Riverhead, which ended in a reversal of the convictions by higher courts and the complete exoneration of the defendants!), prove that the communistic and other subversive, Jewish-Marxistic powers directing these persecutions are in mortal fear of the Bund's red scourge! These persecutions prove definitely that the German American Bund IS the most outspoken and uncompromising and therefore the most EFFECTIVE Opponent of all Atheistic Subversion in the Country today!

The Bund is an Organization of American Citizens unequivocally committed to the Defense of the Flag, Constitution and Sovereignty of these United States and therefore to the Defense of the right and duty to proportionate representation in the conduct of the Nation of the more than 100,000,000 Aryan (WHITE GENTILE) Americans, as being the ONLY means of preserving the Independence and the Christian Culture and Civilization of this our Country!

The usual means of informing the Public NOT being at our disposal, more and more MASS DEMONSTRATIONS are essential to awaken the Nation! The Bund's packed meetings and the record attendance of 35,000 to 40,000 people at its affairs at Camp Siegfried and Camp Nordland prove it to be constantly growing and gaining recognition and support!

We cordially invite you to participate at our PRO-AMERICAN RALLY and George Washington Birthday Exercises at Madison Square Garden on Monday, February 20th, 1939, at 8 P. M. The Doors will be opened at 7 P. M. General Admission 40c, reserved seats 75c and $1.10, Tax incl. Tickets obtainable at 178 East 85th St., Room 6, New York City, BUtterfield 8-8347, 8-8797.

Free America!

German American Bund
P. O. BOX No. 75, STATION K, NEW YORK, N. Y.

A Jewish man named Isadore Greenbaum ran on the stage and was beaten unconscious by the Storm Troopers. He had to be carried off stage by police. The Bund was against Jews, Communists and anyone else who opposed the Nazi regime.

A group photo of a national convention of the Bund. The banner above states: One Nation · One Union · One Leader. This same photo could have been taken just as easily in Germany as in the United States. NA

Another view of a major gathering of male Bund members. A photo such as this should have been considered a serious threat to the U.S. government, as it would be today. NA

Bundesführer Fritz Kuhn parades on stage in front of jack-booted young Bund members. NA

A Bund member sews a flag for the Reading, Pennsylvania, unit in 1934. NA

James Wheeler Hill, a Bund leader in New Jersey, 1938. NA

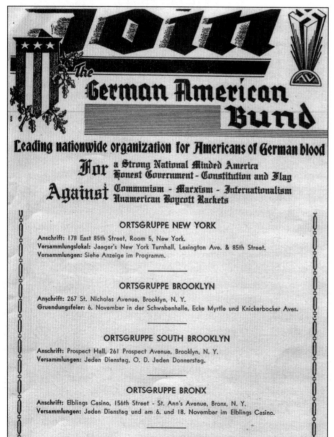

Join the German American Bund

Leading nationwide organization for Americans of German blood

For a Strong National Minded America
Honest Government - Constitution and Flag

Against Communism - Marxism - Internationalism
Unamerican Boycott Rackets

ORTSGRUPPE NEW YORK

Anschrift: 178 East 85th Street, Room 5, New York.
Versammlungslokal: Jaeger's New York Turnhall, Lexington Ave. & 85th Street.
Versammlungen: Siehe Anzeige im Programm.

ORTSGRUPPE BROOKLYN

Anschrift: 267 St. Nicholas Avenue, Brooklyn, N. Y.
Gruendungsfeier: 6. November in der Schwabenhalle, Ecke Myrtle und Knickerbocker Aves.

ORTSGRUPPE SOUTH BROOKLYN

Anschrift: Prospect Hall, 261 Prospect Avenue, Brooklyn, N. Y.
Versammlungen: Jeden Dienstag, O. D. Jeden Donnerstag.

ORTSGRUPPE BRONX

Anschrift: Elblings Casino, 156th Street - St. Ann's Avenue, Bronx, N. Y.
Versammlungen: Jeden Dienstag und am 6. und 18. November im Elblings Casino.

ORTSGRUPPE GLENDALE, L. I.

Anschrift: 105-33 - 134th Street, Richmond Hill, L. I.
Versammlungslokal: Woodward & Gates Avenues, Ridgewood, L. I.

ORTSGRUPPE HUDSON COUNTY

Anschrift: 754 Palisade Avenue, Union City, N. J.
Versammlungslokal: City Hall Tavern, 754 Palisade Avenue, Union City, N. J.
Versammlungen: Jeden Freitag.

ORTSGRUPPE JAMAICA

Anschrift: Saengerbund Hall, 168-15 - 91st Avenue, Jamaica, L. I.
Versammlungen: Jeden Mittwoch um 8.30 abends im obigen Lokal.

ORTSGRUPPE NASSAU COUNTY

Anschrift: German American Bund, 621 Fifth Avenue, New Hyde Park, L. I.

ORTSGRUPPE NEWARK, N. J.

Anschrift: P. O. Box 65, Irvington, N. J.
Versammlungen: Jeden vierten Mittwoch im Monat in der Schwabenhalle, 593 Springfield Avenue, Newark, N. J.
O. D. Zusammenkuenfte: Regelmaessig jeden Freitag im gleichen Lokal.

ORTSGRUPPE NEW ROCHELLE

Anschrift: P. O. Box 724, New Rochelle, N. Y.
Versammlungslokal: Alps Hall, 240 Huguenot Street, New Rochelle, N. Y.
Versammlungen: Jeden 2. Dienstag des Monats.
O. D. und Frauenschaft: Jeden 2. Mittwoch um 8.30 abends.

ORTSGRUPPE STAMFORD—NORWALK, CONN.

Versammlungslokal: Liedertafel Halle, 45 Greyrock Place, Stamford, Conn.
Sprechabende: 2 Mal Monatlich.
Postanschrift: 99 N. Hill Street, Springdale, Conn.

ORTSGRUPPE STATEN ISLAND

Geschaeftsstelle: 15 Florence St., Great Kills, S. I., N. Y.
Versammlungen: Jeden 1. und 3. Freitag des Monats in der Atlantic Rotisserie, 191 Canal St., Stapleton, S. I.
O. D. Zusammenkuenfte: Jeden 2. und 4. Freitag in Alma Guenthers Restaurant, 35 Broad Street, Stapleton.

ORTSGRUPPE WHITE PLAINS

Anschrift: P. O. Box 813 WHITE PLAINS.
Versammlungslokal: Oscars Tavern, North White Plains.

Camp Nordland in New Jersey on German People's Day, 1939. *In der Einheit liegt die Macht* translates to In Unity lies Power. NA

CAMP NORDLAND

ANDOVER, New Jersey

Phone: Newton 9296

SUSSEX COUNTY

●

Winter und Sommer geoeffnet!

Dem Deutschtum gewidmet

Der groesste und schoenste

Ausflug und Erholungsplatz in New Jersey

●

Freunde des Wintersportes herzlich willkommen.

The Bund purchased 200 acres with buildings near Lake Iliff in Andover Township, New Jersey, in 1937. It became Camp Nordland and opened on July 30, 1937, with a parade of 500 Bundists. A "beer blast" was held afterwards. It was estimated that 1,000 residents of New York City and surrounding areas arrived every weekend for political rallies, speeches and recreation. The Bund and Klu Klux Klan held a joint rally at the camp. NA

Inauguration ceremony of new Bund members at Camp Siegfried, June 24, 1939. As with the Nazi party in Germany, the German-American Bund in the United States exploited the young and unemployed during the Great Depression to turn to the extreme right. NA

Twenty thousand Bund members and followers gathered at Camp Siegfried at Yaphank, Long Island, to attend the second annual German Day celebration in 1937. Five hundred half-barrels of beer were consumed at the rally. FDR

Bund members at Camp Siegfried built a mock cannon with a sign that reads: Attention: Speciman of ARMED NAZI MIGHT discovered at Camp Siegfried By Repr. Dickstein Automatically shoots all Bluffers, Liars and Parasites NA

Members of the German American Bund.
German American Men and Women.

Let me extend to each and everyone of you, both from near and afar, a most hearty welcome to our Eastern District Annual Rally. We hope that your stay in our city will be a pleasant one and that you will take back with you an everlasting memory of this day. Let this day imprint in your minds the high ideals for which your bund has fought and suffered.

A year ago we met in Philadelphia and since that day many a battle has been fought with a great success. We are proud to say that we have been the victors. You will remember not so long ago, certain people started a very vicious campaign against our camps. They attacked them in every form and manner, but our organization stood up for its rights and to prove to the American people that this bund is not engaged to spread foreign or unamerican propaganda, we demanded Congress to investigate this organization to satisfy themselves as to the good work that is being done by us.

We have also stated through the press that our aim is to preserve the Constitution of the United States of which we are all proud citizens. Let us again manifest at this rally that we are loyal American citizens and that never at any time would any one of us do anything that would harm our country. As in the past we are going to continue demanding of our fellow citizens and political leaders the right to help build up our country and to help fight international radicalism and bolshivistic propaganda in this country. This, my German American friends, is our aim, although there are people who think we are out to do only evil.

We further wish to emphasize that we will always work to create the most friendly relations between our America and Germany, a nation with whom we are at peace.

Let us at this meeting add one more task to our already numerous ones. Let us protest most emphatically against the unlegal, unconstitutional and unamerican Jewish boycott against German goods and German Services which, in our mind, has harmed to such great extend the American working-men. Let us once more protest against the international poisoners of public minds which has gone so far as to say that we are working to overthrow the Government of the United States. This statement is the most ridiculous of them all. We, like our ancestors have always been loyal and true Americans and we cannot believe that the common sense of our fellow citizens will allow them to take a statement like that seriously.

Our fight will go on regardless what the obstacles will be and in that spirit let us al conduct our "Gautag Ost 1937."

RUDOLF MARKMANN,

Eastern District Leader.

Lend Your Support to the Cause!

ATTEND FOLLOWING IMPORTANT AFFAIRS:

TUESDAY, MAY 18th, 1937
Mass-Meeting

The Edmondson Case

reviewed

JEWS vs. CHRISTIANS IN COURT!

Speakers: George L. Pafort - Franklin Thompson
Fritz Kuhn

8:30 P. M. at Main Ball Room — New York Turnhall

TUESDAY, MAY 25th, 1937

It's Here — At Last!   First showing in New York!

Official Reichssport-Behoerde

OLYMPIA 1936

Sound Motion Picture

Tickets available in advance at the New York Unit Office, 178 E. 85th St.,
Room 5 or at the Yorkville Kanzlei, 208 E. 86th St., New York City
Begin: 8:30 P. M. at the Main Ball Room, New York Turnhall

SATURDAY, MAY 29th, 1937

Comradeship-Night

of the O. D. New York

DANCING — SURPRISES — ENTERTAINMENT

Music by: KURT HEISE and his Eastern Area O.D. Band
Main Ball Room, New York Turnhall   Begin: 8:00 P. M.

Above program subject to change without notice. All affairs are held at
the Main Ball Room of the New York Turnhall, Lexington Avenue and
85th Street, New York City

German American Bund, N. Y. Unit

Office:
178 EAST 85th STREET Room 5
New York City

Mail Address:
P. O. BOX 75, Sta. "K"
New York, N. Y.

The New Germany Under Hitler

Its Political, Social, Economic and Nationalistic Aspects
as Reflected by the Testimony of Foreign Observers,
Writers and Statesmen.

Edited by

Frederick Franklin Schrader

Author of "The Germans in the Making of America",
"German-American Handbook", "1683-1920", Etc.

Published by

Deutscher Weckruf und Beobachter

P. O. Box 24—Station K.

New York, N. Y.

PRICE, 15 CENTS

We Must Stay out of Europe's Wars and Hatreds

"No Ism but Americanism"

ANTI-WAR RALLY

UNDER THE AUSPICES OF THE

Protestant War Veterans

OF THE

United States Inc.

EDWARD J. SMYTHE

National Commander, Presiding

Protestant Chaplains Association	Patriotic Order Founders of America
Ladies Auxillary of the Protestant War Veterans of the U.S.	Loyal Order of Americans
	Federation of Christian Americans
American Patriots	United Christian Front

MASS MEETING

Friday Eve Sept. 22nd

EBLING'S CASINO MAIN BALLROOM

742 St. Anns Ave. at 156th Street

Bronx, N.Y.   8:30 P.M.

Come and Hear....Nationally Known Speakers Who Will Be Announced Later
Sound A Warning To All Americans!

The Youth of America must not be slaughtered again

Admission Free   All Seats Reserved

There were many organizations in the U.S. that ran counter to the principles of the Bund and other subversive groups. The Louis-Schmeling fights evolved into more of political battles than sports fights. German fighter, Max Schmeling knocked out Black fighter, Joe Louis on June 19, 1936, in the 12th round. Schmeling was hailed as a hero and an example of Nazi ideals. In a rematch on June 22, 1938, in New York City, Louis knocked out Schmeling in the 1st round. Schmeling returned to Germany the fallen hero.

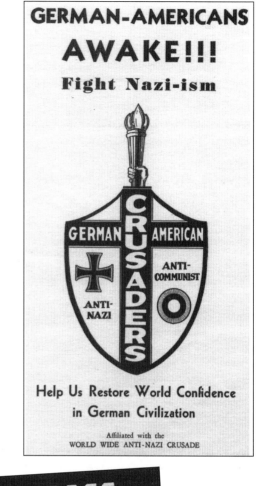

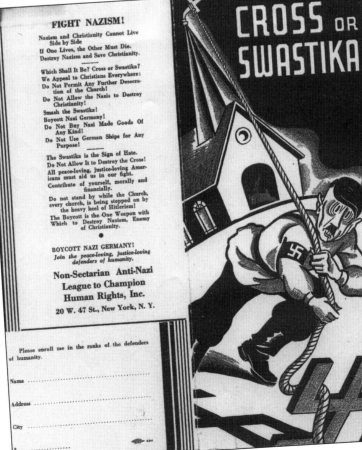

SPIES AND SABOTEURS IN THE UNITED STATES

DURING THE 1930s AND early 1940s hundreds of German spies and sympathizers roamed the United States gathering military, industrial and even personal information. By many methods, (radios, letters to third parties in Portugal, and even diplomatic courier) this information was sent to the Abwebr, (German Military Intelligence Service) in Germany.

In addition, there were thousands of German-Americans who sympathized with the new Nazi government. Many belonged to the German-American Bund or several other neo-Nazi organizations in the United States. Most of the members of Operation Pastorius, (the 1942 landings in New York and Florida), were members of the Bund during their stay in the United States.

It is beyond the scope of this book to follow every spy or sympathizer who operated in this country, but a few of the more important ones are described within. Two stories, which involve some of the most important pre-war German spies, are included as they have a connection to author Stan Cohen's hometown, Missoula, Montana. There are many good books on the major German spy rings that operated in the United States that the reader can obtain for a fuller understanding of the menace that these groups poised to the security of all the American people.

A POSSIBLE GERMAN SABOTAGE EFFORT

The 1939 New York World's Fair held at Flushing Meadows, Corona Park was so successful that it was opened again in 1940. By this time Germany had invaded Poland and World War II was in full swing. Germany was excluded from participating in the 1940 fair.

Shortly after 3:00 p.m. on July 4, 1940, an electrician at the British pavilion on the fairgrounds discovered a ticking suitcase on the pavilion's third floor. Members of the New York Police Department's Bomb and Forgery Squad were called in to assess the situation.

Detective Joseph Lynch of the squad carefully carried the suitcase out of the pavilion and placed it on a grassy area away from people. Another de-

tective named Ferdinand Socha was close by. Lynch carefully opened the suitcase and told his partner, Socha, "This looks like the real goods." The suitcase immediately exploded, killing Lynch and Socha and severely injuring two other detectives standing close by. There was not enough left of the suitcase to trace the bomb's makers.

It was speculated that a German spy or possibly a Nazi sympathizer set the bomb. The mystery remains today as to who actually placed the suitcase in the pavilion.

A plaque to the memory of the two dead detectives is located on a stone a few feet from the front entrance of the Queens Museum of Art at the world's fair site at Flushing Meadows Park.

ADMIRAL WILHELM CANARIS AND THE ABWEHR

GERMANY'S MAIN MILITARY INTELLIGENCE service most commonly used it abbreviated name, "Abwehr," (the Intelligence Department of the German Armed Forces High Command). When Admiral Canaris became its head in January 1935, he began the make-over of the service. He set up three different functional groups. The old *Geheimer Meldedienst,* charged with secret service, gathering intelligence and conducting espionage, was enlarged and became Group I. Group II was established to conduct sabotage operations, foment insurrections and spread false information in foreign countries (this section was in charge of the landings on America's east coast). Group III was responsible for counterespionage.

The head of Abwehr was born on Jan. 1, 1887, near Dortmund, Germany. He entered the Imperial Naval Academy in Kiel in 1905 and went to sea during World War I. His career in the next few years reads like an adventure novel. He was caught in the Battle of the Falkland Islands and was interned in Chile. He escaped to Argentina, and, in the guise of a young Chilean named Reed Rosas, took passage on a Dutch ship to Rotterdam. He eventually got to Hamburg, Germany and was subsequently sent to Spain on his first spy mission.

In February 1916, while attempting to return to Germany to train for U-boat service, he was arrested in Italy (at that time at war with Germany) and held as a suspected spy. He escaped from prison by killing the prison padre and returned to Spain. He spent the rest of the war in U-boat and other naval service.

After the war he remained in the navy but was involved in many political intrigues, including the attempt to undermine the Weimar Republic. He welcomed Hitler's takeover of the government in 1933. During World War II, Canaris increased the Abwehr's network staff tenfold and obtained sweeping powers in the Nazi bureaucracy including close friendships with SS Chief Heinrick Himmler and SD Chief Reinhard Heydrich. As the war progressed, however, Canaris became disillusioned with the Nazi regime and worked behind the scenes against it. After the July 20, 1944 plot to kill Hitler, Canaris was arrested and sent to Flossenberg concentration camp where he was executed on April 9, 1945, just weeks before the camp was liberated. The Abwehr dissolved after July 20 and its operations were taken over by Himmler's SS.

Canaris walking to Hitler's office on the Russian front on June 30, 1942, to explain the capture of the Operation Pastorius saboteurs three days earlier. With him are two key aides, Gen. Erwin Lahousen (left), the Abwehr's head of sabotage, and Col. Hans Piekenbrock, the Abwehr's chief of espionage. PHPC

Admiral Wilhelm Canaris. PHPC

Gerhard Wilhelm Kunze was very active in the German-American Bund and would succeed the defrocked Fritz Kuhn as the Bund's new Fuehrer (leader) in 1940. Kunze was also in the employ of the German Abwehr II and a confidant of Willumeit. In July 1942 he was arrested by the FBI and sentenced to 15 years in Federal prison. NA

Otto Willumeit was the Chicago German-American Bund leader in 1940 and an agent of the German Abwehr. He was arrested in 1940 and pleaded guilty to espionage charges and sentenced to serve five years in Federal prison. NA

Otto Herrmann Voss was a German aircraft mechanic who had spied for his native land since the late 1920s. In the 1930s he worked for the Seversky Aircraft Company, the builder of U.S. Army Air Corps airplanes. In 1938 he was fingered by the elusive spy Ignatz Griebl and eventually sentenced to six years in Federal prison for stealing plans for army aircraft. NA

Erich Glaser was a 28-year-old army private and a native of Germany. Rumrich knew him in the Panama Canal Zone. In 1937 Glaser was stationed at Mitchel Field on Long Island and supplied Rumrich with the army's confidential "Z-code" which was being used in communications between the navy's fleet and shore batteries on America's coast. He was arrested by the FBI along with other German spies in June 1938 and sentenced to Federal prison. NA

GREATEST SPY ROUNDUP IN U. S. HISTORY PRODUCES A GREAT GALLERY OF FACES

TITLE I, Sec. 2 (a) *Whoever, with intent or reason to believe that it is to be used to the injury of the United States or to the advantage of a foreign nation, communicates, delivers, or transmits . . . to any foreign government . . . any document, writing, code book, signal book, sketch, photograph, photographic negative, blue print, plan, map, model, note, instrument, appliance, or information relating to the national defense, shall be pun-*ished by imprisonment for not more than twenty years.

Since the Espionage Act containing this provision was passed in 1917, only 19 people have been convicted of violating it. The fascinating collection of faces on these pages belong to 32 men and women who, in a concerted FBI swoop, were arrested under it last week. Five were already in jail for other offenses. The eleven marked with asterisks promptly removed all doubts

"SPY"

Frederick Joubert Duquesne, 63, called "professional spy" by Hoover, claims to have plotted the sinking of Kitchener's cruiser in 1916.

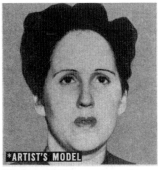

*ARTIST'S MODEL

Lilly Barbara Stein, 26, was born in Vienna. Ex-U. S. Vice Consul Ogden H. Hammond Jr. once denied improper relations with her.

*PORTER

Axel Wheeler-Hill, 40, Russian-born brother of jailed Bund Leader James Wheeler-Hill, had short-wave transmitter in apartment.

*STEWARD

Adolph Henry Walischewsky, 50, German-born American, steward on SS *Uruguay,* was courier for agents in U. S. and Latin America.

MACHINIST

Carl Reuper, 37, German-born American, worked for Westinghouse Electric in Jersey City, N. J. helped to found the German-American Alliance.

*WAITER

Erich Strunck, 31, of 1809 East Olive St., Milwaukee, is a U. S. citizen born in Altona, Germany. He was a waiter on the SS *Siboney.*

BUSINESSMAN

Edmund Carl Heine, 50, U. S. citizen born in Zeulenroda, Germany, represented Ford and Chrysler companies in Germany and Spain.

*BAKER

Franz Stigler, 34, German-born American formerly chief baker on the SS *America,* was arrested last month on Registration charge.

SHIPPING CLERK

Rudolf Ebeling, 42, born in Wittenstock, Germany, became a U. S. citizen and was living in New York's Yorkville district when arrested.

*PAINTER

Leo Waalen, German citizen born in Danzig on Dec. 7, 1907, was described by Hoover as a "particularly active member" of the spy ring.

BARBER

Oscar R. Stabler, 36, was born in Stuttgart, Germany, became U. S. citizen, lived in Brooklyn, was ship's barber on the SS *Excambion.*

IRONWORKER

Paul Bante, 50, a U. S. citizen born in Lennup, Germany, also worked as a tool and die maker, a good trade for learning defense secrets.

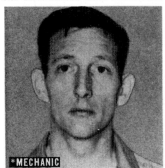

*MECHANIC

Alfred E. Brokhoff, 39, a U. S. citizen born in Bielefeld, Germany, could watch ship movements while he worked on U. S. Lines piers.

*SEAMAN

Hartwig Richard Kleiss, 44, U. S. citizen who was born-in Frankfurt, Germany, worked on the *President Harding, Manhattan, America.*

*ENGINEER

Everett Minster Roeder, 47, New York-born, worked for Sperry Gyroscope Co. Inc., maker of bombsights, other vital defense devices.

COOK

Paul Fehse, 51, a German citizen, pleaded guilty to violating Federal Registration Act last April, was sentenced to year in Atlanta.

Life Magazine's July 14, 1941 issue had a two-page spread on a roundup of a major spy ring in the United States.

about their identity as spies by pleading guilty as charged.

Properly proud of the patient, dangerous, two-year investigation which led to the arrests, FBI Chief J. Edgar Hoover called it the greatest spy roundup in U. S. history. Chary of revealing details until he had placed his evidence before a grand jury, he even omitted to name the "foreign government" to which

they were accused of passing on U. S. defense secrets. But he did point out that 25 of them were born in Germany. All but five of these were naturalized citizens.

Headquarters of the ring, said Mr. Hoover, was the nondescript Little Casino Bar Restaurant on East 85th Street in New York's German-populated Yorkville. One member of the ring, a Viennese-born artist's model named Lilly Barbara Carola Stein, was said to have

moved in New York "social circles." But most moved in the humble circles where spies really do the most good: in defense factories, on waterfronts where ship movements can be observed, on ships or planes by which information can be carried and spy pay brought back. Mastermind of the ring, according to Mr. Hoover, was Frederick Joubert Duquesne, 63, whose checkered career of anti-British intrigue dates back to the Boer War.

MACHINIST

Herman Lang, 39, a German-born American, worked for Carl L. Norden, Inc. as inspector of the famed super-secret Norden bombsights.

PHOTOGRAPHER

Josef August Klein, 37, commercial photographer born in Düsseldorf, Germany, had taken out his first papers to become a U. S. citizen.

CONVICT

Bertram Wolfgang Zenzinger, 36, Austrian-born Briton, was given 18-month jail sentence last April for violating the Registration Act.

CAFE OWNER

Richard Eichenlaub, 36, U. S. citizen born in Herxheim, Germany, was proprietor of Little Casino Restaurant, alleged ring headquarters.

CARPENTER

George Gottlob Schuh, 54, U. S. citizen born in Hochdorf, Germany, was a camper at German-American Bund's Camp, Nordland, N. J.

MUSICIAN

Heinrich Stade of 604 West 140th St., New York City, was born in Hanover, Germany, on Jan. 3, 1901, is a naturalized U. S. citizen.

BOOK SALESMAN

Paul A. W. Scholz, 41, a German citizen born at Reichenbach, sold books for the Germania Book and Specialty Co. of New York City.

*STEWARD

Conradin Otto Dold, 37, German-born American, second steward on SS *Excalibur*, was arrested as ship reached New York from Lisbon.

COOK

Heinrich Clausing, 33, German-born American, vegetable cook on SS *Argentina*, was put in brig as his ship docked at Santos, Brazil.

STENOGRAPHER

Else Weustenfeld, 42, U. S. citizen born in Essen, Germany, worked at German Consulate in New York, was called a ring paymaster.

*BUTCHER

Erwin Wilhelm Siegler, 31, a German-born American, ex-chief butcher on *America*, was arrested last month on Registration charge.

SODA JERKER

Felix Jahnke, 38, was born in Breslau, Germany. If guilty, this soda jerker living in The Bronx had a practically perfect camouflage.

*STEWARD

Rene Mezenen, 36, American citizen born in Paris, steward on transatlantic planes, was arrested last month for smuggling platinum.

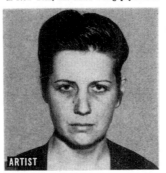

ARTIST

Evelyn Clayton Lewis, 38, born in Fayetteville, Ark., calls herself an artist, sculptress and playwright, lived at Duquesne's address.

STEWARD

Heinrich C. Eilers, 42, German-born American, former library steward on SS *Manhattan*, was called chief of ring's transatlantic couriers.

CLERK

Max Blank, 38, German citizen, was employed at the German Library of Information which President Roosevelt recently ordered closed.

Headlines such as this would be common in American newspapers in the 1930s and early 1940s.

Seattle Post-Intelligencer

SEATTLE, MONDAY, OCTOBER 17, 1938

TWENTY PAGES — DAILY 5c, SUNDAY 10c

VOL. CXV, NO. 45

U. S. NABS 4 GERMANS AS SPIES

Planes Crash in Mid-Air; 5 Die

NAZIS CAUGHT WITH CAMERA IN CANAL FORT

Quartet Permitted to Enter Fortified Area at Panama, Then Are Held by Soldiers

GLARE OF SUN BLAMED FOR AIR TRAGEDY

Ruth Etting Blames Jealousy in Shooting

Former Husband Declares He Fired in Defense

BRITISH LAUNCH NEW DRIVE TO CRUSH ARABS

Lake Dragged For Missing Boy, 7

Child Last Seen Playing on Wharf

JAPAN ADVANCE TO KEY RAILWAY LINE REPORTED

Hitler Scored By Churchill In Talk

British Leader Urges Strong Stand

Johanna Hofmann was a 27-year-old hairdresser on the German passenger liner *SS Europa* and a member of Rumrich's spy ring. She was a courier for the ring between the U.S. and Germany. She was arrested by the FBI in June 1938 and sentenced to four years in Federal prison. NA

RENE MEZENEN, TRANSATLANTIC CLIPPER STEWARD AND A MEMBER OF THE DUQUESNE SPY RING. ALL PICTURES TAKEN BY FBI AGENTS WITH THE EXCEPTION OF THE INDIVIDUAL PHOTOGRAPH OF MEZENEN IN UNIFORM.

Rene' Mezenen was a steward on a Pan American Airways clipper aircraft and a courier for the Duquesne spy ring. On the left are FBI movie stills of Seabold's "prop" office in Manhattan. NA

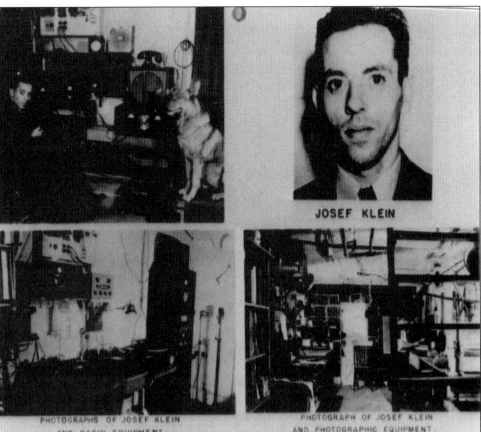

JOSEF KLEIN

PHOTOGRAPHS OF JOSEF KLEIN
AND RADIO EQUIPMENT.
PHOTOGRAPH FOUND IN KLEIN'S APARTMENT
WHEN ARRESTED.

PHOTOGRAPH OF JOSEF KLEIN
AND PHOTOGRAPHIC EQUIPMENT.
PHOTOGRAPH FOUND IN KLEIN'S APARTMENT
WHEN ARRESTED.

Josef Klein, a commercial photographer, was another member of the Duquesne spy ring who operated a short wave radio and had photographic equipment in his Manhattan apartment in 1941. NA

Dr. Wolfgang Ebell was a naturalized American citizen practicing medicine in El Paso, Texas, in 1940. He was a confidante of Otto Willumeit and was involved with passing vital information to Nazi conspirators in Mexico. He was arrested by the FBI in early 1942 and sentenced to seven years in Federal prison. NA

Laura Ingalls was an eccentric but prominent social-ite, aviatrix, actress and dancer. She was a rabid anti-war activist in the late 1930s and used her airplane to drop anti-war leaflets, even over the White House. She also became part of a German spy organization. In early 1942, the FBI picked her up along with other suspected German spies. Ingalls was sentenced to a prison term of from eight months to two years for failure to register as a Nazi agent. She was sent to the Women's Federal Penitentiary in Alderson, West Virginia. NA

While not a spy per se, Max Stephen, seen here between two U.S. Federal officers was the first American to be found guilty of treason since 1794. Stephen was a naturalized U.S. citizen whose Detroit restaurant was a gathering place for members of the German-American Bund. He was convicted in 1942 of helping an escaped Luftwaffe pilot prisoner-of-war from Canada with money and an escape plan to Mexico. Lt. Hans Peter Krug escaped from a POW camp in Ontario, made his way to Windsor, Ontario, and crossed the Detroit River to Detroit, Michigan. Stephen bought Krug a bus ticket to Chicago from where he would proceed in stages to the Mexican border. A hotel clerk in San Antonio recognized Krug from an FBI wanted poster and called the police. Stephen was sentenced to death but President Roosevelt commuted his sentence to life imprisonment. NA

GUENTHER GUSTAV RUMRICH "CROWN"

GUENTHER GUSTAV RUMRICH IN 1938 was known by his German codename "Crown." He was born on Dec. 8, 1911 in Chicago to Austrian parents. In 1913, his father, an Austro-Hungarian diplomat, was transferred from Chicago to Germany and Guenther grew up in the aftermath of World War I. Being a natural-born American citizen, he moved back to the United States in 1929 and worked at various jobs until he joined the U.S. Army in 1930.

After six months of service, he deserted. Guenther was soon broke and turned himself in as a deserter and was sentenced to six months in a military prison.

Released after four months, the army took him back and he became a surgical technician. He was posted to duty in the Panama Canal zone and after promotion to sergeant was sent to the army hospital at Fort Missoula, Missoula, Montana, which was treating Civilian Conservation Corps enrollees.

His six months in Missoula was marked by living beyond his army salary and getting married to a 16-year-old girl who lived near the fort. Rumrich began stealing money from the hospital fund and near discovery, he again deserted the army and his new wife and eventually wound up in New York City.

After his arrest on Feb. 27, 1938, the FBI pieced together enough evidence to determine Rumrich was actually the elusive "Crown" they had been aware of for some time. Rumrich finally decided the game was up and after several days and nights of questioning, he confessed to being "Crown" and implicated his other agents in the U.S.

Eighteen persons were indicted for spying for Germany on June 20, 1938, by a federal grand jury. Only four, including Rumrich were in custody. On Oct. 14, 1938, the four were tried in New York City and found guilty. Johanna Hoffmann was sentenced to four years in federal prison, Otto Voss to six years, Erich Glaser to two years and Rumrich, because of his cooperation with the government, to two years.

Rumrich's wife, who he had brought to New York after he was established as a spy, moved back to her Missoula, Montana home with their two children and divorced him.

Rumrich died in the Buffalo, New York area in 1983.

Guenther Gustav Rumrich. NA

After Rumrich's arrest, an FBI search of his apartment turned up a letter from Rumrich inviting an army buddy, Erich Glaser, to become a spy. Glaser was also arrested.

HOSPITAL MISSOULA. MONT.

The army hospital at Fort Missoula in the 1930s. It still stands and houses a mental health clinic. PHPC

- 27 -

KURT LUDWIG*

As a result of the investigation instituted by the Federal Bureau of Investigation in January of 1941, Kurt Frederick Ludwig, an established German spy operating in the United States, and eight of his associates were sentenced to terms of imprisonment ranging from five to 20 years after their convictions on charges of espionage in the United States District Court in New York City in March 1942.

Exhaustive efforts were continued by the Federal Bureau of Investigation to determine the identity of the individual designating himself as (censored). The first big break in the solution of the case occurred on March 18, 1941, when two men, one a tall middle-aged person wearing horn-rimmed spectacles and carrying a brown brief case, attempted to cross a busy street in the vicinity of Times Square in New York City. The middle-aged man carelessly stepped in front of a taxi and was fatally injured. His companion, apparently unconcerned over the fate of his friend, grabbed the brown brief case and swiftly disappeared into the crowd. The injured man, it was ascertained, was Julio Lopez Lido, and his body, unclaimed for a time, was finally buried by the Spanish Consulate in New York. The unknown man who ran from the scene of the accident called the hotel of his injured companion and asked that the room used by him be kept intact until further notice. In the meantime, the local authorities were notified by the hotel management and they began checking the mysterious circumstances surounding the traffic accident. Coming upon material in the hotel room confirming the mystery involved in the death of Lido, the officials notified the FBI immediately and thereby another missing link was discovered in the case which began at Bermuda two months earlier. Lido was none other than Capt. Ulrich von der Osten, a Nazi army officer who had come to the United States by way of Japan only a month prior to his death to direct the activities of a group of spies in the United States. Kurt Frederick Ludwig, an Ohio-born pocketbook maker, was the individual who ran from the scene of the accident with von der Osten's brief case. He stepped in and filled the shoes of the master spy whose career was cut short on the fateful evening of March 18, 1941.

As a result of laboratory examinations conducted by the FBI on specimens from Ludwig's typewriter and specimens of his handwriting, he was identified as the Nazi agent who had been reporting to his principals in the German Reich the number of cargo ships, troop ships, the number, condition, armament and

Kurt Frederick Ludwig. PHPC

location of the United States armed forces and other items of extreme interest and value regarding the United States.

Captain Ulrich von der Osten was in fact one of the chiefs of the German intelligence service among whose duties it was to establish contact with individual agents operating throughout the world. En route to the United States from Shanghai he had reported detailed information concerning national defense preparations of the United States at Pearl Harbor and other vital points in the Hawaiian Islands. In his report on the Hawaiian Islands he mentioned that this information would be of particular interest to "our yellow Allies." This report of von der Osten, fortunately, failed to reach its destination and was ultimately turned over to the FBI.

Captain Ulrich von der Osten.
NA

Following von der Osten's demise Ludwig continued his efforts at securing espionage information for the Reich with greater fervor. His movements were watched by the FBI in order that the full ramifications of his activities might be disclosed. He made a practice of visiting the docks in New York Harbor and along the Jersey coast where, from his observations, he could report information to Germany concerning the identities of ships and the nature of their cargoes. He also visited various Army posts in the vicinity of New York City where he observed the strength of our armed forces, the identities of various armed units, the quality and quantity of the arms with which they were equipped, and other details which he believed would be of interest and value to his principals abroad.

On one occasion during May of 1941, he took an extended trip to Florida at which time he was accompanied by Lucy Boehmler, an eighteen-year-old girl of German nativity who acted as his "secretary" and

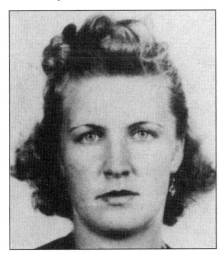

Lucy Boehmler. NA

as a matter of fact assisted him in preparing the secret messages to his superiors and in maintaining detailed records covering his observations. On the trip they availed themselves of every opportunity to pass through Army camps, aviation fields and industrial centers engaged in manufacturing wartime needs.

Upon reaching Miami, Ludwig contacted Carl Herman Schroetter who had been anticipating the call as a result of instructions he had received from a Dr. Ottis during a visit to Germany two years before. It was through Schroetter that Ludwig was able to report to Germany concerning the progress being made in the construction of naval air base facilities in the vicinity of Miami.

Ludwig was assisted in obtaining information to be forwarded to his principals abroad by Rene C. Froehlich, an enlisted man in the United States Army

stationed at Governors Island in New York Harbor. Froehlich in fact assisted Ludwig to the extent of handling his mail which was received through a post office box during Ludwig's absence from the city.

Mrs. Helen Pauline Mayer had previously assisted Ludwig in securing information regarding aircraft construction from plants located on Long Island. Her husband had tried to return to Germany by way of Japan and was apparently stranded in Japan due

Helen Pauline Mayer. NA

to the entrance of Russia into the present conflict. Mrs. Mayer in fact was preparing to follow her husband at the time she was apprehended in connection with her activities resulting in her association with Ludwig.

Hans Helmut Pagel and Frederick Edward Schlosser, two youths of German nativity and Nazi ideologies, also assisted Ludwig in making observations of various docks and military establishments in the vicinity of New York City and in mailing communications to the mail drops abroad.

Karl Victor Mueller was also closely associated with Ludwig and assisted him in mailing letters to foreign addresses for ultimate delivery to Germany.

Last, but not least, of Ludwig's associates in connection with his espionage pursuits was Major Paul Borchardt of the German Army. Borchardt served in the German Army from 1914 until 1933, when he claims to have been discharged because of his non-Aryan extraction. He entered the United States as a refugee, claimed to have escaped from internment in a German concentration camp and to have been aided by friends in fleeing the Reich. Borchardt, however, was found to hold lengthy conferences with Ludwig at Borchardt's residence, a room in an obscure rooming house in New York City, and at the time of Borchardt's apprehension he was found to be in possession of equipment for writing invisible ink messages similar to those transmitted by Ludwig and, in fact, admitted his activities in this regard. During these conferences Ludwig and Borchardt discussed national defense activities in the United States, particularly items believed to be most desired by the Reich, pooling their knowledge, observations and experiences.

During August 1941, Ludwig began a cross-country trek, closely followed by Special Agents of the FBI.

Major Paul Borchardt. NA

He traveled as a hunted man, forcing his car along the country roads through the midwest at a speed of 90 miles an hour. His inborn espionage instincts, however, could not be forgotten and he did not fail to make appropriate note of various Army Camps and other establishments of interest to his superiors. Traveling the lonesome roads across the plains and mountains, however, began to wear on him. He stopped at a cabin in Yellowstone National Park, and apparently because of his fear of being trailed, he endeavored to destroy all incriminating evidence in his possession but was not entirely successful. Proceeding to Missoula, Montana, the next day he stored his automobile, shipped all of his luggage with the exception of bare necessities to relatives in the east and continued his travels to the West Coast by bus. His car was found to have an expensive short wave radio receiver in it.

In view of the indications that Ludwig was contemplating departing from the United States upon reaching the West Coast, apparently in an effort to return to Germany by way of Japan, he was taken into custody by Special Agents of the Federal Bureau of Investigation at Cle Elum, Washington, on Aug. 23, 1941.

Ludwig and his associates were subsequently indicted in Federal Court in New York City on charges of conspiracy to violate the Espionage Statutes. Ludwig, Froehlich and Borchardt received sen-

When Ludwig abandoned his 1941 Ford two door sedan in Missoula, Montana, he left it at Lou's Garage, just behind the local Greyhound Bus Station. After his capture, the FBI came to Missoula to confiscate the radio equipment that was in the trunk of the car. They had no further use for the vehicle so they gave the title to the garage's owner, Lou Croonenberghs. Lou, along with other family members drove the car for years before finally leaving it in a field. In the mid 1980s, Missoula native Craig Dixon bought the car and drove it in stock condition. He eventually did a full body restoration including a Mustang II front end and a Lincoln 9 Ford rear end. He also included disk breaks and a 415-cubic-inch small block Chevrolet engine with aluminum heads. His Montana vanity plates read "I Spy." In the summer of 2002, the car was sold in Reno, Nevada.

tences of 20 years each whereas terms of 15 years each were meted out to Mayer, Mueller and Pagel. Schlosser received a sentence of 12 years while that of Schroetter was 10 years. Lucy Boehmler's term was for five years. Pagel, Schroetter and Boehmler pleaded guilty. The various individuals were sentenced on March 13 and March 24, 1942, and it will be noted that the total sentences amounted to 132 years.

Kurt Fredcrick Ludwig was born in Fremont, Ohio, on Dec. 3, 1903. At the time of his involvement in this case he was approximately five feet and eight inches in height and weighed 140 pounds. His hair was thinning on top and his complexion was slightly ruddy. Ludwig was a fast walker and invariably carried with him a black zipper brief case. He seldom wore a hat.

Ludwig resided in the United States with his parents, who are now deceased, until he was approximately six years of age, when he went to Germany with them. He resided in Munich for several years thereafter and attended the public schools in that city until he was 15 or 16 years of age. He next attended a business school in Munich for several months. According to Ludwig's own statement, prior to his reaching the age of 21, he indicated a desire to remain a United States citizen and thereafter obtained an American passport and returned to the United States in 1924 or 1925. He remained in this country until 1928 and then went back to Germany, returning to the United States in January 1931. He returned to Germany in the fall of 1933 and remained until 1939, when he again came back to the United States. Early in September of 1939, he again left for Germany and remained until March of 1940, when he arrived in New York City.

During the various periods that Ludwig remained in the United States he was employed at intervals by different leather goods companies and worked as a salesman of pocketbooks and various novelties. According to his own statement he was once employed in Munich in the capacity of bookkeeper and manager of a leather company owned by his father.

Very little is known of Ludwig's own background except that he is married, his wife and three children being in Germany. During Ludwig's activities in the United States he was active as a leader in the German Youth Movement in the vicinity of New York City.

In connection with his protracted foreign residence, Ludwig submitted an affidavit in 1937, in which he stated that he lost his job in the United States in 1933 and that his friends in Germany offered him a position there. He alleged that he could not return to the United States since he could not take sufficient funds out of Germany to live on while seeking a job in this country.

Ludwig was arrested at Salzburg, Austria, on Feb. 2, 1938, on suspicion of espionage. At the time, he was taking pictures and notes pertaining to bridges near the Austrian-German border while on a bicycle tour in that vicinity. Ludwig stated that he was not spying at the time and he did everything in his power to put off the trial and managed to delay it for a period of several weeks. He was then released without a trial and without having formal charges placed against him. Ludwig further indicated that the release occurred after Germany invaded Austria and gained control over the particular area in which he was held.

Investigation in this case indicated clearly that Kurt Frederick Ludwig was extremely active in the United States as an espionage agent of the German Reich. His espionage activities covered a wide field. In addition to actually obtaining various national defense information himself and transmitting it to Germany, he recruited a number of other agents to work with him in the United States, some of the latter being quite young. He was able to do this by reason of his former connection with the German Youth Movement in New York City.

It has been reported that Ludwig was a very secretive type of individual and never furnished much information to anyone about himself or his activities. He told one woman acquaintance after his return to the United States in March of 1940, that he was in the leather business and displayed leather products to her as proof of this statement. On a later occasion he claimed to this woman that he was engaged in selling tungsten metal. He explained his frequent trips about the country by stating that they were necessary in connection with his selling activities.

Ludwig told another acquaintance that he had been in a concentration camp in Germany on one occasion, having been imprisoned by the Gestapo. He claimed that he was released on account of his American citizenship. In connection with this matter another individual advised he had been informed by Ludwig that he was at one time in high favor with Hitler. Ludwig allegedly stated, however, that he thought he was still in good graces when he last returned to Germany but that conditions had changed and he found himself more or less ostracized by the party in power. Ludwig also informed this particular individual he had participated in the Munich Beer Hall Putsch with Hitler.

During the course of his activities in the United States, Ludwig purchased some expensive radio equipment which could have been used in communicating with Germany. In connection with the purchase he received a free course at a radio school. He attended classes intermittently over a period of three months and then dropped out entirely apparently without attempting to obtain a license. It is interesting to note that during the course of his attendance at the classes, Ludwig was known by the other students as "Dutch."

From time to time Ludwig expressed in his correspondence some dissatisfaction with his assignment in the United States. Once he indicated that he was doing his best in his business but that many things such as the long separation from his family had caused him disappointment and worry. He indicated that von der Osten's automobile accident was a terrible strain on his nerves. On top of this and other things he indicated that he had many worries about his family and his health. He added, however, that he managed to sleep well, "having a clean conscience–and to eat comparatively well." In connection with his desire to return home Ludwig once received the following secret message from his superiors:

"Please stay there yourself. We have not forgotten your wish to return home soon, but for the moment your task is too important."

Before von der Osten's death, he and Ludwig planned an extensive survey of Army camps on the East Coast and across the Southern States to California. Ludwig, accompanied by Lucy Boehmler, made the proposed tour himself after von der Osten's death. He visited almost every Army camp and airfield on the East Coast of the United States from New York to Key West, Florida. He prepared the data for submission to his principals in Germany through various mail drops by use of secret writing, code and other means. While on the trip to Florida, Ludwig wrecked his automobile in the vicinity of Boone, North Carolina. There were many signs at an intersection and Ludwig became so confused that he ran into one sign and completely wrecked it, and caused considerable damage to his automobile.

As an illustration of the tactics of Ludwig on this and other trips, it might be noted that while returning from Florida he passed a large convoy of trucks in Pennsylvania which were loaded with soldiers. Ludwig remarked to Lucy that he would like to find out where the soldiers were going and from what camp they had come. He thereupon drove slowly beside the trucks while Lucy talked with the soldiers and asked from what camp they had come. The girl was informed the troops were being transferred from a particular camp in the South to a camp in Pennsylvania. After being so advised Lucy located the Pennsylvania camp on the map and advised Ludwig of its location. Ludwig thereupon made notes in a small notebook concerning the number of trucks and the place they were going.

During the FBI's investigation of Ludwig and his activities, information was received indicating a connection with the spy ring headed by Fritz Duquesne which terminated on Jan. 2, 1942, when its 33 members were sentenced to total prison terms exceeding 320 years and were assessed fines aggregating $18,000. Paul Scholz and William Kaercher, two spies involved in the Duquesne ring were apprehended by Special Agents of the FBI in a book store in New York City on June 28, 1941. Ludwig was present at the time but the arresting Agents pretended not to notice him and allowed him to continue with his activities, he being under surveillance, of course, all the time. In speaking of the arrest of these two members of the Duquesne ring Ludwig wrote on July 1, 1941, to his superiors, "I missed a serious accident only by inches."

Shortly after the date of the apprehension of Fritz Duquesne and the 32 other spies associated with him during June 1941, Ludwig went to a summer resort in Pennsylvania and temporarily ceased his activities. While at the resort he seemed to be rather lonely and frequently sat on the front lawn and engaged in playing chess with individuals he met at the camp. He also at one time engaged in lawn bowling and went on a hay ride with other guests at the resort. In this connection it might be noted that one of Ludwig's hobbies was collecting stamps. On one occasion he objected to a friend over the manner in which some stamps had been taken from the envelopes.

Early in August 1941, Ludwig began an automobile trip to the West Coast alone, he being followed all the time by Special Agents of the FBI. While at a hotel in Frement, Ohio, the place of his birth, Ludwig was observed through field glasses by the Special Agents. He was noted to be writing on small cards and studying material in a magazine.

When in the vicinity of Wright Field, Ludwig was observed changing a flat tire on his car. He was seen to be observing closely the activities at the Field while engaged in the tire change.

In addition to driving as fast as 90 miles an hour on occasions, Ludwig used various other tactics in an attempt to elude anyone who might be following him. In the vicinity of Indianapolis, Indiana, he parked in a parking lot and then on foot surveyed all traffic going by. Within about 10 minutes he got into his car again and drove a few blocks and again parked in a parking lot and repeated the process. Ludwig appeared to be an excellent automobile driver and managed to get in and out of traffic rapidly. He was somewhat careless at times, however, and in Chicago went through three red lights and failed to stop for numerous stop signs. Twice he was cautioned by police officers for disobeying traffic regulations. He always seemed to avoid well-traveled roads while going between large cities but in going into a city he always got back on the main road.

While in the vicinity of Selfridge Field outside of

Mount Clements, Michigan, Ludwig picked up two soldiers. He apparently attempted to impress them with his ignorance concerning aircraft for he asked them whether some pursuit ships which were lined up on the Field could be bought for about $1,200 each. The soldiers laughed and told him that the particular planes sold for approximately $30,000 each. Ludwig next asked if the ships could fly at about the speed of an automobile. There was a large cement mixer along the road near the Field and Ludwig questioned the boys as to whether this was an anti-aircraft gun.

During late August 1941, Ludwig spent one night in a tourist cabin in Yellowstone National Park. During the early hours of the evening, he made two or three trips to his car and apparently carried articles into the cabin. Each time he left the cabin he cautiously opened the door slightly, looked outside and then suddenly opened it wide and quickly looked each way. After leaving the cabin he again cautiously looked in all directions and then went to his car. He kept the fire burning in his cabin for approximately one and one-half hours. It was obvious that he was burning papers and documents and it appeared likely that he intended to leave the United States.

Ludwig continued from Yellowstone National Park to Butte, Montana, where he shipped a handbag to relatives in New Jersey. Ludwig stored his car, which contained in the rear compartment some expensive radio equipment, in Missoula, Montana, and continued by bus to Cle Elum, Washington, near Seattle, where he was taken into custody by Special Agents of the FBI on Aug. 23, 1941.

After Ludwig was apprehended in Washington and as he was being held in the custody of the United States Marshal pending removal to New York, he made a last desperate effort to gain his freedom. Reasoning with one of the guards that if he was worth $50,000, the amount of his bond, to the United States he was surely worth that much to Germany. He offered this sum if the guard would assist him in escaping from custody by making a torch available so that the bars could be cut. The guard pretended to be interested in Ludwig's proposition and asked the source of such a large sum of money. Ludwig replied that a small part of it could be obtained from an address in South America and that with this amount he and the guard could go there and await the balance of the $50,000 which would be forthcoming from the German Reich. The guard finally advised Ludwig that such a scheme was not very inviting.

Ludwig used various clever devices during the course of his activities in an attempt to conceal just what he was doing. In some of his communications, he utilized an 1834 system of shorthand which he did not believe could be read by more than two or three persons in the United States. In listing addresses and telephone numbers Ludwig often used certain letters or symbols for figures. In going through one city on one of his trips Ludwig utilized five mail boxes in different sections of the city in mailing about 20 pieces of mail.

When interviewed after his arrest Ludwig indicated that he was afraid to talk because of fear of possible German reprisals against his wife and three children in Munich by the dreaded Gestapo. So thoroughly cognizant was he of this possibility that he would not even go on the witness stand at the time of his trial. He did, however, furnish some personal information about himself, indicating that he stored his car in Montana because he was too jittery to drive. Upon one occasion Ludwig indicated his sympathy for the Nazi cause by stating that the German system "couldn't be beat," and "No matter what's what, I would never do anything–anything at all–to hurt Germany!" Though he admitted having prepared many letters containing secret writing, Ludwig denied that he specifically intended the secret writing placed on these letter and the espionage information to go to Germany.

When questioned by Special Agents of the FBI Ludwig admitted having been paid for his activities on several occasions by mysterious individuals. He said he would receive a letter from an unknown person instructing him to appear at a particular time at a specified place where he would find a man who could be identified in a certain way as by a white rose in his lapel or a particular kind of newspaper in his hand. After the identification was effected the two of them would sit at a table if in a restaurant and Ludwig would order a cup of coffee. As he drank the beverage, amounts varying from $50 to $500 would be handed under the table or rolled up in a napkin. Ludwig claimed, however, that he did not know the identities of the various men he met in this manner, but that they apparently were "white collar" workers. He admitted that on one occasion he received a foreign remittance in his bank account of $2,000 which came from a Swiss bank. Despite the sums of money which he received, Ludwig seemed to be in need of funds most of the time and frequently complained to his superiors on this score.

Ludwig's trial commenced on Feb. 3, 1942, in the United States District Court, Southern District of New York and on March 6th a verdict of guilty was returned against this individual. On March 13, 1942, he was sentenced to serve 20 years. He was sent to Atlanta Federal prison until he was pardoned in 1957 and deported to Germany. He died in Munich in 1987.

Lucy Rita Boehmler was born at Eltinger, Germany, on June 20, 1923, and came to the United States with her mother on Oct. 30, 1928. She lived in New York and vicinity until her involvement with Ludwig in this case. After attending a public school and a high school for three years Lucy Boehmler pursued a comptometry course in New York City. In fact, at the time of her arrest she was still attending the comptometry school. Prior to her involvement with Ludwig, Lucy Boehmler was employed at various times in department stores in New York City. It might be noted that the girl's parents were also born in Germany.

After her arrest, Lucy Boehmler admitted her participation in the espionage ring headed by Kurt Frederick Ludwig. She was extremely active in Ludwig's espionage activities according to her own admissions and served as Ludwig's secretary. In 1940, shortly after Ludwig returned to the United States from Germany, he was introduced to Lucy Boehmler by another individual. Ludwig became very friendly with the Boehmler family and visited their home on numerous occasions. In the fall of 1940 Lucy Boehmler came in contact with Helen Pauline Mayer who lived near Lucy's home.

In March 1941, at which time Lucy was 17 years of age, Ludwig advised her of his connections with Germany. He also informed her that an individual named Phil Lopez, who was really Capt. Ulrich von der Osten, desired to meet her for the purpose of hiring her as his secretary. Thereafter Lucy Boehmler and Ludwig met Lopez and it was agreed that she would work for him, she knowing at the time that he was engaged in espionage work. Von der Osten died a few days after this meeting and Ludwig approached Lucy Boehmler with the proposition of becoming his own secretary. Immediately thereafter she began working for Ludwig and assisted him in preparing his reports to Germany, writing numerous letters for him on the typewriter as well as in secret writing. Ludwig received correspondence at the girl's home which originated in Germany.

Lucy Boehmler pleaded guilty in connection with this case and during the trial which began on Feb. 3, 1942, she testified for the Government. On March 20th she was sentenced to serve five years in a place of confinement to be designated by the Attorney General. After the Judge had sentenced her he remarked he would make a recommendation to the Attorney General that she be placed in the Women's Federal

Penitentiary in Alderson, West Virginia.

* From a 1941 FBI report, slightly edited

MAN FLEEING U. S. HELD AS ARMY SPY

Arrest First in Which Foreign Agent' Is Accused of Trying to Send Military Data

MUCH SECRECY IN CASE

Suspect Said to Have Listed Men and Equipment—Was Caught Near Seattle

The first specific charges that a foreign agent had attempted to furnish precise information on the strength and location of units of the United States Army to a foreign government were revealed here yesterday. Kurt Frederick Ludwig, who, though born in this country, was said to be of German extraction and to have spent most of his life in Germany, was named as the alleged agent.

United States Attorney Mathias F. Correa disclosed that Ludwig had been apprehended near Seattle last Saturday by agents of the Federal Bureau of Investigation. The G-men caught up with the suspect, Mr. Correa said, while he was trying to escape from the country. Ludwig is now in custody in Washington and Mr. Correa is preparing to obtain his removal to the Southern New York Federal District here to face an indictment handed up Monday, but kept secret until yesterday afternoon.

Part of an article from the Wed., Aug. 27, 1941 edition of the *Seattle Post Intelligencer*.

THE *NORMANDIE*

THE FRENCH LINER, *NORMANDIE,* was the pride of the French nation and was exceeded in length only by Britain's liner, the *Queen Elizabeth*. She was launched in October 1932 and made her maiden voyage from Le Havre, France to New York in May 1935. The 1,029-foot *Normandie* had sailed into New York harbor on Sept. 1, 1939, the day that Germany invaded Poland. She was berthed at Pier 88 and was costing her owners $1,000 per day in charges. Only a small crew was kept on board. No one was particularly concerned or even thought about sabotage.

Weeks before France's surrender to Germany in May 1940, the Abwehr had sent word to its operatives in the U.S. to watch the *Normandie* as it would make a great troop transport if the U.S. were to go to war with Germany.

Kurt Ludwig was watching the ship and reporting its status to the Abwehr in Hamburg. An FBI agent, who was tailing Ludwig in June 1941, wrote in a report: "On June 18, he walked down Twelfth Avenue from 59th Street. He was watching the piers. When he came to the *Normandie*'s pier he stopped for some time. He seemed to be examining carefully. Then he walked on, looking back. At 42nd Street, he took the Weehawken ferry, went to the upper deck and kept watching the *Normandie*."

Soon after Dec. 7, 1941, the U.S. Navy took over the ship, renamed it the *Lafayette* and started converting it to a troop ship capable of carrying up to 12,000 troops. Fifteen hundred civilian workers were working on her but security on the ship was lax.

The conversion was supposed to be finished by Feb. 28, 1942, when she would be sailed to Boston, loaded with troops and would cross the Atlantic under sealed orders.

A reporter for a New York newspaper got on board and wrote an article for his newspaper, which was not published, stating how easy it would be to sabotage the ship. Sure enough on February 9, a fire broke out on board and within an hour the entire ship was ablaze. Some 3,000 workers, crew members and coast guardsmen got off with one fatality and 250 injured.

At 2:32 a.m., the *Normandie* rolled over at its pier due to the amount of water poured into her by fireboats. Several inquiries later ruled out sabotage and said the fire was started by careless workers.

Whether it was sabotage or carelessness, the U.S. lost a valuable asset for the duration of the war. The Navy spent millions of dollars to salvage her, but decided she was not needed after being raised. After the war, she was sold for scrap and cut up between October 1946 and October 1947.

Guns, ammunition and materials for manufacturing bombs were found during the course of a New York City raid on Jan. 14, 1940. PHPC

Right after the Pearl Harbor attack, the FBI raided the home of German aliens in Detroit and confiscated weapons and Nazi paraphernalia. PHPC

The first line of defense on our shores in the early months of the war was the foot soldier. PHPC

AMERICA'S DEFENSES

On the morning of Dec. 8, 1941, this headline appeared in *The Honolulu Advertiser*. Potential saboteurs seemed to be landing in Hawaii and on both American coasts in the first few chaotic days following the Pearl Harbor attack. However, no saboteurs landed on American shores until the night of June 13, 1942. PHPC

The Washington Monument, blacked out except for an airplane beacon on top of the obelisk, right after the Pearl Harbor attack. An anti-aircraft battery can be seen on the roof of an adjacent government office building. FDR

Key areas in Washington, D.C., were placed under heavy armed guard immediately following the Japanese attack on Pearl Harbor. These soldiers stand guard at the entrance to the White House. PHPC & FDR

Anti-aircraft guns, were emplaced around Washington, D.C., shortly after Pearl Harbor to guard against another enemy air attack. PHPC

Many bridges throughout the country were placed under armed guard and every car was checked before crossing. PHPC

An alert guard stands ready for any trouble at a Phelps Dodge Mining Co. copper mine at Morenci, Arizona, December 1942. LC

Even in remote Williams County, North Dakota, a railroad bridge was guarded by members of the local American Legion post from Dec. 5, 1941 to Feb. 1, 1942. LC

This armed civilian guard is standing at a railroad bridge in Tulsa, Oklahoma, in October 1942. This area was far away from either American coast but no one knew if saboteurs were in the country or where they would strike. LC

Even as late as April 1943, the Municipal Office Building in Baltimore, Maryland, was protected by sand bags in case of an enemy air raid. LC

Members of the Civil Air Patrol, Coastal Patrol No. 20 out of Bar Harbor, Maine, set their watches from a time signal before going to their planes, June 1943. LC

A 75mm gun crew guards a beach position some-where along the West Coast, Feb. 12, 1942. PHPC

The Boeing Aircraft factory in Seattle, Washington, went so far as to build a fake town on top of its factory to hide it from a potential air attack. BOEING CO.

Supposedly one of the prime interests of the two spies who landed in Maine in November 1944 was the Manhattan Project, America's production of the world's first atomic weapon. These scenes were taken at a 70-square-mile site near Clinton, Tennessee, which would become Oak Ridge. NATIONAL ATOMIC MUSEUM

THE WORLD WAR II BEACH PATROL*

WHEN THE JAPANESE ATTACKED Pearl Harbor Dec. 7, 1941, it shocked and panicked many Americans. The fear on the West Coast was so great that as late as February 1942, a weather balloon detected over Los Angeles by Army radar, became the target of an anti-aircraft barrage that showered hot metal onto the blacked-out city and caused one fatality—a civilian died of a heart attack.

Meanwhile on the Eastern seaboard, German U-boats began a devastating attack on U.S. merchant shipping. Along the coast, numerous ships sank within sight of the beach, causing a great deal of fear among many Americans.

Since the war now seemed to be on America's doorstep, many Americans feared invasion. The Coast Guard undertook two little-known, but important roles to protect the nation during this period of uncertainty. One role was to protect shipping off the East Coast and another was to prevent enemy infiltration from the sea.

With the threat of war hanging over America, the Coast Guard had the foresight to form an Auxiliary and Reserve in 1939 and 1941, respectively. Using many auxiliarists and reservists, the Corsair Fleet or picket patrol made up of small craft, was formed in May 1941 to protect East Coast shipping and prevent enemy infiltration. It was disbanded in October 1943 when the threat along the coast abated although larger yachts still patrolled until the war's end.

Meanwhile, the USCG Beach Patrol was another means to carry out the aforementioned roles.

During the early years of World War II, fears that German submarines could easily surface and land agents along the many deserted stretches of America's Eastern coastline prompted a need for coastal patrols. Along the West Coast, there were numerous reports of Japanese submarines being sighted.

The basic structure of the wartime beach patrol was set into motion even prior to Pearl Harbor. On Feb. 3, 1941, all coastal areas of the United States were organized into defense divisions known as Naval Coastal Frontiers. Then, on Nov. 1, 1941, under Executive Order 8929, the Coast Guard was transferred to the Navy for the duration of what would soon become, for the U.S., World War II. Naval Coastal Frontiers became Sea Frontiers after Feb. 6, 1942, with Army and Navy personnel in each area to guard the coast and prevent invasion. The Army was charged with the defense of the land areas, while the Navy would maintain inshore and offshore patrols. The Coast Guard, as a part of the Navy, was the logical choice to work along the beaches. With an already long, proud tradition of beach patrols dating back to the days of the 19th century Life-Saving Service, the Coast Guard organized the beach patrol. Its members were quickly dubbed the "sand pounders."

These beach patrols were primarily security forces and had three basic functions:

• To detect and observe enemy vessels operating in coastal waters and to transmit information on these craft to the appropriate Navy and Army commands;

• To report attempts of landings by the enemy and to assist in preventing landings;

• Prevent communication between persons on shore and the enemy at sea.

The patrols also functioned as a rescue agency and policed restricted areas of the coast. Just the rescue function alone more than justified the operation of the patrol.

In the first hectic and confused months of the United States' participation in the war, patrols were conducted in much the same way they were during peacetime. That is, one man, armed only with flares, would patrol the beach. The responsibility for this work was placed under the local Captain of the Port.

Meanwhile, the FBI continued issuing warnings about the possibility of enemy landings. But the work of the beach patrol was not taken seriously until one key incident occurred in June 1942—Operation Pastorius.

The landings in New York and Florida quickly dispelled any further questions about the need for a beach patrol.

On July 25, 1942, Coast Guard Headquarters authorized all Naval Districts that were adjacent to the coast to organize a well-armed and maintained beach patrol, with proper communication equipment to relay messages. Five days later, the vice chief of staff for naval operations informed commanders of the Sea Frontiers that the, "...beaches and inlets of the Atlantic, Gulf, and Pacific coasts would be patrolled by the Coast Guard whenever and wherever possible."

Because the patrol activities were intertwined with the activities of the FBI, and the Army and Navy, Coast Guard Headquarters defined the specific functions of the patrol. "The beach patrols are not intended as a military protection of our coastline, as this is a function of the Army. The beach patrols are more in the nature of outposts to report activities along the coastline and are not to repel hostile armed units. The functions of the Army in this connection is not to guard against surreptitious acts, but rather to furnish the armed forces required to resist any attempt by armed enemy forces or parties to penetrate the coastline by force."

In short, the beach patrol acted as a coastal information system. It was operated under a national Beach Patrol Division in Headquarters under the command of Capt. Raymond J. Mauerman. Each district established its own patrol organization and its own beach patrol officer and operated as a part of port security. Ten districts operated patrols, made up of approximately 24,000 officers and men. The area covered by the sand pounders was about 3,700 miles. The varying nature of America's coastline prevented complete coverage of all beaches. On the Gulf Coast, for example, swamps created obstacles. Where the sand pounders could not walk, boat and motor patrols were established.

Normal foot patrol procedures required men to travel in pairs. The patrolmen were armed with rifles, or sidearms and flare pistols. The pairing of the patrols allowed one man to hold a suspect, while the other went for assistance. Usual distances covered were two miles or less, with the Coast Guardsmen required to report in by special telephone boxes placed along the beaches at about quarter-mile lengths. These phones were obviously not available at every location, especially in isolated regions. In some locales, the men conducted the patrols only at night. In those areas of potential invasion or sabotage activities, around-the-clock vigils were maintained.

The routine of foot patrols was far from exciting or glamorous. A walk along a beach on a bright moon-lit June night might seem pleasurable, but the same beach could also be 20 degrees below zero when the patrolman was plodding it in February. In some areas, steep descents onto the beach could be extremely hazardous on dark, rainy nights. One Coast Guardsman at Duxbury, Mass. said the beach there was usually "covered with round, slippery rocks concealed by slimy kelp, flotsam, jetsam and just plain sludge." In some parts of the south, Coast Guardsmen had to face obstacles like alligators, bloodsucking insects, and poisonous snakes.

But Coast Guardsmen also found some interesting things while patrolling that had washed ashore: life preservers, life jackets, sometimes with bullet holes which bore witness to the fury of the Battle of the Atlantic, messages-in-the-bottle, and, sometimes, even bodies.

In 1942, the Coast Guard recognized that the use of dogs, with their keen sense of smell and their ability to be trained for guard duty, would help enhance the patrols. The Coast Guard eventually received about 2,000 dogs for patrol duties. The dogs and their trainers were schooled on the 300-acre estate of P.A.B. Widener, at the Elkins Park Training Station in Pennsylvania. Others trained at Hilton Head, S.C. The first dog patrols began at Brigantine Park, N.J. in August 1942. The dogs were so successful, that within a year, the animals and their handlers were on duty in all the districts.

Dog patrols were usually conducted at night and consisted of a dog and dog handler. The patrol length was about one mile. Where canine patrols were in effect, the two-man foot patrols were replaced, thus reducing personnel requirements. The animals showed great alertness and were formidable as attackers. A 50-to-75-pound snarling dog could be more frightening than a man with a pistol. They also even acted as protection for Coast Guardsmen themselves. In one case, near Plymouth, Mass. a patrolman was prevented from walking off a cliff on a dark night when his dog refused to advance further. At Oregon Inlet, N.C., Coast Guard dog, Nora, actually saved the life of a Guardsman. Sometimes, however, they were not quite as helpful. On three occasions, in the same area, the dogs led their handlers on what appeared to be the trail of suspicious persons only to find skunks instead!

A year after its inception, with the threat of invasion diminishing, Headquarters ordered a reduction of the dog patrols. Even though the program was reduced 75 percent, many dogs and their handlers were placed on special guard duties.

Because they could cover much larger stretches

of beach very quickly, horses were authorized for use by the beach patrol in September 1942. By October 1942, the first sailors on horseback were patrolling a stretch of eastern Florida. The mounted portion of the patrol soon became the largest segment of the patrol. For example, one year after orders were given to use horses, there were 3,222 of the animals assigned to the Coast Guard. All came from the Army and the Army Remount Service provided all the riding gear required, while the Coast Guard provided the uniforms for the riders. East Coast horses came from the Army Remount Station in Front Royal, Va.; the Gulf Coast horses came from Fort Reno, Okla. and the Pacific Coast supply originated in Fort Robinson, Neb.

At the start of the operation, Army cavalry officers instructed the sailors-turned-riders in equitation basics. Army veterinarians cared for the horses' health needs, and the Fort Reno Remount Station trained a group of Coast Guardsmen as farriers and saddlers before their assignment to duty stations around the country.

When a call went out for personnel, a mixed bag of people responded including polo players, cowboys, former sheriffs, horse trainers, Army Reserve cavalrymen, jockeys, farm boys, rodeo riders and stunt men. The age range was from 17 to 73! Much of the mounted training took place at the sites of the dog training schools, Elkins Park Training Station, Pa., Hilton Head, S.C. and Santa Rosa, Calif.

Horse patrols were not used along the rocky beaches of New England, but from New Jersey south, coastal residents were treated to the rare sight of sailors on horseback. Patrols were conducted with at least two mounted riders and they were usually armed with rifles and sidearms. In some cases, dogs and horses patrolled together. The use of two animals sensitive to strangers added to the ability of the patrol to detect suspects. In addition to covering ground quicker, the use of horses allowed patrols to easily carry the bulky 35-pound radios of the day, an important factor in isolated areas. The patrols were on duty for four hours at a time, two hours on the beach and two hours in lookout towers.

Augmenting the foot, horse and dog patrols, but still considered part of the beach patrol, were other means of coastal surveillance. The jeep was used along with trucks to cover isolated regions. Small boats were used in regions where swamps and other obstacles made passage on foot extremely difficult. The boats were also used to transport foot and dog patrols. Throughout the war, Coast Guardsmen stood watch in lookout towers scanning the beach areas

and water for suspicious activities. The tower watches were kept 24 hours a day.

Housing conditions for the patrols ranged from tents to the luxury of seaside estates and hotels leased for the duration by the Coast Guard. Along the Georgia coast, for example, the mounted units were billeted in private estates and resorts that had previously served McCormicks and Morgans, Pulitzers and Carnegies, Rockefellers and Vanderbilts. At the other extreme were abandoned Civilian Conservation Corps barracks and machinery sheds converted to stables along the Gulf Coast.

Though the Army, Navy and Coast Guard practiced invasion maneuvers repeatedly, both to test the beach patrols' readiness and as drills to prepare servicemen headed overseas, the feared enemy onslaught never came.

By the second year of the United States' participation in World War II, there was a need for more men for sea duty. At the same time, the danger from seaborne invasion was diminishing, especially along the East Coast. So, on Feb. 18, 1944, Adm. Russell R. Waesche, Commandant of the Coast Guard, announced that a 50 percent reduction in beach patrols would be ordered for the West Coast. Dog patrols had already been cut back in the autumn of 1943. By July 1944, only the West Coast had an active patrol, which amounted to only 800 men. Eventually, the mounted division was disbanded, and the horses were sold at local auctions for prices averaging $65 per head on the East Coast and $117 on the West Coast.

Eventually, the Army returned to many of the West Coast's beaches, especially in California. Throughout the remainder of the war, however, Coast Guardsmen continued to man beach lookouts and to carry out some traditional beach patrol activities.

The record clearly shows that in surprise drills, Coast Guard patrolmen inevitably located and reported the enemy. On the other hand, as the service's official history very correctly notes, "there is no way of knowing how many spies, despite all possible precautions, eluded the patrols by slipping into the country via the route of the eight apprehended saboteurs of 1942." We will probably never know whether the beach patrols actually made Germany rethink its plans on putting spies into the United States.

*This article first appeared in the Coast Guard's magazine, *The Reservist*, July 1997. It has been edited.

Operation Pastorius

* This FBI report was released on Nov. 14, 1942.

"This will cost these poor men their lives," Admiral Canaris' statement when signing the final order.

The first outward manifestation of the intention of the German High Command to engage in sabotage activities in the United States was disclosed by the recent apprehension of eight trained German saboteurs by Special Agents of the Federal Bureau of Investigation within two weeks after they had landed in this country from German submarines. These eight saboteurs had been thoroughly trained by the High Command of the German Army in the most modern methods of destruction and had been sent to this country for the specific purpose of interfering with our war effort with particular emphasis being placed on interrupting production at aluminum and magnesium plants.

One group of these saboteurs landed on the beach at Amagansett, Long Island, on the night of June 13, 1942. The second group of four men were landed on the beach a few miles below Jacksonville, Florida, on June 17, 1942. After their landing, these men dispersed to various parts of the United States but they were all in Federal custody by June 27, 1942. The saboteurs were Ernest Peter Burger, age 36, George John Dasch, age 39, Herbert Hans Haupt, age 22, Edward John Kerling, age 34, Richard Quirin, age 34, Hermann Otto Neubauer, age 32, Werner Thiel, age 35, and Heinrich Harm Heinck, age 35. All of these men had been born in Germany and at one time or another had spent a portion of their lives in the United States, during which time they learned the English language and became acquainted with American customs. All of these men with the exception of Burger had returned to Germany since the outbreak of the present conflict. Burger had returned to Germany in 1933, after living in the United States for a period of six years.

Recruitment of Saboteurs

The German saboteurs who were sent to the United States were recruited for this work by one Lieut. Walter Kappe who was attached to Abwehr 2 (Intelligence-2) of the German High Command and in charge of German sabotage in the United States. In addition to his connection with the German Army, Kappe is also an official in the Ausland Institute at Stuttgart, Germany, which organization, prior to the war, was engaged in organizing Germans abroad into the Nazi Party and had the function of obtaining

through Germans living in foreign countries various types of military, economic, political and similar information. Kappe had lived in the United States from 1925-1937, during which time he took part in the organizing of the first Nazi organization in this country at Chicago known as Teutonia. He later was one of the principal organizers and an officer in the Friends of New Germany, which subsequently became the German-American Bund. In the latter organization, Kappe was press agent and in charge of propaganda and was editor of the official Bund paper in the United States. He was ousted from the German-American Bund by Fritz Kuhn as a result of some inner-circle rivalries, after which time Kappe returned to Germany where he was placed in charge of the American section of the Ausland Institute at Stuttgart, Germany.

It is known that periodic meetings are held in Berlin and in other cities throughout Germany of those Germans who had formerly lived in the United States. These groups were known by the name Comradeship U.S.A. Walter Kappe was one of the officials in charge of these meetings, which, it is believed, were held for the purpose of keeping up the morale of these Germans because they were accustomed to a higher standard of living in the United States than that which they have in Germany at the present time. Kappe recruited several of the saboteurs from these groups. The Ausland organization also maintained a list of all Germans who returned to that country from the United States and was advised on all current arrivals. As a result of this information, Kappe was also able to keep in touch with all returning Germans and consider them for sabotage activities.

Another source of recruits for sabotage missions to the United States is the German Army. In three instances, Kappe was able to arrange the transfer of Germans who had been in the United States from the German Army into the sabotage organization. No information has been received to indicate that any of the saboteurs were coerced in any way to engage in sabotage activities in this country. It is known, however, that the German High Command thoroughly investigated the background of the individuals proposed for sabotage training and it is interesting to note that the German government places a high value on an individual who had belonged to the German-American Bund or a similar organization while re-

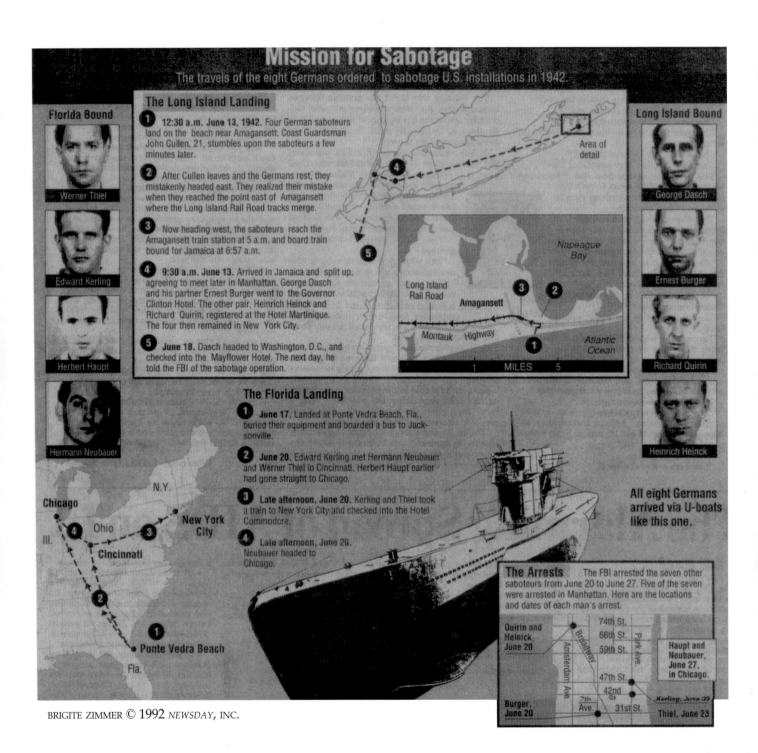

Mission for Sabotage

The travels of the eight Germans ordered to sabotage U.S. installations in 1942.

The Long Island Landing

Florida Bound

Werner Thiel

Edward Kerling

Herbert Haupt

Hermann Neubauer

1 12:30 a.m. June 13, 1942. Four German saboteurs land on the beach near Amagansett. Coast Guardsman John Cullen, 21, stumbles upon the saboteurs a few minutes later.

2 After Cullen leaves and the Germans rest, they mistakenly headed east. They realized their mistake when they reached the point east of Amagansett where the Long Island Rail Road tracks merge.

3 Now heading west, the saboteurs reach the Amagansett train station at 5 a.m. and board train bound for Jamaica at 6:57 a.m.

4 9:30 a.m. June 13. Arrived in Jamaica and split up, agreeing to meet later in Manhattan. George Dasch and his partner Ernest Burger went to the Governor Clinton Hotel. The other pair, Heinrich Heinck and Richard Quirin, registered at the Hotel Martinique. The four then remained in New York City.

5 June 18. Dasch headed to Washington, D.C., and checked into the Mayflower Hotel. The next day, he told the FBI of the sabotage operation.

Area of detail

Napeague Bay

Long Island Rail Road

Amagansett

Montauk Highway

Atlantic Ocean

1 MILES 5

Long Island Bound

George Dasch

Ernest Burger

Richard Quirin

Heinrich Heinck

The Florida Landing

1 June 17. Landed at Ponte Vedra Beach, Fla., buried their equipment and boarded a bus to Jacksonville.

2 June 20. Edward Kerling met Hermann Neubauer and Werner Thiel in Cincinnati. Herbert Haupt earlier had gone straight to Chicago.

3 Late afternoon, June 20. Kerling and Thiel took a train to New York City and checked into the Hotel Commodore.

4 Late afternoon, June 20. Neubauer headed to Chicago.

Chicago

N.Y.

Ohio

Ill.

Cincinnati

New York City

Ponte Vedra Beach

Fla.

All eight Germans arrived via U-boats like this one.

The Arrests

The FBI arrested the seven other saboteurs from June 20 to June 27. Five of the seven were arrested in Manhattan. Here are the locations and dates of each man's arrest.

Quirin and Heinick, June 20

74th St.
66th St.
59th St.

Broadway

Amsterdam Ave.

Park Ave.

Haupt and Neubauer, June 27, in Chicago.

47th St.

42nd St.

Burger, June 20

7th Ave.

31st St.

Kerling, June 22

Thiel, June 23

BRIGITE ZIMMER © 1992 *NEWSDAY*, INC.

Walter Kappe shown in his German Army uniform. He was assigned by the Abwehr, German Naval Intelligence Service, to be in charge of the sabotage missions against the United States. He was born in 1905 and, in 1922, he left the University of Göttingen to join the Deutche Freikorps, an organization which fought Communism and the predecessor of Hitler's Storm Troopers. Later he joined the fledging Nazi party but after the 1923 Beer Hall Putsch in Munich he joined thousands of other party members and curtailed their political activities.

He applied for an American passport and entered the U.S. in March 1925. He worked in a farm implement factory in Illinois but soon went to work for a German language newspaper, the *Chicago Abendpost*, where he wrote stories until 1930 when he was fired. Kappe moved to Cincinnati and became active in various pro-Nazi groups, helping to found the Friends of the Hitler Movement. He was named Press and Propaganda Chief for the movement which three years later

became the German-American Bund.

As editor of the Bund newspaper, *Deutscher Weckruf und Beobachter,* he led an attack to get rid of Bund leader, Fritz Kuhn. When this failed, Kappe resigned and returned to Germany in June 1937.

In Germany he got a job as a propaganda director for a radio station broadcasting to the Americas. He was in the army during the Polish and French campaigns and then was transferred to the Abwehr as a first lieutenant. In late 1941 he was tasked with interviewing repatriated Germans from America for possible missions there if war developed.

Kappe picked the name, Operation Pastorius for the first sabotage mission to the United States in 1942. It was named after Franz Daniel Pastorius, the leader of the first community of immigrant Germans in the U.S. Thirteen families of Mennonites and Quakers had settled in Germantown, Pa., in 1683. NA

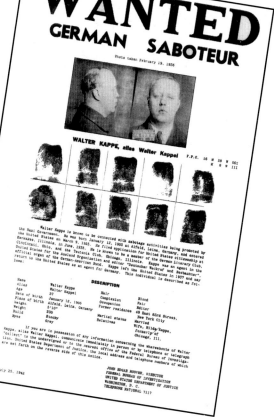

The German-American Bund yearbook for 1937 showing Fritz Kuhn presenting a book to Hitler. Kappe was the publisher of the book.

siding in the United States. It was stated that this indicates to the German government the definite German sympathies of the individual involved. The inducement to these recruits to engage in sabotage activities was the fact that they would be fulfilling their duty to their country. They also were promised good positions in Germany and other rewards upon their return to that country after their mission had been completed. Each saboteur signed a contract with the German Government whereby they were to receive to their credit certain sums each month.

THE EIGHT SABOTEURS
THE LONG ISLAND GROUP I

GEORGE DASCH

Dasch was born in Speyer on the Rhine, Germany on Feb. 7, 1903. He entered a Catholic convent in 1916 to study for the priesthood but was drafted to perform emergency war work in Speyer in 1917. In the latter part of the year he joined the army and spent time in France. After the war he served as an interpreter for his hometown with the army of occupation.

In 1920 Dasch continued his Catholic education but soon left the convent to seek employment in Holland and Germany as a seaman. Unsuccessful at this he moved to Hamburg where he stowed away on an American vessel, the *S.S. Carroll*, which was heading to the United States.

Dasch arrived in Philadelphia on Oct. 4, 1922, and worked for awhile as a dishwasher before moving to New York City. In New York he worked at various hotels and restaurants. Between 1923 and 1927 Dasch worked at various jobs in New York and Florida and made a short trip back to Germany.

In 1923 he took steps to make his entrance into the U.S. legal. Immigration officials allowed him to pay a head tax and gave him an alien seaman identification card. To make his initial entry entirely legal, he returned to Germany employed as a mess boy on the *S.S. Montclay* in September 1923 and returned in October, where he was discharged as a member of the crew.

In August 1927 Dasch enlisted as a private in the U.S. Air Corps and spent a little over a year in service before he bought himself out and received an honorable discharge.

For the next few years he worked at hotels in California and New York and made another trip to Germany. On Sept. 18, 1930, he married Rose Marie Guille, a native of Walston, Pennsylvania, in New York.

During the decade of the 1930s, Dasch and his wife made a trip to Europe and upon their return to the U.S. in 1931 worked at various jobs in Illinois, Missouri, Florida and New York. While in New York he became involved with the Bartender and Waiters International Union but discontinued his union activities when he found that the union was dominated by Communists.

Dasch decided in late 1940 that he wanted to return to Germany to inspect conditions in his native country. On March 22, 1941, he left for San Francisco, then caught a Japanese steamer to Tokyo and then a German freighter, finally arriving in Berlin on May 13. After he arrived he offered his services to the Foreign Office which assigned him work as a monitor in a listening station for all foreign broadcasts. After working in this position for awhile he was approached by the Abwehr to begin training for a sabotage mission to the United States.

At the time of his landing in Long Island, Dasch was 39 years of age and the leader of the eight man mission.

ERNEST PETER BURGER

Burger was born on Sept. 1, 1906, in Augsburg, Germany. He studied to be a machinist and worked at the trade in Germany until arriving in the U.S. in 1927. He was employed in the country in various machine shops until the fall of 1933 at which time he returned to Germany.

As early as

1924 he was a member of the Nazi party in Germany and upon his return to Germany, he resumed party activities in the position of group leader, writer and propagandist. He remained an active member of the Party until March 1940 when he was arrested by the Gestapo because of certain criticisms which he had made concerning party policies and activities. He spent 17 months in a concentration camp before being released and drafted into the army.

While Burger was employed in the U.S., he enlisted in two different National Guard units in Wisconsin and Michigan and became a U.S. citizen in 1933. Burger was 33 at the time of his capture in the U.S. and made a statement to the FBI that he joined the sabotage mission as a means to leave Germany and return to the U.S. and to get even with the Nazis for his confinement in a concentration camp. He apparently left a wife in Germany when he returned to the U.S. in 1942.

WISCONSIN NATIONAL GUARD
Co. K, 127th Inf. W. N. G.
(ORGANIZATION)

Milwaukee, Wis.
(STATION)
September 30, 1933.
(DATE)

Mr. Ernest Burger,
Volklant Str. 8,
Augsburg, Germany.

My dear Ernest:

I received your letter of September 18th, 1933, and was very happy to hear that you are getting along nicely.

I read your letter to the entire organization. The boys in return are sending you many happy wishes and are hoping to see you again.

I have forwarded your final check for $1.95 to Miss Fink as requested in your letter. No doubt you will hear from her shortly.

I am enclosing herewith your honorable discharge and I have no doubt but what you will be proud of same to show your family and friends of your excellent service in the National Guard. Quite a change has taken place in the organization since you left. Your friends from South Milwaukee are not members any more. They obtained positions and are working such long hours that I thought it best to discharge them.

The employment situation has improved a great deal. Practically all the members of the organization are now working. It appears to me th t you left at the wrong time.

Hoping to hear from you in the near future, and with best wishes, I remain

Sincerely yours,

W. J. Szulakiewicz
Capt. Comdg. Co. K.127th Inf.

ROBERT QUIRIN

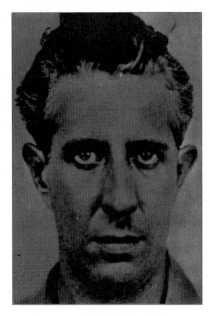

Quirin was born in Berlin, Germany on April 26, 1908. He studied to be a machinist and worked in Germany until he emigrated to the U.S. in October 1927. For three years he worked as a mechanic at the General Electric Company in Schenectady, New York. From 1930 to 1939, he worked at odd jobs in Chicago, New York and Florida.

In 1929 Quirin made application for citizenship papers but never followed through with it. In 1936 he married German-born Anna Sesselman in New York. During the 1930s, Quirin joined the Friends of New Germany and the Nazi party, although this party was not allowed to meet in the U.S.

He and his wife decided to return to their homeland in 1939 and the German government, at the time, was paying passage to German-born citizens who wanted to return home. Shortly after his return to Germany, he was employed in the Volkswagenwerk in Braunschweig. He worked there as a toolmaker until selected for the sabotage mission.

Quirin was 32 years old at the time of the mission. He was executed on Aug. 8, 1942.

HEINRICH HARM HEINCK

Heinck was born in Hamburg, Germany on June 27, 1907. He worked as a machinist's helper and oiler for the Hamburg-American Lines. He made several trips to the U.S. and Heinck jumped ship in New York in the summer of 1926. From that time to July 1938, he was employed in various restaurants and factories in New York City. In July he worked for the C.L. Norden Company as a tool and die maker but had no knowledge of the company's development of the famous Norden bombsight.

During 1934 and 1935 Heinck was a member of the German-American Bund and the Ordungs Dienst. He left the Bund when it was ordered that only American citizens could belong. In March 1939 he got married and he and his wife returned to Germany

at the expense of the German goverment.

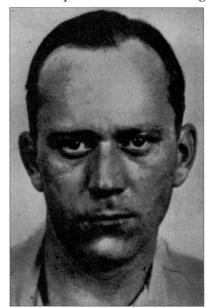

Upon his return, he obtained a job through the German Labor Front in the Volkswagenwerk in Braunschweig where he met Richard Quirin.

Heinck was 35 at the time of the mission. He was executed on Aug. 8, 1942.

THE FLORIDA GROUP II

EDWARD JOHN KERLING

Kerling was the leader of the Florida group. He was born in Weisbaden, Germany, on June 12, 1909. He attended Friedberg University for two semesters before leaving school for the U.S. in March 1928. He travelled to New York as a tourist under a quota on the *S.S. Dresden*. For the next four years he worked in packing houses in New York and then as a chauffeur for several years.

In October 1931, he married Marie Sichart, a native of Munich, Germany. The couple held a variety of domestic jobs, although they were let go several times because of Kerling's rabid Nazi symphazies. He was a member of the Nazi Party in Germany and the German-American Bund. He and his wife made a visit to Germany in 1933 and Kerling made a trip alone to the 1936 Berlin Olympics.

Wishing to return to Germany to join the army, Kerling, his wife and a number of German friends purchased a sloop named *Lekala* with the intention of sailing it to Germany. Due to the war, U.S. authorities would not let them sail across the Atlantic and Kerling sold the sloop in Miami, Florida, and booked passage for himself alone, on a Spanish ship bound for Europe in June 1940.

He reached Lisbon, Portugal, and finally Germany and went to work as a civilian for the army in France translating records of English broadcasts. He later returned to Berlin to work for the Propaganda Ministry where he stayed until he was picked for the Pastorius mission.

After his capture in the United States, he agreed to take the FBI to the site on the Ponte Vedra Beach where the group had buried their explosives. Kerling was 33 at the time of the mission. He was executed on Aug. 8, 1942.

WERNER THIEL

Thiel was born on March 29, 1907, at Essen, Germany. He was trained as a machinist but unable to find steady work in Germany, he travelled to the U.S. in April 1927 as a quota immigrant. He went straight to Detroit, Michigan, to work and applied for American citizenship. He never followed through with it, however.

From 1927 until he left for Germany in March 1941, Thiel worked for various automobile and machine shops as a tool and die maker and machinist in Detroit, Los Angeles, Indiana, Pennsylvania and New York City. For a short time in 1937 he had an interest in a bakery in Fort Myers, Florida. The business failed.

While in New York in 1933, Thiel became a member of the Friends of New Germany. In 1938 he applied for, and in 1939, he received membership in the Nazi party.

On March 27, 1941, he left San Francisco for a long trip back to Germany at the German government's expense. He had to travel to Tokyo, Manchuria, Moscow and finally made it to Berlin in May 1941. Thiel worked as a machinist in Berlin until he was picked for the mission in April 1942. He was 35 at the time of his landing in Florida. He was executed on Aug. 8, 1942.

HERMAN NEUBAUER

Neubauer was born on Feb. 5, 1910, in Hamburg, Germany. He was employed as a cook on the *S.S. Hamburg* of the Hamburg-American Lines and made a number of crossings to New York City. In July 1931 he jumped ship in New York and went to work on the *S.S. Leviathan* of the United States Lines. He obtained a quota immigration visa and legally entered the U.S. on Nov. 13, 1931.

After a short period of employment in a Hartford, Connecticut hotel he signed on with the Matson Lines and worked as a cook for several years. In the spring of 1933 he cooked at the Chicago World's Fair and other Chicago hotels and restaurants into 1936.

Neubauer joined the German-American Bund until resigning because he was not an American citizen. He also joined the Nazi Party while in the U.S.

Neubauer married Alma Wolf, an American-born citizen on Jan. 10, 1940 in Miami, Florida. They were part of the ill-fated *Lekala* affair with their friend, Edward Kerling. The Neubauers left New York on July 11, 1940 for Lisbon, Portugal and Germany. Upon his return to his native land, he was drafted into the army and sent to Poland where he was seriously wounded.

While recuperating in a hospital in Stuttgart, Germany, he was recruited for the Pastorius mission. Newbauer was 32 at the time of the mission. He was executed on Aug. 8, 1942.

Haupt was born on Dec. 21, 1919, in Stettin, Germany. His father, Hans Max Haupt was a soldier in the Germany Army during World War I and emmigrated to the U.S. in 1923. Herbert entered the U.S. with his mother in March 1925 and derived American citizenship through the naturalization of his father in 1930.

Haupt was brought up in Chicago and left high school in 1936 to work as a apprentice optician. As an American citizen he was eligible to join the German-American Bund. He also joined the U.S. Army Reserve Officers Training Corps.

In June 1941, Haupt apparently got his 23-year-old girlfriend, Gerda Stuckmann pregnant. For one of several reasons, he decided to take a trip to Mexico with his best friend, Wolfgang Wergin, who was also born in Germany. Perhaps he was having a last fling before settling down or he really wanted to escape the prospect of being a father.

In either case the two young men ran out of money and were turned back at the U.S. border for selling their car without paying Mexican taxes on it. They boarded a Japanese freighter at Manzanillo, Mexico, on a trip that was suppose to stop in California. Unfortunately, the ship went straight to Japan where the two men tried to get a ship back to the U.S. Unable to do this they contacted the German consulate who got them on a ship bound for Germany.

The day the freighter docked in Bordeaux, France, Dec. 10, 1941, Germany declared war on the U.S. Now stuck in occupied Europe and being American citizens they were eventually sent to stay with their relatives in Germany.

Wergin was drafted into the German Army and spent two years on the Russian Front before being sent to France and taken prisoner by the Americans.

Haupt was approached by Walter Kappe to join the Pastorius mission because of his knowledge of the United States. Haupt stated at his trial that he had no choice but to join as he was told his life and that of his friend, Wergin, would be in danger if he didn't.

Haupt was 22 at the time of the mission. He was executed on Aug. 8, 1942. His friend, Wolfgang Wergin was denied a visa to return to the U.S. because of his service in the German Army. He and his family moved to Columbia and eventually were allowed to return to the U.S. in 1956. His parents were in Chicago to meet him. He became an American citizen again in 1962 and worked as a professional photographer for nearly 40 years in Las Vegas.

Fake Social Security card issued in Germany to Herbert Haupt under his own name.

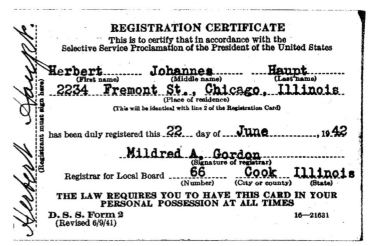

A fake Selective Service card issued in Germany to Herbert Haupt, again using his real name.

SABOTAGE TRAINING

The saboteurs were trained for their mission in a school specifically used for the training of sabotage agents by the German High Command. This training school was located on what had formerly been a private estate belonging to a Jewish family on Quentz Lake, Brandenburg, near Berlin, Germany. The building on this estate had been remodelled to accommodate the instructors and students and one building was equipped as a laboratory. Accommodations were available at this school for approximately 16 to 20 students and it is known that this school had been used to train German sabotage agents for some time. The saboteurs received three weeks of intensive sabotage training and were instructed in the manufacture and use of explosives, incendiary material and various forms of mechanical, chemical and electrical delayed timing devices. This training was both theoretical and practical. Considerable time was spent by the instructors with the saboteurs in developing complete background histories which they were expected to use in the United States. They were encouraged to converse together in the English language and to read American newspapers and magazines in order that no suspicion would be directed to them in the event they were interrogated while in this country. The following is an outline of the subjects in which the saboteurs received training:

General chemistry
Easily ignited incendiaries—methods of igniting these incendiaries.
Incendiaries difficult to ignite—methods of igniting these.
Explosives, detonators and primers.
Mechanical, chemical and electrical timing devices.
Study on concealing identity in the United States, adoption of appropriate background, personal history, etc.
Practical sabotage training. (After preparing incendiaries or explosives, the saboteurs were obliged to use them under realistic conditions.)
Secret writing.

After the completion of the training school, the saboteurs were taken on a three day tour to aluminum and magnesium plants, railroad shops, canals, river locks and other facilities for additional instructions as to the most vital spots to be sabotaged, as well as to learn the vulnerability of these facilities to various types of sabotage.

Lieut. Walter Kappe was in charge of this school. The technical training, however, was given by two professors who were attached to the Technical Section of Abwehr 2. The saboteurs were not permitted to make any permanent notes which they could bring with them to the United States. All of their instructions had to be memorized. While at the school, maps of the United States were exhibited to them, showing the important railroads and the places where sabotage would be most likely to cause a serious interruption in the transportation of raw material. They were also shown maps on which were located the principal aluminum and magnesium plants, as well as the locations of other important war industries. Similar maps outlining the important canals and waterways and the location of the important locks were also called to the attention of the saboteurs.

SABOTAGE EQUIPMENT

Each group of saboteurs brought with them to the United States four waterproof cases containing a large quantity of high explosives, bombs which were disguised to look like large pieces of coal, a considerable number and type of fuses, detonators and primers, as well as mechanical and chemical timing devices. One of the groups was also supplied with a considerable quantity of abrasive material for use in destroying railroad engines and other machinery. It was estimated that the explosives and other equipment furnished these men when utilized in connection with their training in preparing additional explosives and incendiary material would last the saboteurs two years. It is noted that no incendiary material of any kind was brought to the United States. It was expected that the saboteurs would be able to purchase in this country the necessary ingredients to prepare their own incendiary material.

The saboteurs were supplied with large sums of money in American currency which was to be used by them for their expenses in carrying out their work of destruction. Most of this money was placed in secret compartments of small bags and pieces of luggage by the Technical Section of Abwehr 2. Smaller amounts were given to each saboteur in money belts. The leader of each group was furnished with the sum of $50,000 as a general fund. Each saboteur was given $4,000 in his money belt and in addition, approximately $400 in small bills for immediate use after their landing in the United States. The sum of $5,000 was also given to the group leader for each man in his group. This sum was to be turned over to the individual saboteurs as required. Practically all of this money was in $50 bills, none of which were counterfeit. At the time the saboteurs were apprehended by the FBI, $174,588.62 of their funds were seized.

In connection with the money furnished to the saboteurs, it is interesting to note that the German High Command made two errors. They included in the sum of money furnished to the individual saboteurs American gold notes which are no longer in circulation in the United States. They also were furnished some bills on which Japanese letters had been placed or other foreign markings which would have aroused suspicion if they had been tendered in this country.

SABOTAGE OBJECTIVES IN THE UNITED STATES

The importance of the aluminum and magnesium industries, the so-called "light-metal" industry, to our war effort was emphasized to the saboteurs, and these industries were the primary objectives of the two groups of saboteurs. The saboteurs had received special training with respect to the destruction of this type of plant. The saboteurs were informed that if the production of aluminum and magnesium could be interrupted, it would have a serious effect on the number of military aircraft produced by the United States, which would have a definite effect upon the outcome of the war.

In addition to the aluminum and magnesium industries, certain other objectives were suggested to the saboteurs. A list of the objectives of the saboteurs is set forth hereinafter, but it is pointed out that this list was not expected to be all-inclusive and the leaders of the two sabotage groups were instructed to use their discretion as to the places where their acts of sabotage should be committed, always keeping in mind, however, that they should endeavor to commit sabotage at such vital places as would seriously retard the production or transportation of war materials.

THE LEKALA AFFAIR

In late September 1939, there occurred an incident off the New Jersey coast involving a sloop named *Lekala* and eight German aliens. Edward Kerling, who would later be the leader of the four Florida saboteurs, purchased the sloop in Baltimore, Maryland, along with his wife and six other Germans. They planned to sail the sloop to Germany to join the Nazi cause.

Agents of the Coast Guard, Customs Service, Immigration and Naturalization, and the FBI boarded the sloop at Sandy Hook. The members of the group first stated they were planning on going to Miami to spend the winter, but later admitted that they were planning to return to Germany. At that time, Kerling stated he was very anxious to return to Germany to serve his country. Also on board was another member of Kerling's Florida landing party, Herman Neubauer. After an examination by the government officials, the sloop and it's occupants were released.

The *Lekala* was again taken into custody by the Coast Guard at Topsail Inlet, North Carolina, on Dec. 5, 1939. As captain, Kerling maintained the group was merely sailing to Florida for the winter season to look for jobs. Kerling did state at that time that he had no intention of becoming a citizen of the United States. All the members of the crew were fingerprinted and prints were sent to the FBI. Since none of the crew had a criminal record, the Germans were once again released.

When the crew got to Miami, restrictions, due to the war in Europe, prevented them from crossing the Atlantic Ocean and they were forced to sell the *Lekala* in Miami in May 1940.

The FBI already had some of the crew under scrutiny including Kerling. He eventually got back to Germany via Lisbon, Portugal, on the *S.S. Erochordia* in June 1940. He would return to the United States by submarine on June 17, 1942.

June 24, 1942

M E M O R A N D U M

Re: GEORGE JOHN DASCH, et al;
SABOTAGE
(Objectives of Sabotage Groups)

During the questioning of George John Dasch in connection with the two groups of potential German saboteurs, one of which was landed near Amagansett, Long Island, New York, and the other near Jacksonville, Florida, during the week end of June 13, 1942, it was ascertained that no set plans as to their method or manner of operation were dictated to them. When they arrived here, the two group leaders, George John Dasch and Edward Kerling, were to meet on July 4, and plan the best method of attack. General instructions were that surveys were to be made of the following facilities and the most effective methods of sabotage which they were taught before leaving Germany were to be applied in an attempt to cripple or destroy the facilities:

1. The light metal industry in the United States with special mention of the Alcoa plant in Tennessee (Knoxville Field Division), and the Cryolite plant in Philadelphia, Pennsylvania (Philadelphia Field Division).

2. The railroad system of the Chesapeake and Ohio Railroad Company with main offices at Cleveland, Ohio (Cleveland Field Division). The vulnerable spots along the railroad right of way, such as bridges, tunnels, and so forth, were to be attacked.

3. The new Pennsylvania Railroad Depot at Newark, New Jersey (Newark Field Division).

4. The Hell Gate Bridge between Long Island and the Bronx (New York Field Division).

5. The canal system and inland waterways with particular mention of the sluices (locks) between Cincinnati and St. Louis. This undoubtedly means the locks on the Ohio River (Cincinnati, Louisville, Indianapolis, Springfield, and St. Louis Field Divisions).

6. The Aluminum Company of America plant at Massena, New York (Albany Field Division).

7. The Aluminum Company of America plant at East St. Louis (Springfield Field Division, but newspaper publicity undoubtedly from St. Louis Field Division).

8. Any miscellaneous form of sabotage which might be considered effective by the individual operator such as: (a) Placing detonating bombs in locker rooms of large railroad stations to intimidate and excite the public, and (b) placing bombs in Jewish department stores.

The method recommended for crippling the Alcoa plant was to damage the power lines so that the electrolytic process would be interrupted for a period of at least six to eight hours. It was estimated that in doing this the production at the Alcoa plant would be frozen for a period of from one to three months.

* The Pennsylvania Railroad's Horseshoe Curve near Altoona, Pennsylvania, was also a possible target.

The Pennsylvania Railroad station in Newark, New Jersey, as it looks today. Its elevated tracks sat on a choke joint in what is now called the Northeast Corridor. BILL LEVY, NEWARK, NEW JERSEY

The Cascade Tunnel on the Great Northern Railroad east of Seattle, Washington. *CLASSIC TRAINS*

The Hell Gate Bridge carried the main traffic into Manhattan from the north. *CLASSIC TRAINS*

A steam-era photo of Horseshoe Curve shows Pennsylvania Railroad's four-track mainline, the Kittaning Point Station, Altoona's city reservoirs, a pair of since-abandoned branch lines, and an eastbound passenger train passing a freight. *CLASSIC TRAINS*

Walter Kappe (foreground), Reinhold Barth (center, back row) and two associates posed for this photo in Germany. Burger stated in his confession: "During the [training] course, a man named Reinhold Barth gave a lecture on the American railway systems. He used...photographs, plans and drawings, which he showed around the class. A lecture about railroads consisted of a description of the main railroad lines of the United States. All of the major terminal points were shown to us, and we were given information as to the condition of the rolling stock on the various railroad lines. Barth also illustrated the different types of engines used, their average speed, and the average speed of freight trains used in general throughout the United States." He also demonstrated various ways to sabotage railroad equipment. Barth was a German citizen and a resident of the United States from 1929 to 1938. He had worked as a draftsman for the Long Island Railroad and was an active member of the German-American Bund. His tenure with the LIRR, a Pennsylvania Railroad connection, could explain the prominence of PRR and New York-area targets for Operation Pastorius. *CLASSIC TRAINS*

If the story of intended Nazi sabotage on Horseshoe Curve rings a bell—but you can't figure out why—you may have read *The Long Trains Roll* as a kid. Loosely based on the intrigues of Operation Pastorius, it was the 1944 work of Stephen W. Meader, an award-winning author of juvenile fiction. Copies can still be found from rare-book dealers—or from garage sales, if you're really lucky.

The story is set in fictional Gaptown, Pa., a railroad berg astride a four-track main line at the foot of the Allegheny summit. Gaptown is home to a huge shop and yard complex, and to Randy MacDougal, the teenage son of a railroad family. Together with his friends and coworkers, he foils a Nazi attempt to disrupt traffic on "the big curve" near his home. Without giving away the plot, suffice it to say the Nazis get a lot further in Meader's book than they did in real life.

The Long Trains Roll is a great adventure yarn for kids, but it also depicts a railroading life that's long gone in many ways. From the banter of the characters—heavily laced with railroad slang—to the brakemen riding the roofwalks of boxcars, to the grimy boarding houses, the book evokes a lost world. And through it all runs a young man's devotion to the iron road and his easy camaraderie with its people. We can well understand why he feels as he does, and why he strives to protect them.—*Peter Hansen*

THE LANDINGS

TWO SABOTAGE TEAMS WERE ready to go to America in late May. If this plan worked more teams would follow, and when finally operational, Kappe would also go to America and lead their missions.

The Florida team, led by Kerling, boarded U-584 at Lorient, France on May 26, 1942, under command of Capt. Joachim Deeke. The Long Island team boarded U-202, under command of Capt. Hans-Heinz Linder two days later.

Upon landing in the U.S. both teams were to bury their boxes on the beach where they could be obtained later, and then travel to New York or Chicago and blend in with the population. On July 4th they were to all meet in Cincinnati, Ohio and plan their sabotage missions.

After 15 days at sea, U-202 made landfall on June 12 at 11 p.m. off Amagansett, Long Island, about 100 miles east of New York City. The original plan had the submarine surface at East Hampton, to the west of Amagansett. Two armed sailors brought the four saboteurs to the landing site on the beach. All the men wore complete or partial German naval uniforms to ensure they were treated as prisoners of war rather than spies if captured.

The landing went undetected. While three of the men were burying their boxes and uniforms, (they were to change into civilian outfits if not caught on the beach), Dasch went over a small sand dune to check the area. Suddenly, he noticed a Coast Guardsman walking directly toward him. Dasch walked towards him to keep him from seeing the other three and told the young man, John Cullen, that his group were fisherman from Southampton who had run aground. Cullen suggested that they accompany him back to his guard station to get warm and dry, and wait for daylight.

Burger, not seeing that Dasch was talking to someone when he approached, spoke in German, and their cover was blown. Dasch then offered Cullen money to keep quiet, (Cullen was unarmed at the time), first, $100, which Cullen refused, then, $300 which he accepted. After a few more words, Cullen said he would keep quiet and left in a hurry to report his encounter.

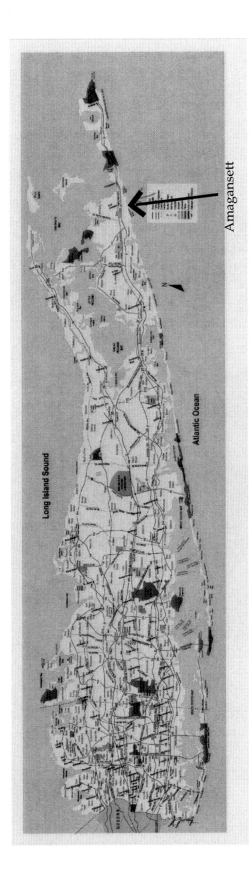

Long Island Sound

Atlantic Ocean

Amagansett

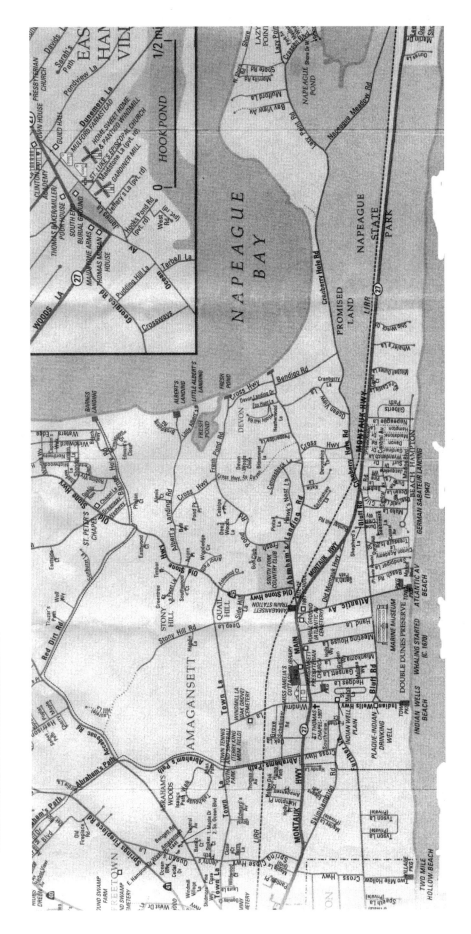

The beach at Amagansett as it looks today.

The Long Island Railroad stop at Amagansett as it looks today. The small building was not there in 1942.

U-202
TypeVII-C Standard Combat Boat
Built by Krupp's Germania Werft in Kiel
Launched 10 February 1941
Assigned to the 1st U-Bootflottille based in Brest, France
Ships sunk by *U-202*

     230 ton British trawler *LADYLOVE* near Iceland 27 August 1941;

     1,980 ton Swedish steamer *SCANIA* on 11 September 1941;

     2,022 ton British steamer *FLYNDERBORG* on 3 November 1941;

     4,586 ton British steamer *GRETAVALE* on 3 November 1941;

     4,000 ton (est.) unidentified ship on 3 November 1941;

     4,000 ton (est.) unidentified ship on 3 November 1941;

     8,882 ton British motor tanker *ATHELVISCOUNT* on 22 March
          1942 — only damaged, not sunk;

     5,249 ton British motorship *LOCH DON* on 1 April 1942;

     4,864 ton Argentinean steamer *RIO TERCERO* on 22 June 1942;
     (although a neutral ship, she did not display neutral markings)

     5,861 ton American steamer *CITY OF BIRMINGHAM* 1 July 1942;

Above were sunk by *U-202* under command of Hans Linder.

     1,815 ton Netherlands steamer *ACHILLES* on 1 October 1942;

     7,191 ton American steamer *JOHN CARTER ROSS* on 8 October
          1942 along with *U-201*;

     9,811 ton British tanker *EMPIRE NORSEMAN* on 23 February 1943;
       (this ship was damaged, not sunk)

     8,482 ton American tanker *ESSO BATON ROUGE* on 23 February 1943;

These five were attacked under command of Günther Poser who joined the new German Navy (the Bundesmarine) and retired as a Konter (Rear) Admiral with two stars and was in charge of intelligence for NATO.

U-202 was sunk 1 June 1943 by *HMS STARLING* 315 miles south of Cape Farewell with the loss of 18 men.

Surface Speed 16 Kts
14 Torpedoes

Type VII (500 tons)
Standard Atlantic Boats
Nearly 700 built
actual tonnage 769

— 3·5" gun

I Stern T.T.

4 bow T.T.

JOHN C. CULLEN

When John Cullen, a native of Bayside, New York, joined the U.S. Coast Guard in December 1941 he never dreamed he would be involved in one of the most bizarre incidents of World War II.

At 0010 on June 13, 1942, Seaman 2nd Class John C. Cullen, 21 years old, left the U.S. Coast Guard station at Amagansett, Long Island for his nightly patrol along the beach. The night was particularly dark with fog rolling across the beach from the ocean. Back at the station the man in charge was Boatswain's Mate second class Carl Ross Jenette. The commanding officer, Warrant Officer Oden had left the station for liberty several hours earlier. On this stretch of beach lay sand dunes covered with long grass which stretched for several hundred yards to the beach road winding among a few small cottages and fisherman's shacks. Cullen had proceeded only 300 yards along the beach toward Montauk when he almost stumbled over three men working beside a small boat at the waterside.

One of them, dressed in civilian clothes, was on shore; the other two, wearing bathing suits, stood in the surf up to their knees. The conversation which follows is taken from the official U.S. Coast Guard report:

"Cullen called out, 'What's the trouble?'

"Nobody answered. The man on shore started toward Cullen.

"Cullen called again, 'Who are you?'

"There was no answer. The man kept advancing.

"Cullen reached to his hip pocket for a flashlight. The man saw the motion, and apparently thinking the Coast Guardsman was reaching for a gun, cried out, 'Wait a minute. Are you the Coast Guard?'

"Cullen answered, 'Yes. Who are you?'

"'A couple of fishermen from Southampton who have run aground.'

"'Come up to the station and wait for daybreak.'

"Cullen recalled later that the weather

Coast Guardsman Cullen during the war.

seemed to get worse and the fog closed in.

"The spokesman snapped, 'Wait a minute–you don't know what's going on. How old are you? Have you a father and mother? I wouldn't want to have to kill you.'

"A fourth man in a bathing suit came up through the fog, dragging a bag. He started to speak in German.

"Cullen spoke up, 'What's in the bag?'

"'Clams.'

"The man in civilian clothes said, 'Yes, that's right.'

"Cullen knew there were no clams for miles around.

"Cullen's pretended gullibility appeared to influence him. In a friendly voice he said, 'Why don't you forget the whole thing? Here is some money. One hundred dollars.'

"Cullen said, 'I don't want it.'

"The man took some more bills out of his wallet. 'Then take $300.'

"Cullen thought fast. He answered, 'O.K.'

"The stranger gave him the money, saying, 'Now look me in the eyes.'

"As Cullen explained to his superiors later, he said he was afraid he might be hypnotized. The stranger insisted. Cullen braced himself and looked directly at the man. Nothing happened, to Cullen's relief. As he looked at him, the stranger kept repeating, 'Would you recognize me if you saw me again?'

"When Cullen finally said 'No,' The man appeared satisfied."

A few weeks later Cullen was called to Washington, D.C. to testify at the military trial of the eight saboteurs. The evening before he appeared he was led to the cells to see if he could recognize George Dasch. He did and also picked out Dasch in the trial the next day.

After his brush with destiny in 1942, Cullen traveled throughout the eastern United States for the Coast Guard doing public relations work. He regretted, in some ways, his involvement in the historic event since his notoriety kept him from seeing action. His requests for transfer to a seagoing ship were always denied. The war effort needed its heroes. It was frustrating he said in a newspaper interview.

Cullen got out of the Coast Guard in 1946 with a 1st Class rating and moved to Westbury on the island were he worked in the dairy business until 1985. He and his wife then moved to Chesapeake, Virginia, to be near one of their children. Cullen received the Legion of Merit and the Victory Medal while in the service.

Cullen was made an honorary chief and had a street named after him at the Portsmouth, Virginia, Coast Guard Station in 2001.

CARL JENNETT SR.

One of the Coast Guard players on the beach at Amagansett was Carl Jennett Sr. He was born in 1912 in Cape Hatteras, N.C., the son of a lighthouse keeper. After graduating high school in 1931, he joined the Coast Guard and was assigned to the Montauk Station at the eastern tip of Long Island.

While stationed at the Shinnewak Station in September 1938, he survived the worst hurricane to ever hit New England. He was the duty officer at the Amagansett Station in the early morning hours of June 13, 1942, when Seaman Cullen burst into his room and announced, "Two Germans held me up on the beach." Jennett got the crew up, armed them and raced, in a heavy fog, to the site. They didn't find the Germans but did hear a submarine's engines as it apparently was trying to get off a sandbar.

During the 1940s Jennett was a star pitcher for the Coast Guard team in the Sunrise League. He retired in 1957 and worked at Guild Hall, a museum and theater in East Hampton. He died in 1999, preceded by his wife, Marie in 1968 and his son, Carl Jr.

Burger and the other two were very concerned about the encounter but Dasch said to them, "Now boys, this is the time to be quiet and hold your nerves. Each of you get a box and follow me." Burger then dragged his sea bag to a burial site, deliberately leaving a trail. He also left his bathing suit and cigarette tin on the beach.

Cullen raced to his station at Napeague and sounded the alarm. Armed seamen came back to the landing site and as Cullen stated, "We saw a blinker light and smelled diesel oil." U-202 was just pulling away after hanging up on a sandbar.

The four saboteurs had already left the area trying to find their way to the Amagansett Long Island Railroad Station. After traveling the wrong way for a mile and bumping into a trailer court they finally arrived at the station in time to catch the 6:30 a.m. train for Jamaica, just east of New York City.

Upon arriving at Jamaica they bought new clothes, changed in the men's room at a nearby restaurant and assimilated into the Queens Borough neighborhood. Jamaica, at the time, had a sizable number of German immigrants and it was easy for the saboteurs to walk around, unnoticed.

Meanwhile, the Coast Guard had alerted the FBI and by early morning, all the saboteurs boxes, and Burger's items on the beach had been found. All of the items were taken to the area Coast Guard headquarters at Governors Island near Manhattan. There, the boxes of explosives and the other items were examined and cataloged. The FBI now took over the investigation. Its director, J. Edgar Hoover, informed Attorney General Francis Biddle of the events. Agents were placed on the highest alert in an effort to find the saboteurs. The four saboteurs left Jamaica for Manhattan. When they arrived, Dasch and Burger checked into the Hotel Governor Clinton. Dasch used the name George John Davis. Burger used his own name. Heinck and Quirin registered at the Hotel Martinique. Heinck used the name Henry Kaynor and Quirin used the name Richard Quintas.

With the money that was provided each man, it didn't take long for them to experience the freedom of America. Dasch wrote in his book, "There was nothing in the way of Nazi surveillance to prevent me from taking the money I'd been provided with and fading into a happy and luxurious obscurity." Things were soon to turn out differently for Dasch and his compatriots.

Four days after the Long Island landings, four more saboteurs left U-584 and stepped ashore at Ponte Vedra Beach, about 25 miles south of Jacksonville, Florida. This landing occurred without incident. After burying their boxes in a secluded spot just off the beach, the four saboteurs walked to a store on Highway 140 and caught a bus for Jacksonville. As one story goes, police were checking vehicles, including buses going into Jacksonville, but the saboteurs passed without being questioned. In town, they split up and Kerling and Neubauer, using the names Kelly and Nicholas, checked into the Seminole Hotel. Haupt and Thiel checked into a different one. They went out that afternoon and bought new clothes and accessories. The next morning, Haupt and Thiel were on a Cincinnati bound train, and Kerling and Neubauer were en route to Cincinnati also, but on a different train. Haupt went on to Chicago where he contacted his family. Neubauer left Cincinnati for Chicago on June 20. Kerling and Thiel went on to New York City.

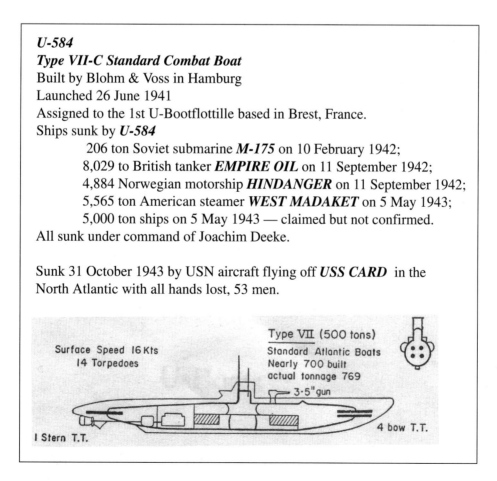

U-584
Type VII-C Standard Combat Boat
Built by Blohm & Voss in Hamburg
Launched 26 June 1941
Assigned to the 1st U-Bootflottille based in Brest, France.
Ships sunk by *U-584*

  206 ton Soviet submarine *M-175* on 10 February 1942;
  8,029 to British tanker *EMPIRE OIL* on 11 September 1942;
  4,884 Norwegian motorship *HINDANGER* on 11 September 1942;
  5,565 ton American steamer *WEST MADAKET* on 5 May 1943;
  5,000 ton ships on 5 May 1943 — claimed but not confirmed.
All sunk under command of Joachim Deeke.

Sunk 31 October 1943 by USN aircraft flying off *USS CARD* in the North Atlantic with all hands lost, 53 men.

Surface Speed 16 Kts
14 Torpedoes

Type VII (500 tons)
Standard Atlantic Boats
Nearly 700 built
actual tonnage 769

3·5" gun

I Stern T.T.

4 bow T.T.

U-584 at Brest, France. This sub brought the four saboteurs to Ponte Vedra Beach.

BUNDESARCHIV, KOBLENZ, GERMANY

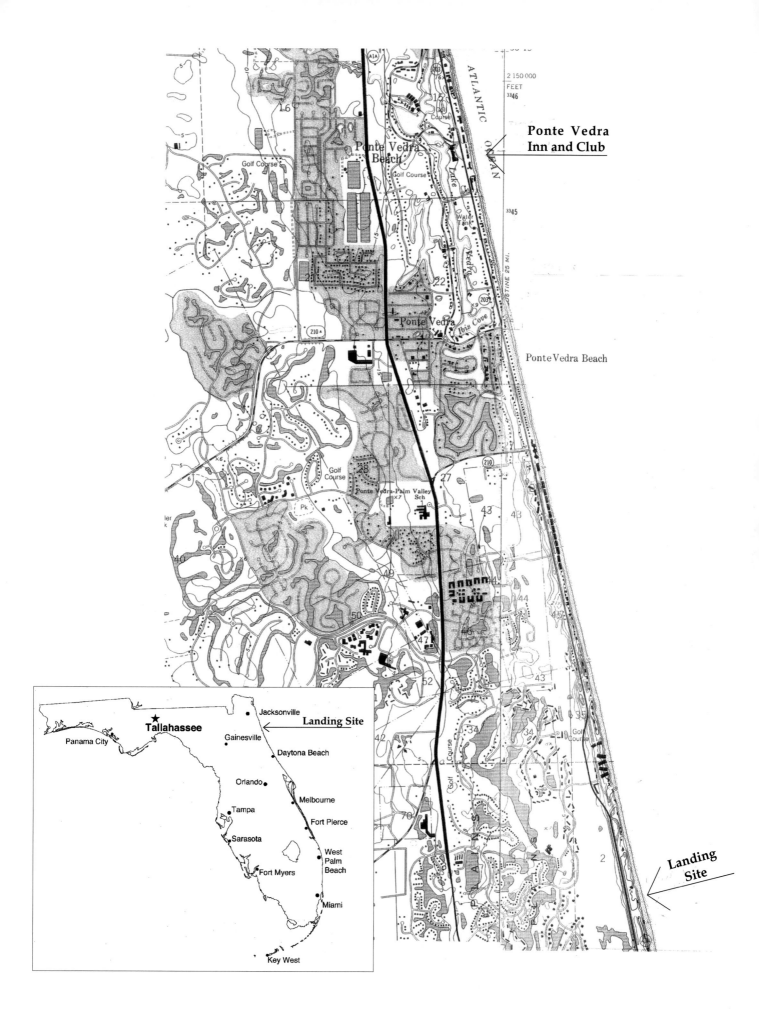

PONTE VEDRA BEACH

The first person to land on what is known today as Ponte Vedra Beach was Ponce de Leon, a Spanish explorer best known for his pursuit of the legendary "fountain of youth." He landed on April 2, 1513. Some settlement took place through the next three centuries but it wasn't until 1914 that two chemical engineers discovered that the area's beautiful beaches contained over a dozen industrial minerals, including rutile and ilmenite, components necessary for the production of titanium and zirconium, that the area had its first boom.

Titanium was a key component in the manufacture of poison gas and Germany controlled much of the world's titanium supply. The U.S. government ordered as much titanium mined from the beaches as possible during World War I. The area had been named Mineral City.

In 1928, the owners of Mineral City, the National Lead Company, rechristened their town Ponte Vedra after the city in Spain, Pontevedra.

The state began work on a road along the shoreline from Ponte Vedra to St. Augustine in 1929, which helped speed up development of the new resort–the Ponte Vedra Inn & Club. Development continued through the Depression years but the area could not match the pace of South Florida as a tourist destination.

World War II erupted in 1941, just when development seemed to be increasing. Blackout curtains were required for every household to deceive the German submarines patrolling off the Atlantic coast. Ponte Vedra residents were among the very few stateside Americans to witness acts of war firsthand as German submarines sank ships within sight of the shore, and oil from torpedoed tankers blackened the beaches.

After the war, Ponte Vedra Beach evolved into a resort community and has come to be considered one of the most luxurious and prestigious recreational and residential destinations in Florida. The area offers some 150 holes of golf along with miles of white sandy beaches.

This historic sign is placed across Ponte Vedra Boulevard from the Ponte Vedra Inn and Club. The original sign was placed 4.3 miles south of the inn at the actual site of the landing. Vandelism caused the sign to be moved to its present site. The saboteurs actually took a bus to Jacksonville and then trains to Cincinnati and Chicago before two of them went to New York.

The Ponte Vedra Inn & Club is directly across the street from the historic sign. PHOTOS COURTESY FRANCES TABER, FERNANDINA BEACH, FL.

Looking east from the beach road to the old foundation path where the saboteurs buried their equipment. NA

Kerling led FBI agents back to the beach after his capture to show them where the buried boxes of explosives were hidden. NA

Ponte Vedra Beach as it looks today near the site where the saboteurs landed.

Left, the beach road that ran past the Ponte Vedra landing site in Florida as it looked in 1942. At right, Ponte Vedra Boulevard as it looks today. NA

THE BETRAYAL

SIX OF THE SABOTEURS were now in New York City. While four of them were out on the town, Dasch and Burger began to talk about their mission and their reasons for coming to the United States. Dasch indicated he really did not belong in Germany and that he signed on to the mission just to get back to America. Burger, who had previous trouble with the Gestapo, also expressed his reservations about the mission.

Dasch, who used the false name George John Davis, told Burger that his real name was Dasch and that he intended to turn the two teams over to the

FBI. Burger confessed that he had left items on the beach in hopes that someone would find them soon after the landing.

Dasch felt he should contact the FBI right away so he could tell them the real reason why he and Burger had signed on to the mission. Burger did not tell Heinck or Quirin what Dasch was up to and asked them to keep a low profile for a few days.

Sunday, June 14, just one day after they landed on Long Island, Dasch telephoned the FBI office in New York. He talked to agent Dean McWorter and said his name was Franz Daniel Pastorius, "a German citizen who has arrived in this country only yesterday morning." He had some very important information for the FBI but wanted to tell it directly to J. Edgar Hoover. He further stated that he would contact the Washington office directly later in the week. McWorter made note of the call but did not relay it to Washington.

Dasch left for Washington by train four days later. Before he left, he paid Burger's hotel bill and left him a note. Upon arriving in Washington he checked into the Mayflower Hotel. The next morning, he telephoned the main FBI headquarters in the Justice Department building.

Agent Duane Traynor took the call and listened as Dasch identified himself by name and indicated he was the leader of eight saboteurs who had recently landed on Long Island and in Florida. At this time the FBI knew only of the Long Island landing. Agents met Dasch in his hotel room and learned of the mission from its conception to that day. He did not know the exact whereabouts of the Florida group, but a handkerchief he carried had some American contacts written on it in invisible ink. He couldn't remember what chemical was needed to bring out the names

but the FBI lab soon figured it out.

All through the interview, Dasch insisted he had no intention of carrying out the sabotage mission and planned to turn in the men long before he left Germany. He also insisted that Burger had the same idea and both were staunchly anti-Nazi in their beliefs. He also, reluctantly, turned over a satchel that contained $83,000 that he brought from Germany to sustain the men for up to two years.

In a few days, the other seven saboteurs were captured and Dasch assumed that he would be hailed as a hero and let go. He even stated, after he was formally arrested on July 3rd, that he was told that he would go to jail for a few months and then receive a presidential pardon. But, to protect himself, he requested that he be jailed with his fellow conspirators so they would not know he had turned them in.

Headlines in newspapers across the country announced the apprehension of all eight saboteurs by the FBI. Not one mentioned that one of the detainees was responsible for the capture. Even President Roosevelt was not told all the pertinent details about Dasch's role in the story.

This letter was written to Burger at the Hotel Governor Clinton by Dasch just before he left for Washington, D.C. to turn in his colleagues.

June 19, 42

Dear Pete!

Sorry for not have been able to see you before I left. I came to the realization to go to Wash'ton & finish that which we have started so far.

I'm leaving you, believing that you take good care of yourself & also of the other boys. You may rest assured, that, I shall try to straighten everything out, to the very best possibility. My bag & clothes I put in your room. Your Hotel Bill is paid by me, including this day.

If anything extra ordinary should happen, I'll get in touch with you directly.

Untill Later
I'm your sincere friend
George

Dasch wrote this letter after checking into The May-flower Hotel in Washington, D.C. on his mission to contact the FBI.

My dear friend Pete!

Got safely into room last night and contacted the responsibly parties. At present I'm waiting to be brought over to the right man by one of his agent.

I had a good night rest, feel fine physical as well as mentally and believe that I will accomplish the part of our participation. It will take lots of time & talking but please dont worry, have faith & courage. I try hard to do the right thing. In the meantime take good care of yourself & of the boys, please dont go all over town, Keep Silent to everybody. I promise you, to keep you posted on the future developments.

Before I left you, I begged the mgr. of your hotel Mr. Weil to take good care of you, for you are a Jewish refugee, so please act accordingly.

Best regards & wishes
Geo. J. Dasch

I'll forward to you my address where you reach me, via mail or phone, soon.

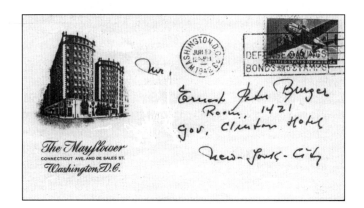

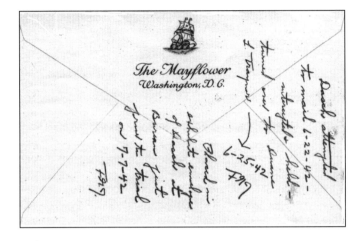

June 22, 1942

My Dear Pete!

I bet you begin wondering why I didn't write to you sooner.

In my last letter to you from here, I stated, that I have found the right way and right persons to tell our story. Since that time things began to happen. I've been working like hell from daybreak untill dawn. What I make for accomplishant is to much to describe here. I can only tell you, that everything is working out alright. Have faith & patience you will hear or see me in the future. Please stick to your role & keep the other boys contented & please don't loose their rights. Also don't tell them, that I've been here, tell them that you have heard from me from Pitsbourgh. I also beg you to destroy this letter after having read it, for it would be awful if Henry & Dick would ever read this letter.

So please Pete take good care of yourself, have fullest confidence that I shall try to straighten everything out to the best of everyone concerned. Untill you hear from me again, accept my best regards & wishes.

Your friend

George J. Dasch

Letter Dasch wrote but did not send to Burger at the Hotel Governor Clinton Hotel in New York City explaining he is taking care of everything (actually turning over the other seven saboteurs to the FBI).

THE ARRESTS

ON JUNE 20 THE FBI put Ernest Burger under surveillance at the Governor Clinton Hotel in New York City. At 2:40 P.M. he left the hotel and proceeded to the Rogers Peet Clothing Store where he met Heinrich Heinck and Richard Quirin. They then proceeded to a restaurant across the street where they stayed for 45 minutes then left and split up at the corner of 40th Street and Fifth Avenue. Quirin and Heinck took a bus north to 72nd Street and Broadway and then Heinck entered a drugstore at the corner of 74th Street and Amsterdam Avenue. Quirin was arrested near 76th Street. Heinck was taken into custody soon afterwards.

On the evening of June 20 Burger was arrested in room 1421 at the Governor Clinton Hotel. Only after the other seven saboteurs were apprehended, was George Dasch officially arrested on July 3.

As a result of reading the secret writing on Dasch's handkerchief, the name and address of Helmut Leiner appeared. He lived on 37th Avenue in Astoria, Long Island, and on June 23 he was placed under surveillance. In the afternoon, he met Edward Kerling at a bar and they later separated. Both men were followed. Kerling went to another bar at 44th Street and Lexington Avenue where he was joined by Werner Thiel and Anthony Cramer. Kerling left them and proceeded to the Shelton Hotel on Lexington Avenue where he was arrested. Thiel and Cramer separated late that evening and Thiel was immediately arrested.

Herbert Haupt was also under surveillance in Chicago and was arrested there on June 27 at an elevated train station on Webster Street. Haupt said that Herman Neubauer would probably be registered as H. Nicholas at a hotel in Chicago. He was found at the Sheridan Plaza Hotel on Sheridan Road. At 6:45 P.M. on the 27th he was arrested. The two were taken to New York City to join the other six saboteurs. Once there the FBI started an intensive interrogation period before the entire group were taken to Washington, D.C. for trial.

Wants Medal for Hoover

WASHINGTON, July 6 (AP)—Award of a Congressional Medal to J. Edgar Hoover, director of the Federal Bureau of Investigation, for the capture of eight alleged Nazi saboteurs, was proposed today by Senator Mead.

A bill introduced by Senator Mead would authorize the President to award the medal in the name of Congress.

Haupt Planned to Marry
Special to THE NEW YORK TIMES.

CHICAGO, June 28—Mrs. Gerda Melend, 24-year-old brunette, who was to have been married next week to Herbert Hans Haupt, accused as a German spy and saboteur, told today of her reunion Tuesday with Haupt after a year's mystery absence and of her hunch that something was wrong.

She met Haupt, 22, a former R. O. T. C. cadet, about three and a half years ago. They fell in love, she said, and while not actually engaged, had discussed being married.

"I knew he liked Hitler's policies," Mrs. Melend said, "but that was a couple of years ago and we weren't in the war."

About a year ago, she said, Haupt suddenly announced that he wanted to visit California. He was a bit vague on details, she said, and after a postcard from St. Louis she heard no more. But on Tuesday Haupt's mother, Erma, telephoned the beauty shop where Mrs. Melend, a widow, is employed, saying that Herbert had returned.

"I saw him at dinner that night in his parents' home, and he was very nervous. I thought maybe it was because he hadn't registered for the draft, but he told me he'd gone down and registered that day and that they'd been awfully nice to him. I asked him how he came back and he didn't say anything.

"He called me every day after that, but I wouldn't see him. I had a hunch there was something wrong, and I said I'd see him Saturday, figuring if there was something wrong they'd have him by then. He had mentioned marriage Tuesday, and we'd agreed to be married this week."

She added that she arrived at the Haupt home Saturday night and that, although the Haupts told her their son had been arrested, they insisted they did not know why. She said she herself didn't know until operatives of the Federal Bureau of Investigation questioned her this morning.

Lone Coast Guardsman Put FBI on Trail of Saboteurs

By LEWIS WOOD
Special to The New York Times.

WASHINGTON, July 15—The discovery of the daring saboteur invasion of this country came when a solitary young Coast Guardsman on the Long Island shore saw two Germans emerging from the sea at midnight and another standing on the beach, the United States Coast Guard revealed today in a graphic story of the incident.

The men in the water were in bathing suits, obviously landing at Amagansett from a U-boat, seen dimly through the fog and whose engines were heard roaring.

The 21-year-old Coast Guardsman, John C. Cullen, seaman second class, was threatened with death by one of the Nazis in a bathing suit, who offered him a bribe of $300. But almost immediately, the young Coast Guardsman "accepted" the bribe, only to report the incident at once to his superiors. Later Cullen found that he had been short-changed by $40.

[Vice Admiral R. R. Waesche, Coast Guard commandant, promoted Cullen to coxswain tonight, according to The Associated Press.]

Cullen indubitably was one of the Coast Guardsmen testifying at the opening of the saboteur trial that has now gone through its seventh day in secret. Most of today was consumed by reading a "very long statement which had been made by one of the accused to the FBI," and assumed to come from George John Dasch, credited with assistance to the government in the case.

Florida Residents Startled
Special to The New York Times.

JACKSONVILLE, Fla., June 28—Florida East Coast residents were electrified today by the disclosure of the Nazi saboteurs' landing at Ponte Vedra Beach, but if there was any one who knew more about it than the F. B. I. chief told he was keeping mum.

The consensus, however, is that the landing was made somewhere along the desolate thirty miles of beach stretching southward from Ponte Vedra toward St. Augustine. Northward the beach is lined with screened-out resort homes for eight miles, and civilian defense workers have maintained a twenty-hour watch there for several weeks.

Close behind the low sand dunes lining the beach southward runs State Highway 78 from Jacksonville to St. Augustine. Back of this, a mile of scrub timber and marshland reaches across to the intracoastal waterway. Vehicular traffic along this stretch of road is prohibited, but three miles north of Ponte Vedra, at Jacksonville Beach, buses and autos with dimmed lights are allowed to use the road inland to Jacksonville.

Some persons ventured the opinion that the four Germans landed here walked into a trap and were shadowed from the time of their arrival. Officials had no comment, but the subject was on the lips of thousands of week-end visitors, including service men from Camp Blanding and the Naval Air Station.

GUEST COPY

SHERIDAN PLAZA HOTEL

SHERIDAN ROAD AT WILSON AVE.

Chicago, 6/27 1942

Received of _Nicholas_

$ 2—00   ROOM 1230   FROM   TO   BAL. DUE

IN FULL ON ACCT. 2 00   AMT. RENT   AMT. PHONE   MISC.   CHECK ☐   CASH ☐

DEMAND RECEIPT
RECEIPT OF ANY KIND VOID UNLESS ON THIS FORM

THE CASHIER EXECUTING THIS RECEIPT HAS NO AUTHORITY TO BIND THIS COMPANY, OTHER THAN TO ACKNOWLEDGE RECEIPT OF SUCH FUNDS.

THIS RECEIPT IS ISSUED CONTINGENT UPON PAYMENT OF PRESENT AND FUTURE CHECKS THAT MIGHT BE CASHED.

WE APPRECIATE YOUR PATRONAGE AND TRUST THAT THE SERVICE AND ACCOMMODATIONS FURNISHED DURING YOUR STAY WITH US HAVE BEEN ENTIRELY SATISFACTORY. WE HOPE YOU WILL COME TO REGARD THE SHERIDAN PLAZA AS YOUR CHICAGO HOME.   THE MANAGEMENT

SHERIDAN PLAZA HOTEL

No. 11678   By _Ruger_

Neubauer's registration receipt from the Sheridan Plaza Hotel in Chicago.

Room 2250
F.B.I., Dept of Justice Building
Washington, D.C.
June 25, 1942

The following personal property was taken from my person and turned over to Special Agents F. G. Johnstone and M. W. Mills on June 25, 1942:

a) one $50.00 bill serial # B 00799008 A
b) one $50.00 bill serial # B 01747014 A
c) one $20.00 bill serial # B 18235731 A
d) one $10.00 bill serial # B 78705231 B
e) one $10.00 bill serial # A 82123204 A
f) one $10.00 bill serial # E 30646743 A
g) one $5.00 bill serial # J 71022294 A
h) one $1.00 bill serial # W 89443275 B
i) one $1.00 bill serial # X 38595447 B
j) one $1.00 bill serial # X 37267214 B
k) one $1.00 bill serial # X 37267213 B
l) ~~Silver~~ in amount of $1.17.
m) Shaeffer pen and pencil set
n) Gold Lord Elgin men's wrist watch with leather strap.
o) Red address book
p) Chain containing gold knife and 3 keys.
q) one tie clasp.

Geo. J. Dasch

2 keys on pen knife chain given to F. G. Johnstone on 6/27/42 by M. E. Singleton. The other key is being attached to brief case.

6-25-42
FMW

Dasch filled out this list of property which was on his person when he turned it over to the FBI on June 25, 1942.

Room 2250, FBI
Washington DC
June 25, 1942

The money bundled as reflected on the reverse side of this paper was found by Special Agents N. D. Wills and F. G. Johnstone in a brown leather accordion type brief case having white stitching on June 25, 1942 in possession of George John Dasch. This brief case was unlocked by George John Dasch in Room 2250 of the U.S. Dept of Justice Building, Washington, D.C., and the same turned over to Agents Wills and Johnstone for counting and listing the serial numbers. The date this money was counted, the amount contained in each bundle and the agents initials appear on the wrapper to each bundle; also, the envelopes containing the bundles of money have been dated and initialed by the agents in my presence. This is all the money George John Dasch has except that in his person

I read the above statement a found to be correct.

George John Dasch

Witness: N. D. Wills - Special Agent
F.B.I., N.Y.C.
Frank G. Johnstone - " "

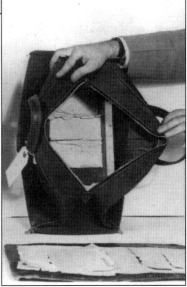

Affidavit signed by
George Dasch as to the
contents of the zippered
brief case at right.

Manila Envelope #1

7 X $50.	———	350.00 ✓
40 X 50.	———	2000.00 ✓
100 X 50.	———	5000.00 ✓
101 X 50.	———	5050.00 ✓
101 X 50.	———	5050.00 ✓
98 X 50.	———	4900.00 ✓
		$ 22 350.00 ✓

Manila Envelope #2

96 X $50.	—	$ 4800.00 ✓
98 X 50.	—	4900.00 ✓
100 X 50.	—	5000.00 ✓
100 X 50.	—	5000.00 ✓
100 X 50.	—	5000.00 ✓
95 X 50.	—	4750.00 ✓
		$ 29 450.00 ✓

Manila Envelope #3

100 X $50.	$ 5000.00 ✓
99 X 50.	4950.00 ✓
99 X 50.	4950.00 ✓
99 X 50.	4950.00 ✓
99 X 50.	4950.00 ✓
99 X 50.	4950.00 ✓
	$ 29 750.00

Letter envelope (Gov. Clinton Hotel) # 4 - 20 X 50 $ 1000.00 ✓

Grand total in $ 82 550.00

letter envelope (Gov Clinton Hotel) # 5 - Contains no money, only a note
dated 6/18/42

A list of money that was contained in the brief case carried by Dasch and
deposited with the FBI in Washington, D.C. on June 25, 1942.

THE OTHER CONSPIRATORS

THE HANDKERCHIEFS

THE GROUP LEADERS (DASCH and Kerling) each had a handkerchief in their possession with the names of American contacts written in secret ink. By prior arrangement, each group leader had exchanged addresses by which the other could be contacted at a later date. Dasch's handkerchief was confiscated when he surrendered to the FBI but he would not, or could not, reveal the chemical formula for bringing out the names. Eventually, the FBI lab exposed it to ammonia fumes and the names became visible.

The names and addresses on the handkerchief proved invaluable to the FBI in apprehending the Florida saboteurs. The name Maria da Conceico Lopez in Lisbon, Portugal, was a mail drop for the saboteurs to communicate with the Abwehr, since there was no direct mail service to Germany. Portugal was a neutral country during the war and had mail service to both Germany and the United States. The initials F.D.P. were also found on the handkerchief. They stood for the code name of the mission, Franz Daniel Pastorius.

The following 16 individuals were involved with

This handerkerchief was carried by Kerling at the time of his arrest in New York City. When treated with a certain chemical, it revealed the saboteur's contact in Lisbon and potential contacts in the United States.

the saboteurs and their eventual disposition, when known, is given.

Pas Krepper's name was on the handkerchief. He was born in Germany and came to the United States in 1909. He was a Lutheran pastor in Philadelphia. During World War I he was investigated for engaging in German activities. In the 1930s he lived in New Jersey, attended Rutgers University and held a minor political office. He also made a trip to Germany where he apparently embraced the Nazi doctrine.

On Jan. 20, 1942 the FBI received an anonymous letter. It stated that Pastor Carl Krepper is an American citizen and that although he had been in the United States for 32 years, he had gone back to Germany for a visit which lasted four or five years. It was stated that he should be watched inasmuch as he had no respect for the United States, which had fed and clothed him during his stay in that country. Walter Kappe gave Krepper's name to the saboteur's leaders.

Gene Frey's name was on the handkerchief as well. He was born in Philadelphia to German parents. Frey held various jobs in New Jersey. They ranged from running a gas station, to being a tax collector, to being a factory worker. He was the stepson of Pastor Carl Krepper.

Walter Froehling's name was on the handkerchief. He was Herbert Haupt's uncle and a resident of Chicago since 1929. He was the main contact for the saboteurs if they needed help in the Chicago area. Herbert Haupt contacted him upon arriving in the city and gave him $9,500 to hide in his house. Froehling married his wife, a German national, in 1930 and they had two children. In November 1942, Walter was sentenced to death, and Lucille to 25 years in prison for helping Haupt. In June 1943 the convictions were overturned. Lucille was released and Walter was sentenced to five years in prison for another crime of treason.

Hans Max Haupt was the father of saboteur Herbert Haupt. He immigrated to the United States in the early 1920s and became a naturalized citizen in Chicago in 1930. During the 1930s he was very active in several pro-Nazi organizations. He was also a World War I German Army veteran. His son went to his family's home upon arriving in Chicago and told them that he had come by submarine to the United States. Hans Haupt was sentenced to death in November 1942. The conviction was overturned and, after another trial in June 1944 he was sentenced to life in prison plus a $10,000 fine. He was released in 1957 and deported to Germany.

Erna Froehling Haupt was a native of Germany and married Hans in 1919. Both of them worked as servants for a couple in Glencoe, Illinois, for several years in the 1930s. Erna was naturalized in 1940. In November 1942 she was sentenced to 25 years in prison and a $10,000

fine. The sentence was overturned in June 1943 and her citizenship was revoked. She remained in Federal prison until 1946 when she was deported to Germany.

Helmut Leiner's name was on Dasch's handkerchief. He came to the United States from Germany in 1936 to join his father who resided in Astoria, Long Island. Leiner was a friend of Kerling through their mutual association in the German-American Bund. Leiner was to be repatriated to Germany on June 10, 1942, as he was a German National but he did not board the boat. After Kerling got to New York he contacted Leiner to have him change some of his large denomination American money and to ask for assistance in contacting other Nazi sympathizers. It was through this contact that Kerling was arrested by the FBI. Leiner was eventually sentenced to 18 years in prison but was released on parole in 1954. He was deported to Germany in 1956.

Marie Kerling was the wife of Edward Kerling, leader of the Florida landing party. She entered the United States in 1924 and married Edward in 1930. Both worked for a family in Short Hills, New Jersey, for four and one half years. She was to be repatriated to Germany on June 13, 1942, but did not show up at the time of the sailing. Mrs. Kerling spent a year as an internee on Ellis Island and four years at an alien detention camp in Texas, before being released in late 1947.

Hedwig (Hedy) Engemann was Edward Kerling's mistress. She was born in Brooklyn, New York, in 1907 to German parents. Kerling met Engemann in Florida in 1939 and she was his first contact upon returning to the United States. He told her he had just landed from a submarine, and wanted her to help him with his mission and to accompany him on his travels in the United States. He also wanted her to rent an apartment in New York City so he would have a place to stay while there. Engemann told the FBI, after Kerling's arrest, that she did not turn him in because of the relationship she had with him. On June 30, 1942, she was arrested and held by the FBI for four weeks. The charge against her was

misprision of treason, or to have known of the treason committed by another person but not acted on it. As the only American-born conspirator arrested, she was in a difficult position and finally pled guilty. She spent a year in the Women's House of Detention in New York City and was then sent to the Federal Penitentiary for Women in Alderson, West Virginia, where she was released on parole in 1945. Hedy Engemann died in 1988.

Ernest Herman Kerkof, a native of Hanover, Germany, became a naturalized citizen in 1932. He was a close friend of Marie Kerling and an important contact for the saboteurs. He was arrested on June 23, 1942 while on board a repatriation ship bound for Europe. He was never tried for treason.

Lucille Froehling was a native of Berlin and became a naturalized citizen in 1935. She was married to Otto Froehling and knew of Haupt's mission to the United States. She was charged with treason in October 1942 and sentenced to 25 years in prison and a $10,000 fine. A new trial was held in June 1943 and in 1944, she made a deal with the government and was set free.

Anthony Cramer was an old friend of saboteur Werner Thiel. Thiel went directly to Cramer's home after he arrived in New York and put $3,000 in Cramer's safety deposit box at his bank. The FBI arrested Cramer for his association with Kerling and Theil. He was convicted of treason, but the United States Supreme Court overturned the conviction citing a lack of conclusive evidence. He eventually pled guilty to "trading with the enemy" and was sentenced six years in Federal prison.

Harry Jaques jumped ship (*SS Hamburg*) in New York in 1924. He moved to Chicago and became friends with saboteur Neubauer through his wife, Alma. Neubauer left $3,600 hidden in a coffee bean jar in Jaques' house. Jaques and his wife were never tried but were interned and later deported to Germany.

Emma Jaques came to the United States from Germany in 1925 with her then husband, Adolph Wiek. That same year, she left her husband and moved with Harry Jaques to Chicago. She was a good friend of Alma Neubauer.

Otto Richard Wergin was a German Navy veteran of World War I and came to the United States in 1926. In 1936 he became a naturalized citizen. Wergin was an active member of the German-American Bund and other pro-Nazi organizations and offered help to Herbert Haupt when he arrived in Chicago. Wergin's son, Wolfgang, had gone to Mexico with Haupt in the 1930s. In July 1942, Otto Wergin was indicted for treason and in November was sentenced to death. After a new trial in June 1943, Otto was re-sentenced to five years. After the war he managed a bar in Chicago before retiring in California.

Kate Martha Wergin entered the United States in 1927 and became a naturalized citizen in 1934. She was also an active member of several pro-Nazi organizations. In November 1942 she was sentenced to 23 years in prison and a $10,000 fine. A new trial was held in June 1943 and she was set free.

Herman Heinrich Faje came to the United States in 1928 from Hamburg, Germany. He worked as a hairdresser in New York and lived in Astoria, Long Island, with his wife, Hildegard. The couple was friends with saboteur Heinrich Heinck when he lived in the United States and helped him hide money after his landing. Faje was sentenced to five years in Federal prison.

THE TRIAL

WHEN THE PROSPECT OF a trial was made public in late June, the reaction around the country was predictable. Newspapers and radio commentators demanded no mercy for the men who had come to America's shores to destroy vital war industries. President Roosevelt did not want a public trial and indicated that he expected a verdict of guilty and a sentence of death for all eight conspirators. He did not know at the time of Dasch's involvement in the capture of the other seven men. A normal trial would entail too many sensitive details ending up in the public records and a death sentence was not absolutely assured, as no actual occurrence of sabotage had been carried out. The eight men were thus tried before a military tribunal although the defendants were not U.S. military personnel.

As a precedent, the government used the 1865 trial of the conspirators who assassinated President Lincoln. They were declared enemies of the state and most of them were executed by hanging. Four major generals and three brigadier generals were assigned to be judges with Maj. Gen. Frank McCoy as president. Attorney General Francis Biddle was to be the lead prosecutor, assisted by Maj. Gen. Myron Cramer, the Army's Judge Advocate General. Gen. Albert L. Cox was the tribunal's provost marshal. Defense lawyers for seven of the defendants were Col. Cassius M. Dowell and Col. Kenneth C. Royall. Col. Carl Ristine of the Army's Inspector General Office represented Dasch separately.

Votes of five of the seven generals were required for conviction and sentencing, but President Roosevelt had the final decision over all the members' recommendations.

The eight Germans were transported from New York to the District of Columbia jail in Washington, D.C. on July 4, 1942. They were held in separate jail cells and had very spartan living conditions, partly to prevent the men from attempting suicide. Assembly Room #1, on the fifth floor of the Justice Department building, was selected as a courtroom. It was secluded and easy to guard. Room 5235 led to the courtroom that was used by the FBI.

On July 8, 1942 the trial began. Each day the eight men were transported to the Justice Department by a convoy of vans manned by U.S. Marshals and FBI agents. Armored cars manned by heavily armed soldiers escorted the vans. The defendants were always guarded in the courtroom and were dressed in the clothes they had bought upon arrival in the United States.

The defense council made a strong defense statement:

"In deference to the commission and in order that we may not waive for our clients any rights which may belong to them, we desire to state that, in our opinion, the order of the President of the United States creating this court is invalid and unconstitutional Our view is based on the fact that the civil courts are open in the territory in which we are now located and that, in our opinion, there are civil statutes governing the matters to be investigated."

They further argued that since the defendants were not U.S. citizens, (actually, some were naturalized citizens), the articles of war did not apply to them and they had committed no acts of sabotage since landing on America's shores. Biddle responded:

"This is not a trial of offenses on law of the civil courts, but is a trial of the offenses on the law of war, which is not cognizable by the civil courts. It is the trial, as alleged in the charges, on certain enemies who crossed our borders, and who crossed in disguise and landed here. They are exactly and precisely in the same position as armed forces invading this country."

John Cullen, the Coast Guardsman who first saw Dasch, gave damaging testimony. (Dasch had brought up the fact to the FBI that he had orders to kill anyone that discovered the men on the beach, but had let Cullen go). All of the defendants, testifying in their own defense, stated that they had second thoughts about committing any sabotage, but had not turned themselves in because of fear that the Gestapo would harm their families back in Germany. Biddle did tell Roosevelt that should the defendants be sentenced to death that Dasch and Burger be given some clemency for their earlier help in apprehending the other six.

The defense rested on July 27, but Royall decided to challenge the President's order for the military tribunal and demanded a writ of habeas corpus for his clients. The Supreme Court was not in session in July but decided to convene a special session to rule on the case. They rejected the defense's arguments and upheld the jurisdiction and authority of the military tribunal.

On August 3 the tribunal reached a verdict. It was delivered to President Roosevelt and stated that all eight men were found guilty and recommended death by electrocution. It did ask, however, that Dasch and Burger's sentences be commuted to life in prison. Four days later, instructions were received to execute all defendants except Dasch and Burger the next day.

The sentences were carried out starting at noon on August 8. They were electrocuted in the District of Columbia jail and buried in a pauper's cemetery at Blue Plains Potters Field in the District. Six wooden headboards were placed on the graves marked simply 276, 277, 278, 279, 280 and 281.

This ended the story of the only sabotage landings on America's shores in World War II. The Maine landing two years later was mostly a spy mission.

The arrests of the saboteurs triggered the roundup of hundreds of German aliens thought to be Nazi sympathizers and the sale of assets of Axis controlled companies. When it was learned that three of the saboteurs had worked as waiters in the United States before the war, the FBI ordered the dismissal of all German and Italian nationals working as waiters, barbers, busboys, housemen and maids in Washington's hotels, restaurants and clubs. The theory was that they might be spies and may overhear something of military importance from their customers or employers.

George Washington Helps Prosecute the Saboteurs

Special to The New York Times.

WASHINGTON, July 15 — George Washington is helping Attorney General Biddle in the prosecution of the eight Nazi saboteurs.

The nearest collateral descendant of the first president is an attorney on the staff of Oscar Cox, Assistant Solicitor General, who cooperates with Mr. Biddle and Major Gen. Myron C. Cramer, Judge Advocate General, in handling the government case.

Mr. Washington, a direct descendant of Colonel Samuel Washington, brother of the original George, is also, said the Department of Justice, "somewhat deviously related" to Abraham Lincoln inasmuch as the government lawyer's grandmother, Jane Todd Washington, was a cousin of Mary Todd Lincoln.

Thirty-four years old and a Yale and Oxford graduate, Mr. Washington practiced law in New York for some years before joining the Cornell Law School faculty, from which he is now on leave.

New York Times, July 16, 1942

WAR DEPARTMENT

WAR DEPARTMENT GENERAL STAFF
MILITARY INTELLIGENCE DIVISION G-2
WASHINGTON

June 28, 1942.

MEMORANDUM FOR THE SECRETARY OF WAR:

Subject: Disposal of Saboteurs Landed on
Eastern Seaboard.

1. On June 13 it was reported that four men were landed from a submarine near Amagansett, Long Island, the preceding night. A Coast Guardsman contacted these men who bribed him to keep silent. He reported to his superiors and during the day of the 13th of June there were found buried on the Beach two wet uniforms identified as the kind worn by German sailors. In addition there were unearthed three cases of TNT, detonators, and incendiary pencils. Representatives of the Eastern Defense Command, Second Corps Area, Federal Bureau of Investigation, Coast Guard, United States Secret Service, and Navy Department cooperated in the search.

2. At 10:30 a.m., on June 19, an officer of the Military Intelligence Service contacted an individual (Johan-Dasche alias George John Davis) who admitted his participation in the landing near Amagansett. The Counterintelligence Group, MIS, was notified and turned the man over to the FBI. As a result of the FBI investigation of this man's story, the remaining three members of the first group were seized and four additional men who were members of a second group, which landed June 17 at Ponte Vedra Beach, south of Jacksonville Beach, Florida, were seized. The last arrest was made yesterday in Chicago. Material for sabotage, similar to that buried near Amagansett, was found at Ponte Vedra Beach.

3. As a result of the arrest in Chicago yesterday, the newspapers became aware of the story and Mr. Hoover, Director of the FBI, was compelled to release the story, which appears in substantially correct form in the press this morning.

4. The premature breaking of the story has wrecked our plans for seizing two additional groups of four men each who apparently are scheduled to land on our shores in August. In consequence, the only benefit to National Defense that can be obtained is the deterrent effect upon possible sabotage by the prompt trial and execution of the eight men now in the hands of the FBI.

-1-

This communique issued on June 28, 1942, shows the confusion created by the quick capture of the eight saboteurs, the premature news release and their ultimate legal determination.

5. It is understood that the Attorney General is insistent that these men be tried by civil courts as saboteurs, and not be tried by military authorities under the provisions of the 81st or 82d Article of War as spies.

6. It is believed that insofar as the war effort is concerned, it would be highly desirable that these eight cases be handled by a military commission in spite of the fact that, although operations against the enemy are proceeding on the Atlantic seaboard, no technical state of martial law as such has been declared. The exigencies of the present situation appear to demand drastic action without too much deference to the technical rights which might be accorded, under the Constitution, to enemy aliens coming to our shores with the admitted intention of crippling our defense effort, and with the training and means adequate to accomplish that end.

7. Opinion of the Judge Advocate General herewith.

GEO. V. STRONG,
Major General,
A. C. of S., G-2.

June 28, 1942.

SPJGW 383.4

MEMORANDUM for the Assistant Chief of Staff, G-2.

Subject: Trial of Ernst P. Burger and other alleged saboteurs.

1. You have called attention to the account in this morning's papers of the capture by the F.B.I. of eight persons of German birth, two of whom are naturalized citizens of the United States, who, it is stated landed four on a beach at Amagansett, Long Island, New York, and four at Ponte Vedra, near Jacksonville, Florida, with explosives, weapons and money with the object of sabotage in industrial plants in the United States important to the war effort. The article in the papers leaves it to be inferred that these men landed in uniform but changed to civilian clothing on the beach. It states that they buried the material which they brought with them on the beach and that five of them have been captured at New York, one at Chicago, and the place of capture of the other two is not stated. You have correctly said that there are two questions, first whether these men may lawfully be tried by military tribunal and second whether such trial is advisable.

2. Between the time when you asked my advice on the matter and the time at which you requested this memorandum be delivered to you, I have been unable to make a thorough search of the files of this office and other legal authorities but the present statements are my views based on such consideration and research as have been possible.

3. There are two Articles of War having more or less bearing on this subject as follows:

"ART. 81. Relieving, Corresponding With, or Aiding the Enemy.- Whosoever relieves or attempts to relieve the enemy with arms, ammunition, supplies, money, or other thing, or knowingly harbors or protects or holds correspondence with or gives intelligence to the enemy, either directly or indirectly, shall suffer death or such other punishment as a court-martial or military commission may direct.

"ART. 82 Spies.- Any person who in time of war shall be found lurking or acting as a spy in or about any of the fortifications, posts, quarters, or encampments of any of

FOR VICTORY
BUY
UNITED STATES
WAR
BONDS
AND
STAMPS

the armies of the United States, or elsewhere, shall be tried by a general court-martial or by a military commission, and shall, on conviction thereof, suffer death."

It would seem that the men recently arrested do not fall within the first clause of Article 81 since so far as appears they have not relieved or attempted to relieve the enemy with arms, supplies, etc., nor have they harbored enemies. It is possible that they may have held correspondence with the enemy since their landing although that is not stated to be the fact.

The 82nd Article denounces the crime of acting as a spy as thus defined in Article 29 of the Hague Regulations, published in FM 27-10, paragraph 202:

"Spies.- a. General. - A person can only be considered a spy when, acting clandestinely or on false pretenses, he obtains or endeavors to obtain information in the zone of operations of a belligerent with the intention of communicating it to the hostile party."

It is also very doubtful whether the men under arrest are guilty of spying since their purpose appears to have been to destroy factories and commit sabotage rather than to obtain information which is the essence of spying.

If they are to be tried by a military commission, my opinion is that a conviction would be more likely to be obtained by charging them with violation of the unwritten laws of war in that they appeared in the territory of their enemy with hostile intent in civilian clothing and there conspired together to destroy his arms, munitions, and factories engaged in making the same. There is precedent for trying persons violating the unwritten laws of war by military commissions as for example the trial, conviction and executed death sentence of Vwirz, the keeper of the Confederate prison camp at Andersonville, Georgia, in the Civil War, for cruelty to the prisoners under his charge.

The most serious objection to the trial of the men now under arrest by military tribunal is the doubt as to the jurisdiction of such a tribunal. You will observe that the 82nd Article of War above quoted provides for criminal liability only if the offence is committed "in or about any of the fortifications, posts, quarters, or encampment of any of the Armies of the United States, or elsewhere". In 13 Opinions of the Attorney General, 356, the Attorney General held that under the

Hague Regulations and the laws of war there must be a showing that the spy operated in the zone of operations, and he held that Nogales, Arizona, was not in such a zone. In a later unpublished opinion in the same case, a copy of which is in the files of this office (CM 119966), after it had been pointed out to the Attorney General that the alleged spy was arrested within half a mile of an encampment of the United States Army, the Attorney General held that he might lawfully be tried under this Article in view of the changed state of facts disclosed to him. However, the Attorney General withdrew nothing in principle that he had said in his earlier opinion.

Two of the leading and soundest writers on martial law, Fairman and Wiener, hold that the words "or elsewhere" must be limited to the general vicinity of fortifications, posts, etc., and to the theater of operations (Fairman, Law of Martial Rule, sec. 39; Wiener Practical Manual of Martial Law, sec. 130). There is some authority to the contrary, U.S. ex rel. Wessels v. McDonald, 256 Federal 754; Ops. JAG 1918, vol. 2, p. 252.

In the Milligan case, 4 Wallace 2, it was held that a military commission may sit only in the theater of actual operations; and that Indiana in 1864, even though that state had been invaded the preceding year, was not a part of that theater. Though often attacked, that case has never been overruled. It may, of course, be argued that changes in tactics and particularly the invention of the airplane and its adaptation to the uses of war have extended the meaning of the "theater of war". However, there is as yet no judicial authority for such a view, though strong argument can be made for it.

My conclusion on this branch of the discussion is that it will be possible to draw one or more specifications stating offenses against the laws of war cognizable by courts-martial or military commissions, which offenses these prisoners appear to have committed; and for which trial by military commission is probably lawful; but that the jurisdiction of military tribunals over them is open to very serious doubt and would almost certainly be attacked by application to a U.S. District Court for the writ of habeas corpus.

4. The second question is as to the advisability of trial by military tribunals. The district courts of the United States unquestionably have jurisdiction of the offenses committed by these prisoners. The general rule with respect to concurrent jurisdiction is that that jurisdiction which first attaches should be allowed to carry the case through to a conclusion. The jurisdiction of the district courts has attached by the arrest of the accused by agents of the F.B.I. and presumably by swearing out of warrants on which the prisoners were arrested. That jurisdiction could only be ousted by consent of the

- 3 -

Department of Justice or by a direct order from the President to the Attorney General to turn over the prisoners to the military authorities.

The principal objection to trial by a U. S. District Court is that, so far as I have been able to ascertain in the brief time at my disposal, that court would be unable to impose an adequate sentence. It could impose a sentence of two years confinement and a fine of $10,000 for conspiracy to commit a crime against the United States, and could also punish the prisoners for violation of the immigration laws in entering the country clandestinely and of the customs laws in bringing articles into the United States otherwise than through the custom house. The maximum permissible punishment for these offenses would be less than it is desirable to impose. It may be that the officers of the Department of Justice, who, of course, are more familiar than I with the statutes applicable to crimes triable in the district courts, have in mind some theory on which a severer punishment may be imposed.

5. My recommendation is that no determination be reached at the present moment with respect to the tribunal which should try these accused; but that representatives of this office be authorized to confer with the proper officers of the Department of Justice and in consultation with them to explore the subject, discussing both the jurisdiction of the civil and military courts and the punishments which they may impose. It is to be hoped that at such a conference the officers of the Department of Justice and of this office will be able to make a recommendation upon the appropriate procedure, subject of course, to confirmation by the Attorney General and the Secretary of War.

Myron C. Cramer,
Major General,
The Judge Advocate General.

Three of the four boxes found on June 13 on Long Island. Both landing parties had basically the same types of materials in the four boxes.
NA

The four wooden boxes each had an inner tin box tightly packed with the group's sabotage equipment: brick-shaped blocks of explosives, safety and detonating fuses and bombs disguised as lumps of coal. NA

TNT DEMOLITION BLOCK IN PAPER WRAPPER.
APPROXIMATE WEIGHT 2.2 POUNDS

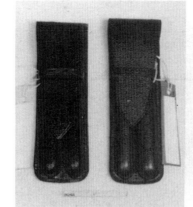

PEN AND PENCIL DELAY DEVICES IN
CARRYING CASES

X-RAY PHOTOGRAPH SHOWING PEN AND
PENCIL SET IN CARRYING CASE

TNT DEMOLITION BLOCK SHOWING HOLE
TO ACCOMODATE A DETONATOR

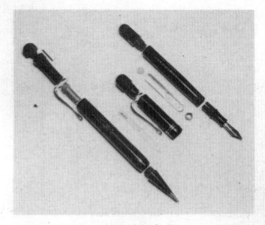

PEN AND PENCIL SET, DISASSEMBLED, SHOWING
COMPONENT PARTS

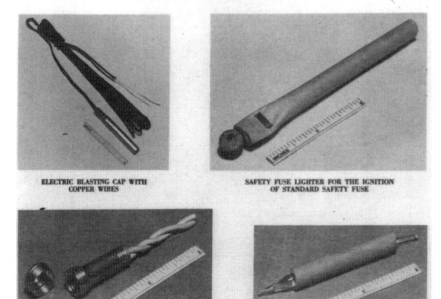

ELECTRIC BLASTING CAP WITH
COPPER WIRES

SAFETY FUSE LIGHTER FOR THE IGNITION
OF STANDARD SAFETY FUSE

ELECTRIC MATCH WITH SCREW CAP REMOVED--USED IN
CONJUNCTION WITH TIMING MECHANISM AND BATTERY

CAPSULE CONTAINING SULPHURIC ACID ENCASED
IN RUBBER TUBING FOR PROTECTION

A disassembled time clock showing a larger coiled driving spring which could be set for as long as two weeks. NA

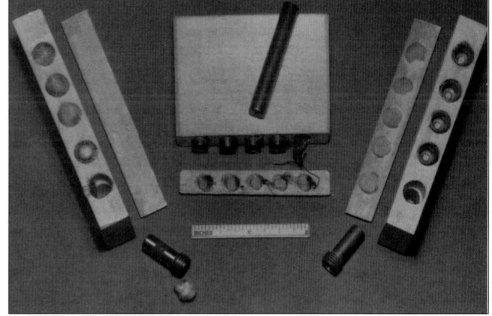

Wooden blocks hollowed out to store detonating items. NA

One of the bombs made to look like a lump of coal. NA

Time clocks and accessories. NA

Various devices for detonating bombs. Left to right on the bottom: Electric match heads; brass adapters for detonators; dummy detonators. On top: fuse lighters; blasting caps, wood block with detonators.
On top: fuse lighters; blasting caps, wooden blocks with detonators insides.NA

An FBI employee shows one of the shovels used to bury the four boxes of explosives. This shovel would be part of the evidence used at the trial. NA

These three photos show clothing items, shovels and other things found in duffel bags buried at both locations. NA

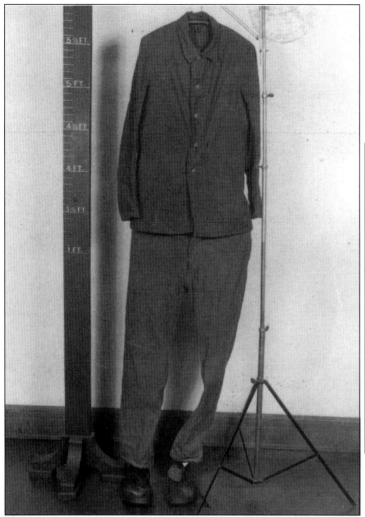

Set of clothes found in a duffel
bag buried on the beach. NA

Shoes worn by Burger found buried
on the Long Island beach. NA

Pair of Jantzen
swimming trunks
worn by Edward
Kerling when he
landed at Ponte
Vedra Beach. NA

The Buried Items on Long Island and Florida.
Four wooden boxes were found at each location. Their contents were as follows:

Amagansett, Long Island

· Two small bags containing 10 fuse lighters. These bags were marked "C. Heinrich Anton Dusberg Reissbanzunder."
· One small bag containing five fuse lighters.
· Twenty-five .30-caliber electric blasting caps.
· Brass tube containing 50 electric match heads.
· Twenty-five small wooden boxes, each containing five detonators.
· A small paper bag marked "25 Brand Kapseln" containing five wooden boxes, each containing five detonators.
· A cardboard box containing 10 brass and plastic devices holding a small charge of a chlorate mixture protected by a paper diaphragm. The box was wrapped in brown paper which was labeled in German "For F.O. Miuntan [sic] H2SO4 EBOINT"
· A box containing:
  - Two leatherette cases each containing two mechanical pen and pencil sets. These items were actually time-delayed detonators marked with pink tags indicating "6 to 7 hours."
  - Two leatherette cases each containing a mechanical fountain pen and pencil set. These items were time-delayed detonators labeled with a blue tag indicating "2-3 hours."
  - One leatherette case containing a mechanical fountain pen and pencil set. This time-delayed detonator was labeled "11-13 hours."
  - Five small brown tablets rolled in tissue paper and labeled:
  "Rhiz Rhei 0,5 - Wehrpresseissanitatspark X."
  - Several scraps of paper with German writing.
· One box containing:
  - Ten clockwork-timing devices.
  - Ten sets of buttons to set firing pins and fasteners for the timers.
· One tin box containing:
  - Eight demolition blocks of TNT, drilled with holes for a cap or fuse.
  - Three rolls of black safety fuse.
  - A cardboard box containing four bombs shaped to look like lumps of coal. Each of these blocks had a hole drilled in one end for a fuse or cap. Also in this box were a roll of safety fuse and a roll of detonating fuse.
· Two tin boxes, each containing 18 (3" x 2-5/8" x 5-5/16") demolition blocks.
· One tin box containing two blocks of TNT.

Ponte Vedra, Florida

· Forty-six blocks of TNT, individually wrapped in paper.
· Four blocks of TNT shaped like coal.
· One coil of detonating fuse.
· Four small coils of detonating fuse.
· A small round paper box containing approximately one pint of Thermite.**
· Ten clockwork-bomb timing devices.
· Ten brass and plastic timing devices marked *"70 Minuten."*
· Five leather cases containing:
  - Timing devices marked "11-13 hours."
  - Timing devices marked "6-7 hours."
  - Timing devices marked "2-3 hours."
· Eleven sealed glass vials containing sulphuric acid.
· Twenty-five fuse lighters, marked, *"C Heinrich Anton, Dulsburg, Beissanzunder 6. 1939."*
· Fifty electric match devices.
· Twenty-five electric blasting caps.
· Fifteen wood blocks containing blasting caps.
· Ten wood blocks containing detonators.
· Five wood blocks marked with red lines containing detonators.

** Thermite is a mixture of powdered aluminum and iron oxide. It was commonly used in incendiary bombs.

Boxes dug up on Ponte Vedra Beach, Florida, 1942. NA

Text of Presidential Orders

Special to THE NEW YORK TIMES.

WASHINGTON, July 2—The texts of President Roosevelt's order establishing a military commission to try the eight Nazi saboteurs, and of his proclamation suspending the right of court trial for enemy aliens who enter the United States to commit sabotage, espionage or warlike acts follows:

THE MILITARY ORDER

WASHINGTON, D. C., July 2, 1942.

By virtue of the authority vested in me as President and as Commander in Chief of the Army and Navy, under the Constitution and Statutes of the United States, and more particularly the Thirty-eighth Article of War (U. S. C. Title 10, sec. 1509), I, Franklin Delano Roosevelt, do hereby appoint as a military commission the following persons:

Major Gen. Frank R. McCoy, president.

Major Gen. Walter S. Grant.
Major Gen. Blanton Winship.
Major Gen. Lorenzo D. Gasser.
Brig. Gen. Guy V. Henry.
Brig. Gen. John T. Lewis.
Brig. Gen. John T. Kennedy.

The prosecution shall be conducted by the Attorney General and the Judge Advocate General. The defense counsel shall be Colonel Cassius M. Dowell and Colonel Kenneth Royall.

The Military Commission shall meet in Washington, D. C., on July 8, 1942, or as soon thereafter as is practicable, to try for offenses against the Law of War and the Articles of War, the following persons:

Ernest Peter Burger.
George John Dasch.
Herbert Hans Haupt.
Henry Harm Heinck.
Edward John Kerling.
Hermann Otto Neubauer.
Richard Quirin.
Werner Thiel.

The Commission shall have power to and shall, as occasion requires, make such rules for the conduct of the proceedings, consistent with the powers of military commissions under the Articles of War, as it shall deem necessary for a full and fair trial of the matters before it. Such evidence shall be admitted as would, in the opinion of the President of the Commission, have probative value to a reasonable man. The concurrence of at least two-thirds of the members of the Commission present shall be necessary for a conviction or sentence. The record of the trial, including any judgment or sentence, shall be transmitted directly to me for my action thereon.

FRANKLIN D. ROOSEVELT.
The White House, July 2, 1942.

THE PROCLAMATION

WHEREAS the safety of the United States demands that all enemies who have entered upon the territory of the United States as part of an invasion or predatory incursion, or who have entered in order to commit sabotage, espionage or other hostile or warlike acts, should be promptly tried in accordance with the law of war;

Now, therefore, I, Franklin D. Roosevelt, President of the United States of America and Commander in Chief of the Army and Navy of the United States, by virtue of the authority vested in me by the Constitution and the Statutes of the United States, do hereby proclaim that all persons who are subjects, citizens or residents of any nation at war with the United States or who give obedience to or act under the direction of any such nation and who during time of war enter or attempt to enter the United States or any territory or possession thereof, through coastal or boundary defenses, and are charged with committing or attempting or preparing to commit sabotage, espionage, hostile or warlike acts, or violations of the law of war, shall be subject to the law of war and to the jurisdiction of military tribunals; and that such persons shall not be privileged to seek any remedy or maintain any proceeding, directly or indirectly, or to have any such remedy or proceeding sought on their behalf, in the courts of the United States, or of its States, territories and possessions, except under such regulations as the Attorney General, with the approval of the Secretary of War, may from time to time prescribe.

In witness whereof, I have hereunto set my hand and caused the Seal of the United States of America to be affixed.

Done at the City of Washington this second day of July, in the year of Our Lord nineteen hundred and forty-two and of the Independence of the United States of America the one hundred and sixty-sixth.

FRANKLIN D. ROOSEVELT.
By the President:
CORDELL HULL,
Secretary of State.

THE TRIBUNAL JUDGES

Maj. Gen. Frank R. McCoy, president of the tribunal board, was from Pennsylvania and an 1897 graduate of West Point. He was aide de camp to Maj. Gen. Leonard Wood when he was military governor of Cuba. McCoy was later military aide to President Theodore Roosevelt and served on the Mexican border in 1916. During World War I he commanded the Sixty-Third Infantry Brigade in France and Germany. He was also commanding general at Governors Island in New York.

Maj. Gen. Walter S. Grant was from New York and won the Distinguished Service Medal while serving in France during World War I. In 1940, he was commander of the Third Army Corps area in Baltimore. In August 1941, he was assigned to duty with the Army Chief of Staff.

Maj. Gen. Blanton Winship was from Georgia. He fought at Vera Cruz, Mexico in 1914, served in France during World War I, and was governor of Puerto Rico. He was also a former Judge Advocate General.

Maj. Gen. Lorenzo D. Gasser was from Ohio and was in the Spanish-American War. He was with General Pershing in Mexico in 1916 and with the 2nd Division at Chateau-Thierry during World War I. Before he retired in 1939, he was Deputy Army Chief of Staff. Later, he was returned to active duty and assigned to the Office of Civilian Defense.

Brig. Gen. Guy V. Henry was from Nebraska. He saw service in the Philippines and became a celebrated Calvary officer. He once commanded Fort Myer, Virginia, and later headed the Calvary School at Fort Riley, Kansas.

Brig. Gen. John T. Lewis was from Illinois and was a Coast Artillery officer. He served in France during World War I and in Hawaii.

Brig. Gen. John T. Kennedy was from South Carolina. He received the Medal of Honor for action in the Philippines. He served in France during World War I and in May 1942 was made commanding general at Fort Bragg.

Four of the seven military judges at the trial, from left, Maj. Gen. Lorenzo D. Gasser; Maj. Gen. Walter S. Grant; Maj. Gen. Frank R. McCoy, president; and Maj. Gen. Blanton Winship. NA

Part of the military judges, from left: Maj. Gen. Walter S. Grant; Maj. Gen. Frank McCoy; Maj. Gen. Blanton Winship and two unidentified officers. NA

July 3, 1942.

MEMORANDUM for the Provost Marshal General, Military
District of Washington.

Subject: Receipt of prisoners.

1. The Secretary of War directs that you receive
and keep in custody until further orders from the Federal Bureau
of Investigation, Department of Justice, the following named
prisoners, to be tried before a military commission:

Ernest Peter Burger,
George John Dasch,
Herbert Haupt,
Heinrich Harm Heinck,
Edward John Kerling,
Hermann Neubauer,
Richard Quirin, and
Werner Thiel.

2. The Secretary of War further directs that
defense counsel for said prisoners may have access to them at
all times prior to their trial and confer with them without the
presence of any other party. The defense counsel, as at present
constituted, are the following officers: Colonel Cassius M. Dowell,
Colonel Kenneth Royall, Major Lauson H. Stone, and Captain William
G. Hummell. On oral representation of either of the senior defense
counsel that officers other than those named herein are of defense
counsel, they may have similar privileges without further permission
being obtained.

J. A. ULIO,
Major General,
The Adjutant General.

A true copy of original signed in my
presence, this 3rd day of July, 1942.

/s/ F. G. MUNSON
F. G. MUNSON
Colonel (J.A.G.D.)A.G.D.

The President

    The White House

The President:

    There has been delivered to us your Order of July 2, 1942 which provides for a Military Commission for the trial of Ernest Peter Burger, George John Dasch, Herbert Haupt, Heinrich Harm Heinck, Edward John Kerling, Hermann Neubauer, Richard Quirin, and Werner Thiel, and which further designates us as defense counsel for these persons.

    There has also been delivered to us a copy of your Proclamation of the same date, which Proclamation provides that a military tribunal shall have sole jurisdiction of persons charged with committing classes of acts set forth in the Proclamation and that such persons shall not have the right to seek any civil remedy.

    Our investigation convinces us that there is a serious legal doubt as to the constitutionality and validity of the Proclamation and as to the constitutionality and validity of the Order It is our opinion that the above named individuals should have an opportunity to institute an appropriate proceeding to test the constitutionality and validity of the Proclamation and of the Order.

    In view of the fact that our appointment is made in the same Order which appoints the Military Commission, the question arises as to whether we are authorized to institute the proceeding suggested above. We respectfully suggest that you issue to us or to someone els appropriate authority to that end.

    We have advised the Attorney General, the Judge Advocate General, General McCoy, General Winship and Secretary Stimson of our intention to present this matter to you.

                    Respectfully,

                      Cassius M. Dowell
              Colonel, United States Army

                      Kenneth C. Royall
            Colonel, Army of the United States

Washington, D.C.
July 6, 1942

                    Copy of a letter to the President from Dowell and Royall, attorneys for the seven defendants (Dasch had a separate attorney).

July 6, 1942.

The Honorable Francis Biddle, Attorney General of the United States, and Major General Myron C. Cramer, The Judge Advocate General of the Army.

1. By direction of the President, the attached charges and specifications, duly sworn to on July 3, 1942, against Ernest Peter Burger, George John Dasch, Herbert Haupt (otherwise known as Herbert Hans Haupt), Heinrich Harm Heinck (otherwise known as Henry Harm Heinck), Edward John Kerling, Hermann Neubauer (otherwise known as Hermann Otto Neubauer), Richard Quirin, and Werner Thiel, are referred to you, for trial before the Military Commission established by an order of the President, dated July 2, 1942, as the Trial Judge Advocates of said Military Commission and the persons designated in said order to conduct the prosecution before said Commission, and, by further direction of the President, you are vested with all the powers and duties of a trial judge advocate of a general court-martial.

2. The employment of a stenographic reporter or firm of reporters is authorized and three copies of the record of trial, for the use of the prosecution, and two copies of said record, for the use of the defense, in addition to the original copy to be submitted to the President, are authorized in each case before the Commission.

By order of the Secretary of War:

J. A. ULIO
Major General,
The Adjutant General.

WAR DEPARTMENT
The Adjutant General's Office
Washington
July 29, 1942.

MEMORANDUM TO ALL UNITED STATES ARMY PERSONNEL IN WASHINGTON, D. C., AND VICINITY.
    (Chiefs of Divisions, War Department General Staff.
    Commanding Generals, Army Ground Forces,
      Army Air Forces, Services of Supply, and
      Military District of Washington.
    Chief of each Arm or Service, SOS.)

1. No officer, warrant officer, army nurse or enlisted man will attend any session of the Supreme Court during the hearings which start this date in connection with the trial of so-called saboteurs, unless they are required to actively participate in such hearings.

2. It is the responsibility of addressees that this memorandum reaches the hands of all military personnel under their respective jurisdictions by 0930, July 29, 1942.

    By order of the Secretary of War:

                    J. A. ULIO
                    Major General
              The Adjutant General.

The two U.S. Army defense counsels for the seven saboteurs (Dasch had his own attorney). On the left is Col. Cassius M. Dowell, a regular Army officer, who advanced from private to commissioned rank prior to World War I, where he was wounded in action. Between the wars, he obtained a law degree and then spent the next 40 years in the Army handling a multitude of legal affairs. He was not a trial lawyer per se so he asked Colonel Royall to be the lead counsel. On the right is Col. Kenneth C. Royall, a World War I veteran, who headed the legal section of the Army's office charged with financial supervision of military contracts. Royall graduated in 1917 from the Harvard Law School, was editor of the *Law Review* and practiced in his native North Carolina. He became president of the state bar association and a prominent member of the state senate. After the war, President Truman appointed him as his Secretary of War and after military reorganization, he became Secretary of the Army until 1949. PHPC

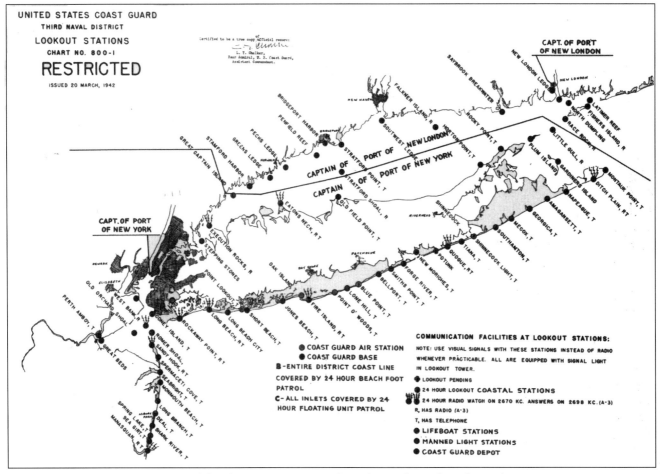

Map used by the prosecution at the saboteur's trial to show the landing site on Long Island **was** included in a military zone. NA

Herman Otto Neubauer
is led into the courtroom.

Richard Quirin is led
into the courtroom. NA

Ernest Peter Burger sits in the
courtroom awaiting his fate.
He would have his death sentence commuted to life imprisonment. In April 1948 he
was deported to Germany on
the recommendation of the
Justice Department and with
President Truman's approval.
He had spent five years and
eight months in prison. NA

Herbert Hans Haupt in the corridor outside the fifth floor courtroom in the Department of Justice Building being led in for the opening of the third day's proceedings. NA

Werner Thiel awaiting the opening of the third day's proceedings. NA

Ernest Peter Burger is led into the courtroom. NA

Henry Harm Heinck and guards in the hallway as Coast Guardsman John Cullen enters in the background.

From left: Thiel, Quirin, a guard, Neubauer and Kerling listen to testimony. NA

Heinrick Heinck awaiting the opening of the third day's proceedings. NA

U.S. Coast Guardsman John Cullen on his way to the trial. Cullen would be one of the main witnesses for the prosecution. NA

On the left, Maj. Lauson H. Stone and Captain Rennel in the fifth floor hallway. Stone was the son of Supreme Court Chief Justice Harlan Fiske Stone and was assigned to the defense team. There was some question as to whether Chief Justice Stone should sit on any appeal to the Supreme Court as his son was part of the defense, but Major Stone was not involved in the habeas corpus proceeding, only in the defense case before the military tribunal. NA

Scene in the court-
room as the seven
judges enter. NA

Assembly Hall No. 1, whose
main entrance was Room 5235
in the Justice Department
Building, was converted for the
trial. On July 9, camera crews
were allowed in the room to
film the proceedings. NA

Attorney General Biddle
questions FBI agent Charles
F. Lanman about a shovel
found with the saboteur's
buried cache of equipment
and explosives. NA

Colonel Dufrenne was appointed medical officer for the defendants. NA

On the left, Gen. Oscar Cox, assistant Solicitor General and assistant prosecutor under Biddle, talks to Major Rivers. NA

Chief prosecutor Francis B. Biddle. Biddle was from a prominent Philadelphia family and a descendant of Edmund Jennings Randolph. He was born in Paris, France, of American parents on May 9, 1886. He graduated from Harvard Law School in 1911 and became the private secretary to Supreme Court Justice Oliver Wendell Holmes. After service in the U.S. Army during World War I, he joined a Philadelphia law firm and in 1939-40 was a judge of the 3rd Circuit Court of Appeals. He was appointed Solicitor General of the United States and in 1941 became Attorney General where he served until June 30, 1945. He was a delegate to the 1944 Democratic National Convention from Pennsylvania and from the District of Columbia in 1942. In 1946, he was appointed as a United States member to the Nuremberg War trials. Biddle retired after the trials were over. On Oct. 4, 1968, he died of a heart attack at the age of 82. NA

Key figures in the trial of the eight saboteurs. Left to right in the foreground: Attorney General Francis Biddle; FBI Director J. Edgar Hoover and Col. Carl L. Ristine. Ristine was a lawyer in the Army's Inspector General office who was appointed as a defense attorney for George Dasch only. While Hoover attended most of the trial sessions, he took no part in the actual prosecution presentation. This photo was taken at the opening of the third day's proceedings. NA

A general view of the entire courtroom on July 15, 1942. The seven men in the background are the U.S. Army generals who comprised the military commission. The prosecutors are at the table on the right and the defense counsel are on the left. The defendants are lined up along the left wall. NA

Maj. Gen. Myron C. Cramer enters the courtroom. NA

Maj. Gen. Myron C. Cramer, Judge Advocate General of the Army and assistant prosecutor, examines a shovel and other pieces of evidence during the third day's proceedings. NA

Haupt, left, and Dasch, right, sit on opposite sides of their guard, Army Lieutenant Meakin, awaiting the opening of the third day's proceedings. NA

Clock - Contact
when spring extracts
contact is make.

+

rubber stick
with
Contact

E. P. Burger
June 23/42

These drawings by Ernest Burger were drawn after his capture by the
FBI. They illustrate several ways he was taught to set off explosives.

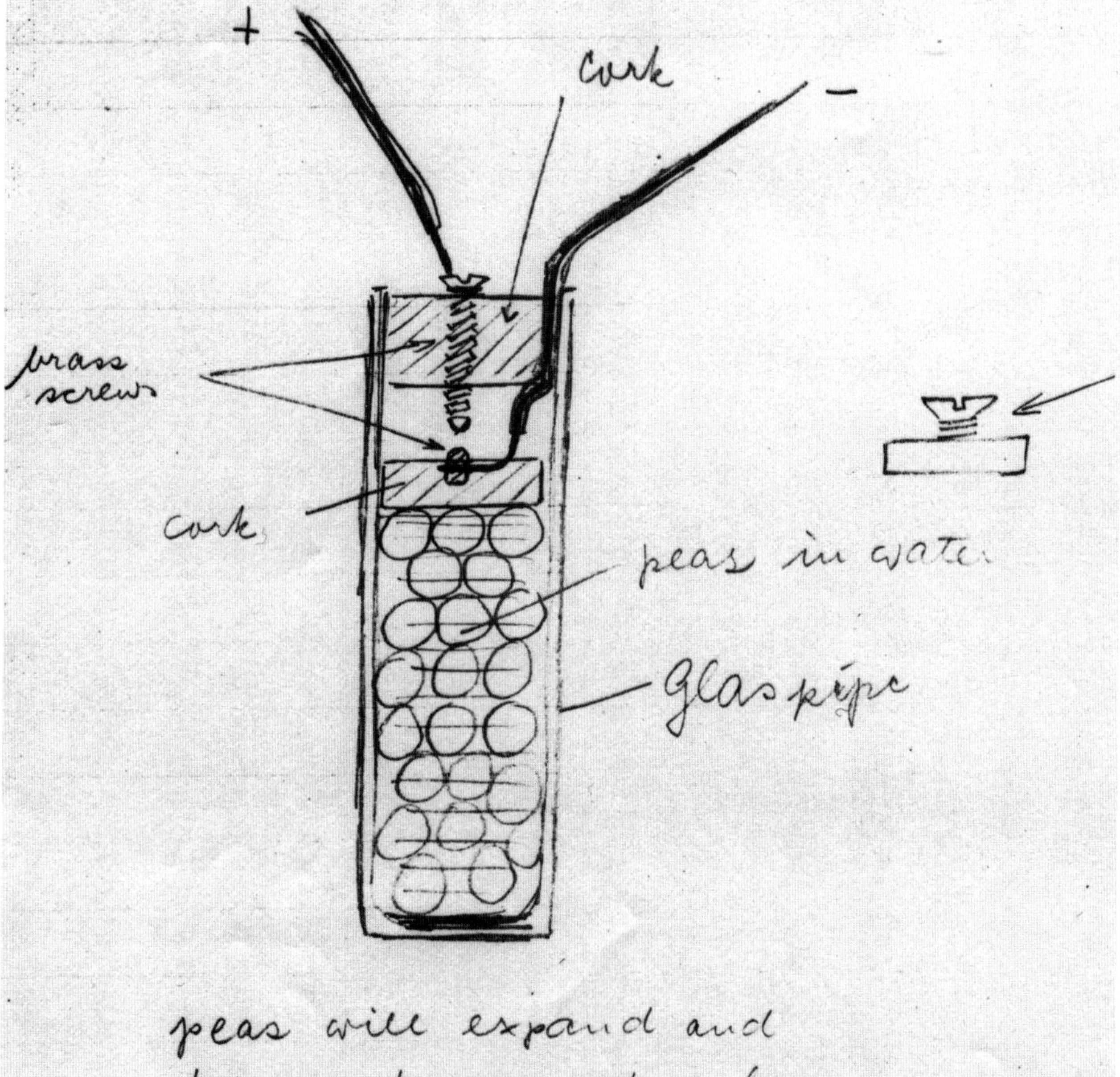

peas will expand and
drive cork upwards – brass screws
will touch and form electrical
contact.

E.P. Berger
June 23/42

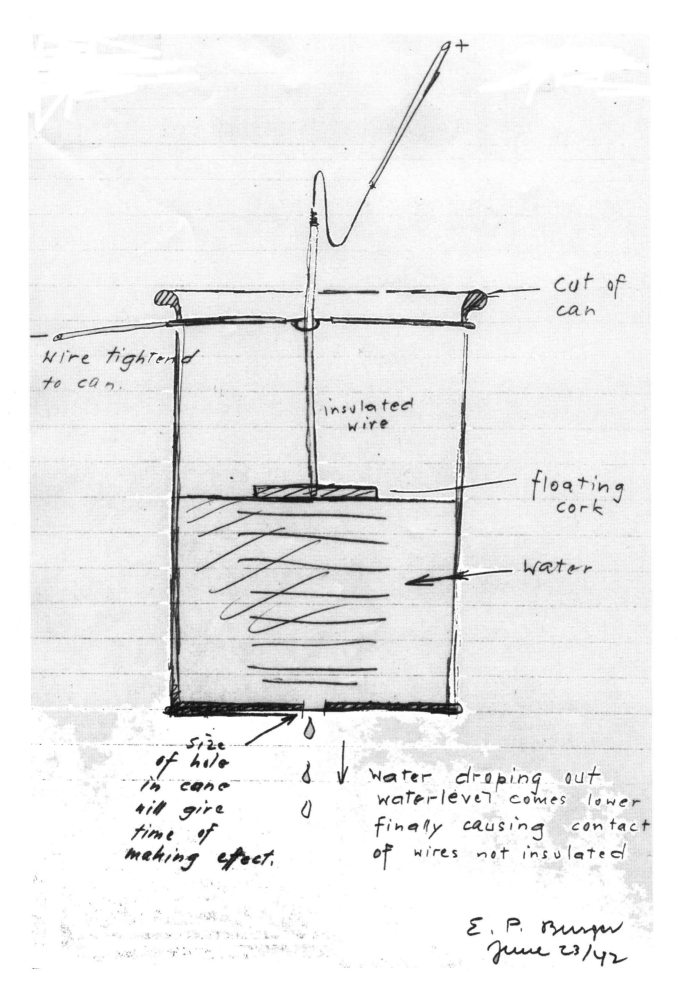

9+

cut of
can

Wire tightend
to can.

insulated
wire

floating
cork

Water

size
of hole
in cane
will give
time of
making efect.

Water droping out
water-level comes lower
finally causing contact
of wires not insulated

E. P. Burger
June 23/42

- 112 -

Police and armed U.S. Army enlisted men guard the elevators in the basement of the Justice Department. NA

A soldier stands guard at the main entrance of the FBI on the fifth floor of the Justice Department. NA

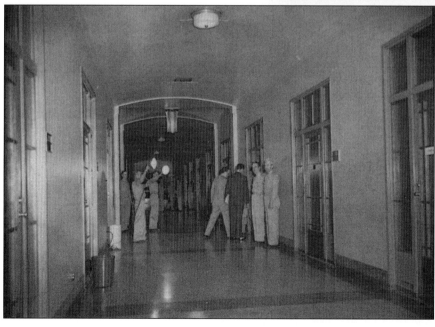

Hallway on the fifth floor of the Justice Department. One of the FBI's lecture rooms, Assembly Hall No. 1, whose main entrance was Room 5235, was converted into a courtroom for the duration of the trial. The hallway was patrolled by armed U.S. Army enlisted men. NA

Defendant Herman O. Neubauer, with his hat pulled over his eyes, enters the U.S. Marshall's prisoner van in the basement of the Justice Department at the end of one of the trial sessions. NA

Ernest Peter Burger is escorted into the Marshall's van. NA

View of U.S. Army scout cars parked in the basement of the Justice Department used to guard the prisoners. NA

More U.S. Army scout vehicles parked in the basement of the Justice Department used to guard the prisoners.NA

The prisoners were brought to the Justice Department each morning from the District of Columbia jail in two U.S. Marshall vans, led by a car of FBI agents and followed by an Army scout car mounted with machine guns and armed soldiers. NA

Newspapers around the country broke the news of the capture of the eight saboteurs on June 27, 1942, although factual information was hard to come by. While the actual trial was closed to the press, daily communiqués were issued and eventually the government did allow reporters into the trial chambers for a period of less than 15 minutes. The U.S. Army Signal Corps did take still photos and silent motion pictures. The official trial proceedings, however, were not declassified until 1960. NA

THE WHITE HOUSE
WASHINGTON

OFFICE OF THE
RECEIVED
AUG 10 1942
ATTORNEY GENERAL

August 8, 1942.

Dear Mr. Attorney General:

I am very anxious that all of the copies of the record, together with the exhibits and photostats thereof of the eight Nazi saboteurs tried by the Military Commission appointed by me July 2, 1942, be physically sealed for the duration of the war.

They should remain sealed unless opened by order of the President of the United States.

Will you please see that this is done with respect to all copies in the possession of the Department of Justice?

Very sincerely yours,

Franklin D. Roosevelt

Honorable Francis Biddle,
The Attorney General,
Washington, D. C.

President Franklin D. Roosevelt's order to seal the records of the trial during the war. Trial records were not declassified until 1960. NA

ARMY'S SPY TRIAL UPHELD BY COURT; CASE NEARS CLOSE

RULING UNANIMOUS

Supreme Bench Backs President's Power Over Invader Saboteurs

GENERALS RESUME TASK

Hear Final Pleas for Nazis— Verdict Due Soon, to Go to Roosevelt for Review

Text of the court's decision will be found on Page 3.

By LEWIS WOOD
Special to THE NEW YORK TIMES.

WASHINGTON, July 31—President Roosevelt's power to order trial of the eight Nazi saboteurs before the military commission instead of in the civil courts was unanimously sustained by the Supreme Court today in a session lasting only four minutes.

Immediately after the special session was reconvened at noon, Chief Justice Stone read a per curiam opinion, short in length but extensive in its implications, holding that the charges against the men alleged offenses for which the President was authorized to order a military trial, that the commission was legally constituted and that the Nazis were held in lawful custody.

In the per curiam opinion the highest court denied the appeal by seven of the eight Nazis for writs of habeas corpus which would have taken them from the control of the Army and the military commission, where they face a generally expected sentence of death by shooting or hanging.

Five of 7 Generals Can Set Nazis' Fate

By The Associated Press.

WASHINGTON, July 31—Five of the seven generals trying the eight Nazi saboteur suspects can seal their fate.

When President Roosevelt created the Military Commission he ordered that "the concurrence of at least two-thirds of the members of the commission present shall be necessary for a conviction or sentence."

But, both as Commander in Chief and as President, Mr. Roosevelt has the power to change the sentence, and it was understood that any announcements of a verdict — possibly next week — will come from him.

The President has directed the commission to send its verdict "directly to me for my action thereon."

SABOTEUR VERDICT GIVEN TO PRESIDENT BY SEVEN GENERALS

He Will Review Findings, Which Will Be Kept Secret Until He Makes His Decision on Them

8 NAZIS HEAR SENTENCES

Commission Informs Prisoners and Lawyers at Brief Session —Clemency Is Seen for One

By LEWIS WOOD
Special to THE NEW YORK TIMES.

WASHINGTON, Aug. 3 — The verdict of the military commission which tried the eight Nazi saboteurs was delivered to the White House today for review by President Roosevelt.

Shortly before, during a two-minute session in the Justice Department Building, the seven generals revealed the sentences to the prosecution staff, the prisoners and their lawyers. But no inkling of the commission's findings was given to the public.

Penalties prescribed by the seven Army officers will, it is expected, be disclosed only by President Roosevelt, final arbiter in the case. This was indicated in the Commission's statement today, which read as follows:

"The commission reconvened at 11:05 A. M. The commission announced that the findings and sentence will not be announced by it. The commission adjourned at 11:07 to meet at the call of the President."

Those familiar with President Roosevelt's methods in criminal cases believe he will withhold his decision until he has delved deeply into the long transcript of the eighteen-day trial, and made up his mind as to approval, modification, or rejection of the commission's findings. Then, should the ruling call for the death penalty, he would fix the time and place for execution.

Clemency Expected for One

It was believed here that not all the Hitler agents would be sentenced to die. Clemency has been suggested for George John Dasch, leader of the Long Island invaders, who is reported to have given the government valuable information on German plans to wreck this nation's war plants. And defense counsel, it has been said in some quarters, have had faint hopes of leniency for Ernest Peter Burger, and in a lesser degree for Herbert Hans Haupt.

Escape from death would probably mean long prison terms, ranging upward from thirty years to life.

Under President Roosevelt's order creating the Military Commission

FEDERAL SERVICES CLASH IN SPY TRIAL

Hoover of FBI Declares That the Coast Guard Fails to Cooperate Properly

VEST OF NAZI AN ISSUE

Officer and Others Alleged to Have Retained the Garment for Several Days

By LEWIS WOOD
Special to The New York Times.

WASHINGTON, July 21 — Friction over the arrest of the four saboteurs on Long Island developed today between the Federal Bureau of Investigation and the United States Coast Guard as the trial of the eight invaders proceeded for the twelfth day.

J. Edgar Hoover, director of the FBI, lodged a protest with the Coast Guard alleging failure to cooperate properly, and, it is understood, said this supposed failure violated the national interest.

The protest was based on what was described as the omission of the Coast Guard to turn over promptly a vest and several other articles belonging to the Germans. Instead, it was said here, the Coast Guard took the vest to a New York tailor to identify a cleaner's mark. In another quarter it was said the vest was taken to the New York Police Laboratory.

The clue, it was added, did not turn out successfully, as it involved a man who was innocent of the saboteur affair. Meanwhile the FBI learned of the existence of the vest, which was not handed over until several days after the landing, it was reported here.

Order on Evidence

According to a Washington version, Coast Guardsmen had been ordered to give all evidence to the FBI but a group including Lieutenant (j. g.) Sidney K. Franken retained the vest despite the order. Eventually the garment was surrendered and is now one of the exhibits in the guarded courtroom of the military commission.

Almost since the trial began there have been behind-the-scenes reports of disagreement between the two government services. One rumor had it that the Coast Guard did not notify the FBI of the Long Island landing for a considerable period. Another was that some of the articles dug up had been handled so much that fingerprint identification was made very difficult, if not impossible.

Inside the secret courtroom one of the saboteurs testified today as the defense started its case, it was revealed by Major General Frank R. McCoy, head of the commission. Both the defense and the prosecution examined the man, assumed to be George John Dasch, 39 years old, leader of the Long Island expedition.

Mrs. Agnes Jordan, mother of a soldier missing at Bataan, and Mrs. Gerda Melind, once the fiancée of Herbert Haupt, one of those on trial, spent some time within the barricaded corridors leading to the courtroom. Whether they will be called as actual witnesses was not made public. For a time they visited the offices of the defense counsel.

Statements by McCoy

The forenoon statement by General McCoy follows:

"The commission reconvened at 10 A. M. Most of this morning's session was spent in argument upon motions by the defense. Thereafter the defense started the presentation of its case by one of the defendants taking the stand. The commission recessed at 12:30 P. M. to reconvene at 1:30 P. M."

The afternoon communiqué read:

"The commission reconvened at 1:30 P. M. The defense concluded its direct examination of one of the accused. The remainder of the session was devoted to the cross-examination of this accused. The commission adjourned at 4:32 P. M. The trial will be resumed at 10 A. M. tomorrow."

While the trial of the saboteurs was proceeding, the District of Columbia grand jury which has been investigating Nazi propaganda activities handed up a sealed indictment.

Army Chaplains Attend

By The Associated Press

WASHINGTON, Aug. 8—Shortly before noon—the time when the executions of the saboteurs began in the District of Columbia jail—a guard reported that six Army chaplains had entered the jail. Close on their heels arrived Dr. A. Magruder Macdonald, the district coroner. To him fell the task of pronouncing the men dead.

Soldiers and a Briton Offer to Shoot Saboteurs

By The United Press.

WASHINGTON, Aug. 8— Three American soldiers and a British sailor volunteered their services today as a firing squad for the Nazi saboteurs.

The quartet marched up to the entrance of the district jail and rang for the chief guard.

John Martin, seaman of North Ireland, told the guard that he and his American friends, all attached to the Army's Bolling Field, thought a firing squad would save the government some electricity.

When told that they needed "authority," Martin said that he would request it of Prime Minister Churchill and, if that failed, would induce his companions to call on President Roosevelt.

EUROPE TOLD OF NAZIS' END

British Broadcast News of Six Executions at Washington

LONDON, Sunday, Aug. 9 (AP) —Beginning at 8 o'clock last night the British radio spread throughout Europe the news that the United States had executed six of the eight Nazi saboteurs seized after they landed from German submarines.

The broadcasts, made in several languages, emphasized the swift capture, trial and death in the electric chair of the men before they could begin their sabotage campaign.

Up to an early hour today the German radio had made no comment on the men's fate.

HAVANA, Aug. 8 (AP)—Havana newspapers today displayed under eight-column headlines the news that six German saboteurs had been executed in the United States. Advance commented.

"In other days wars were fought in gentlemanly fashion."

WALTER REED GENERAL HOSPITAL
Washington, D. C.

Laboratory Service,
August 11, 1942.

This is to certify that the following bodies were received from the Morgue, Walter Reed General Hospital, Washington, D. C., at 6:30 PM, August 11, 1942:

278-Herbert Hans Haupt   278

277- Heinrich Harm Heinck   277

279- Edward John Kerling   279

280- Hermann Otto Neubauer 280

276-Richard Quirin   276

281 —Werner Thiel   281

Carl J. Lind. J.
Major M.C.
_____

Potters Field, District of Columbia
August 11, 1942

Received this date six (6) unidentified bodies in closed coffins, from Major Carl J. Lind. Jr., M.C.,

Otto Kass
Supt of Home for Aged
and Infirm; Potters Field

THE WHITE HOUSE
WASHINGTON

August 12, 1942

MEMORANDUM TO THE SECRETARY OF WAR

The Order of August 7, 1942 to you and the Provost
Marshal with reference to the carrying out of the sentences
against the eight Nazi saboteurs contained a provision that
the sentences of Ernest Peter Burger and George John Dasch
should be commuted to imprisonment. The United States Penitentiary at Atlanta, Georgia was designated as the place of
confinement.

It was the President's intention and desire to have
these two prisoners turned over by you to the Attorney General,
with discretion in the Attorney General to receive them at
Washington, D. C., and to place them in any Federal penitentiary
or other institution, in accordance with the powers given to
him under the applicable provisions of law. Your responsibility
would be ended when you turn these two prisoners over to the
Attorney General in the District of Columbia.

M. H. McINTYRE
Secretary to the President

WALTER REED GENERAL HOSPITAL
ARMY MEDICAL CENTER
WASHINGTON, D. C.

August 14, 1942.

SUBJECT: Disposal of Bodies of Six Saboteurs.

TO: The President of the United States.

THROUGH: Chief of Staff, United States Army.

1. On August 8, 1942, at 4:15 P.M., in accordance with previous secret arrangements, the bodies of:

Herbert Hans Haupt
Heinrich Harm Heinck
Edward John Kerling
Hermann Otto Neubauer
Richard Quirin
Werner Thiel

were brought to Walter Reed General Hospital from the District Jail in two Army Medical Center ambulances. Major Robert S. Higdon, Medical Corps, was in charge of the ambulance detail. The bodies were identified by Colonel Martin F. DuFrenne, Medical Corps, and Major Thomas M. Rives, Assistant Provost Marshal, D. C., who accompanied them from the execution room. Individual name tags were attached to the bodies and they were receipted for by Colonel Paul A. Schule, Medical Corps, of the Walter Reed Hospital Laboratory Section.

2. The six bodies were stored in individual compartments of the refrigerating room at the hospital morgue. An armed guard was present in the morgue day and night until the bodies were removed, to insure that the boxes were unopened and the bodies not seen by any unauthorized person. On the evening of August 10, 1942, each body was embalmed in the hospital morgue by Mr. William G. Durisoe of the Tabler Funeral Home, Incorporated, in the presence of Major Carl J. Lind, Medical Corps, of the Hospital Laboratory Section.

3. At 6:00 P.M., August 11, 1942, the bodies were placed in individual plain pine boxes, identified by name tag, and taken in a light truck, accompanied by Major Lind, Major Harland W. Layer, Medical Administrative Corps, and three armed guards to the Potters Field, Blue Plains, D. C.

4. A detail from Fort Myer, under the direction of Captain Josiah T. Showalter, Medical Corps, had prepared the graves. The bodies were receipted for by Mr. Otto J. Cass, Superintendent of the Home for the Aged and Infirm and

Potters Field. Each box was identified to correspond with the stake to be erected above that individual grave. A combined Protestant and Catholic burial service was provided by Chaplain (Lieutenant Colonel) Charles D. Trexler, Protestant, and Chaplain (First Lieutenant) Edward J. McTague, Catholic. The six bodies were buried at 7:30 P.M., August 11, 1942, and the numbered stakes without names were placed above the graves in the following order:

276 - Richard Quirin
277 - Heinrich Harm Heinck
278 - Herbert Hans Haupt
279 - Edward John Kerling
280 - Hermann Otto Neubauer
281 - Werner Thiel

The precautions taken were such that no information has been given out and no photographs taken during any stage of these procedures so far as known. All concerned with the disposition of the bodies have been warned concerning need for secrecy both present and future.

S. U. MARIETTA,
Brigadier General, Medical Department,
Commanding.

1st Ind.

Office Chief of Staff - August 15 - 1942

A copy of this report will be shown to the Secretary of War and to the Chief of Staff and then filed in the 'secret' files of The Adjutant General's Office.

Colonel, G.S.C.
Secretary, General Staff.

WAR DEPARTMENT
THE ADJUTANT GENERAL'S OFFICE
WASHINGTON

August 14, 1942.

IN REPLY
REFER TO

SUBJECT: Transfer of Prisoners George John Dasch and Ernest Peter Burger to Department of Justice.

Auth: V O T A G

Initials: R H O

Date: 8-14-42

To: The Provost Marshal, Military District of Washington.

1. By direction of the President, you will transfer, at Washington, D. C., to the custody of James V. Bennett, Director, Bureau of Prisons, Department of Justice, who has been designated by The Attorney General as the officer to receive them, the above-named prisoners, George John Dasch and Ernest Peter Burger.

2. A certified copy of the order of the commitment is herewith inclosed, to be delivered to the Director of Prisons.

3. At the same time you will also deliver a copy of this letter to the Director, requesting that receipt therefor be indorsed below, and invite his attention orally to the following paragraph of a memorandum to the War Department from the Secretary to the President, dated August 13, 1942, which reads as follows:

"Please be reminded that this order is a confidential one which has been directed by the President to be sealed and please so inform the Warden of the Penitentiary."

A copy of the memorandum of the Secretary to the President, addressed to the Secretary of War, under date of August 12, 1942, showing the authority to deliver these prisoners to The Attorney General at Washington, D. C., is herewith inclosed, for delivery to the Director with the other papers mentioned herein.

4. You will secure proper receipt for said prisoners which will be transmitted to this office, and thereupon your responsibility for said prisoners will be ended.

By order of the Secretary of War:

J. A. ULIO
Major General,
The Adjutant General.

2 Incls.

Received a copy of this letter:
August 14, 1942. _James V. Bennett_
Director, Bureau of Prisons,
Department of Justice.

PAUL A. F. WARNHOLTZ
ATTORNEY AT LAW
III WEST WASHINGTON STREET
CHICAGO
TELEPHONE RANDOLPH 7657

August 26, 1942

Colonel Arden Freer
Executive Officer
Walter Reed Hospital
Washington, D. C.

Dear Col Freer:

As attorney of Hans Haupt and Erna Haupt, the parents
of Herbert Haupt, I will appreciate if you will
kindly inform me as to the following: Erna Haupt
the mother of Herbert Haupt wishes to take over the
remains of Herbert Haupt. Due to the present physical and mental condition of Hans Haupt, the father,
I have so far not informed him of the death of his
son and neither have the authorities informed him
thereof. However, he will undoubtedly join in the
aforesaid wishes of his wife, as soon as he knows of
the death of his son Herbert.

I will greatly appreciate to have you state to me if
the authorities will permit a cremation of the remains of Herber Haupt and the transmission of the
ashes to his parents here in Chicago. I should like
to know what, if any, costs must be paid in connection
therewith by the parents.

I have also been asked by Mrs. Erna Haupt to inquire
if Herbert Haupt left any statement or letter for his
parents shortly before or at any time before his
death.

I thank you before hand for your courtesy in giving
me early information of the matters herein stated,
and remain,

Very truly yours,

PWW:gs

- 124 -

September 20, 1942

Mr. Paul A. F. Warnholtz,
    111 West Washington Street,
        Chicago, Illinois.

Dear Sir:

    Your letter of August 26, 1942, addressed to the Executive Officer,
Walter Reed General Hospital, Washington, D. C., has been transmitted
to this office for reply. As attorney for Hans Haupt and Erna Haupt,
parents of Herbert Haupt, you inquire whether permission will be granted
for the cremation of the remains of Herbert Haupt and the transmission
of the ashes to his parents in Chicago; and whether he left any statement or letter for his parents.

    This matter has received consideration by proper authority and you
are advised that no action with respect thereto will be taken during
the existence of hostilities. If a further request is made subsequent
to the termination of the war, further consideration will be given to
the matter.

                    Yours very truly,

SEP 21 42 AM

DISPATCHED MISC. DIV., AGO
SECTION

                            H. B. LEWIS,
                            Brigadier General,
                        Acting The Adjutant General.

BASED ON: OPD 095 Haupt, Herbert (8-26-42)
           Sept. 19, 1942.

COMPARED: reh/cjm.

SUBJECT: Remains of Herbert Haupt.

LEGATION OF SWITZERLAND

WASHINGTON, D.C.

DEPARTMENT OF
GERMAN INTERESTS

The Minister of Switzerland in charge of
German interests presents his compliments to the
Honorable the Secretary of State and begs to refer
him to his note of August 26 dealing with the eight
Germans sentenced on August 8 as saboteurs.

In this connection, the Legation has now received an inquiry on behalf of a Mrs. Kerling
relative to:

a. Whether the bodies of the German
Nationals who were executed have
been buried or cremated and where
the remains are kept at present;

b. What happened to the personal belongings of the executed German
Nationals and how they can be recovered.

Mrs. Kerling based her request on Articles 76 and
77 of the Geneva Convention.

The Minister would be very much obliged to be
favored with a reply in this matter, if feasible,
as well as information in general as to what has
happened to the bodies and personal belongings of
these executed Germans, which, according to a
newspaper article in the Washington Times-Herald
of August 17, allegedly are to be claimed by
families, relatives or possibly the protecting
power.

WCB:ac

Washington, D.C.,

September 29, 1942.

The Honorable,

The Secretary of State.

Dear Mr. Secretary:

Receipt is acknowledged of your letter of November 13, 1942 (SD 862.20211/3528), with which was inclosed a copy of a note dated September 29, 1942, from the Minister of Switzerland, in charge of German interests, relative to an inquiry on behalf of Mrs. Kerling, said to be the widow of Edward John Kerling, one of the executed saboteurs, regarding the whereabouts of the bodies of the German nationals who were executed and the disposition of their personal belongings. The inquiry is predicated upon Articles 76 and 77 of the Geneva Convention of 1929 with respect to Prisoners of War (FM 27-10, pars. 162,163).

For the reasons stated in letter of this Department, dated October 21, 1942, the eight saboteurs did not fall within the category of prisoners of war, but were unlawful belligerents. This conclusion has been upheld and emphasized by the opinion of the Supreme Court in the saboteurs' case, Ex parte Quirin et al., handed down on October 29, 1942. Consequently, the cited provisions of the Geneva Convention are inapplicable and do not furnish any basis for granting Mrs. Kerling's request. It is suggested that the Minister of Switzerland, in charge of German interests, be so advised. If the request is renewed after the end of the war, it will then be reconsidered.

For your own information, the President has reserved to himself the question of disclosing any information connected with the trial in question or its sequel. Consequently, the War Department is not free in any event to furnish the desired information in the absence of specific Presidential direction to that effect.

Sincerely yours,

(Sgd.) HENRY L. STIMSON

Secretary of War.

Copy - The A.G.

- 127 -

September 18, 1942.

Dear General Cramer:

I think it is fitting that I should
express to you and your associates in the recent
trial of the eight saboteurs my gratitude and
appreciation for the manner in which you have all
performed your difficult duties.

As you know, I followed the matter
very closely and am familiar with the many obstacles and
difficulties with which you were confronted and I therefore realize the skill and care with which those difficulties
were surmounted and the case brought to a successful
conclusion with dignity and efficiency.

I think a valuable precedent has been set
which will have great influence in the protection of
the national interests against dangerous and subversive
attacks. I send you my hearty thanks.

Very sincerely yours,

HENRY L. STIMSON

Major General Myron C. Cramer,
The Judge Advocate General,
War Department,
Washington, D.C.

Major General Cramer was the assistant prosecutor in the case. Henry Stimson (1867-
1950) was Secretary of War during World War II and also held the same position earlier
under President William Howard Taft. He was in action in France during World War I.
NA

George Dasch is shown in Germany in 1948 shortly after his 30-year sentence was commuted and he was deported to Germany. He was sent to Danbury Federal prison and in early 1943 to Atlanta Federal prison. In 1945, he was sent to Leavenworth Federal prison. He wrote a book in 1959 entitled, *Eight Spies Against America* in which he tried to justify his action of turning in his compatriots. Dasch tried repeatedly to return to the United States but was always rejected. He and his wife attempted to set up a business in several German cities, but each time public hostility against him would not allow it since he was branded a traitor to Germany. In a 1952 *Associated Press* interview Dasch said he wanted to return to the U.S., which he still considered him "home." He insisted when he saw Cullen appear on the beach, he quickly told him to "Beat it." His instructions from his superiors had been to kill any witnesses, he said. Then they were to load the body on the U-boat and dump it at sea. "I saved that kid's life," he said. Dasch died in 1991 without ever returning to his "home." AP/WORLD WIDE PHOTOS

Ernest Burger, one of the two saboteurs not executed, tells newsmen at Ludwigsburg, Germany, of his part in the U.S.'s biggest spy case. He was first sent to Danbury Federal prison and in early 1943 to Atlanta Federal prison. In April 1948, he was pardoned by President Truman and deported back to Germany where he faded into obscurity in postwar times. AP/WORLD WIDE PHOTOS

WANTED

GERMAN SABOTEUR

Photo taken October 18, 1940

JOSEPH SCHMIDT, with aliases

Paul Schmidt; Jerry Swenson

F.P.C. 17 L 1 2 9
M 1 Ut

Joseph Schmidt formerly resided in Canada where he spent many years as a woodsman and trapper in the Province of Alberta prior to the outbreak of the war between England and Germany. Shortly thereafter, he fled to Mexico and later went to Germany. Schmidt, as Jerry Swenson alias Paul Schmidt, is reported to have received training as a saboteur in Germany and may be sent to the United States by Germany to commit sabotage in American plants. This individual is known to have been at Lorient, France, during May, 1942. Schmidt is described as follows:

DESCRIPTION

Name	Joseph Schmidt, with aliases, Paul Schmidt, Jerry Swenson	Teeth	Tobacco stained
		Beard	Light, smooth shaven
Age	33-34	Speech	Speaks English with high pitched
Height	6' 1-2"		voice and Swedish accent. Face
Weight	200 pounds		flushes when he laughs.
Build	Medium		Frequently interrupts his con-
Hair	Dark blond, straight, parted on left side		versations with a peculiar laugh.
Eyes	Blue	Hands	Big, strong hands covered with
Features	Broad receding forehead; normal eyebrows; long narrow slightly humped nose; thin lips; thin firm chin		freckles. Has been known to do tricks of bending metal with his hands.
Complexion	Ruddy	Occupation	Farmer, hunter, and trapper. Formerly resided in Province of Alberta, Canada.

If you are in possession of any information concerning the whereabouts of Joseph Schmidt, alias Jerry Swenson or Paul Schmidt, communicate immediately in person or by telephone or telegraph "collect" to the undersigned or to the nearest office of the Federal Bureau of Investigation, United States Department of Justice, the local address and telephone numbers of which are set forth on the reverse side of this notice.

JOHN EDGAR HOOVER, DIRECTOR
FEDERAL BUREAU OF INVESTIGATION
UNITED STATES DEPARTMENT OF JUSTICE
WASHINGTON, D. C.
TELEPHONE, NATIONAL 7117

July 25, 1942

After the East coast landing in mid-June 1942, the FBI put out the word that there could be more German saboteurs either in the country or on their way by submarine or some other method.

Operation Pelican

The Panama Canal was of vital importance to the Allied war effort. The canal is 50 miles long and has six double locks, each 330 yards long and 36 yards wide. If it was closed for any length of time, warships and merchant ships would have an 8,000-mile longer trip from point to point on both coasts of the United States. The war effort could be drastically reduced.

It was a tempting target for both the Germans and Japanese. It was, however, a long way from any Axis base and was heavily defended by surface and air forces.

It was 1943 and the war was not going well for Germany on land or sea. Erich Gimpel, a trained German spy, who would take part in the last spy mission to the United States the following year, was tasked with the almost impossible mission of planning an attack on the Panama Canal. As he stated in an interview after the war: "I had long since accustomed myself not to have any personal opinions about the instructions I received from my new Department. An attack on the Panama Canal? Splendid! Why not land on Mars? Why not kidnap President Roosevelt from the White House? I tried to give an impression of confidence while I gambled on the conviction that *Operation Pelican* would end up as a piece of paper in a desk drawer just as so many other plans had ended."

Although Gimpel was opposed to this project he did find out that it was indeed possible to put the canal out of action if everything went according to plan. He was sent to Breslau to discuss a plan with an old engineer named Hubrich, who lived in Panama at the turn of the century and later became one of the leading engineers of the canal construction and still had all the plans in his possession.

Gimpel thought that if a plane or planes could somehow get to the canal (a distance of many thousands of miles) they could launch an attack on the Gatun locks and put the canal out of order. However, Hubrich had a better idea—If bombs were to destroy the Gatun dam instead, the water behind it would sweep over the canal and flow into the sea. The canal has a steep gradient; in fact that was the difficulty in its construction. There would be nothing to hold back the water and it could destroy everything in its path. It could take years to repair the damage.

The attack would have to be made by aerial bombardment. Gimpel now thought that it just might be possible to make a real contribution to Germany's war effort if only he could get several dive bombers close enough to the canal and the dam.

He flew to Luftwaffe headquarters in Berlin to try and obtain the two aircraft (Stukas), which, because he had been given authorization for any military equipment he needed, were given to him. He next went to Kiel, to the staff headquarters of Grand-Admiral Dönitz to obtain the services of two U-boats. Then he rented a long lakeside site on the Wannsee and made it a military area. Here he built an exact model of the Panama Canal and the two Stuka pilots, after practicing take offs and landings on sandy soil, dropped dummy bombs on the canal model.

Then came the most difficult part of the undertaking. Mechanics practiced dismantling the Stukas and putting them together again, and finally managed to do their jigsaw puzzle in two days. In Kiel, the U-boat crews made a systematic and practical study of stowing the parts in the hull.

The plan was to penetrate into the Caribbean Sea with the two U-boats with the Stukas stowed on board. At a certain time, the boats would surface near an uninhabited island and the aircraft parts would be put ashore and assembled in two days. Two high explosive bombs were allocated for each plane which would then take off, fly at a low altitude to the dam and drop them on the spillway. After the attack, the two pilots were to fly to a neutral South American country and ask for asylum. The U-boats would have already started on their long journey home.

Everything was ready in the fall of 1943, the aircraft stowed, the boat crews on board in Kiel and Gimpel resigned to a long voyage but a successful one. However, he received a telegram just before leaving Kiel. It read: "Operation Pelican called off. Report to Berlin at once."

In Berlin he was told, "It's a good thing that we could still get hold of you, otherwise we'd have had to call you back over the high seas. We have it from a

Gatun Dam spillway with a great
volume of water released.

reliable source that the whole thing has been given away. There's no doubt about it. You wouldn't have gotten very far. You can congratulate yourself that we made our discovery in time."

That was the end of Operation Pelican. The questions never answered are on what island would the Stukas have been put together and who betrayed the operation or how did American authorities find out about it? Would Gimpel's plan have worked if he could have gotten the planes to the canal? Luckily the United States never had to find out.

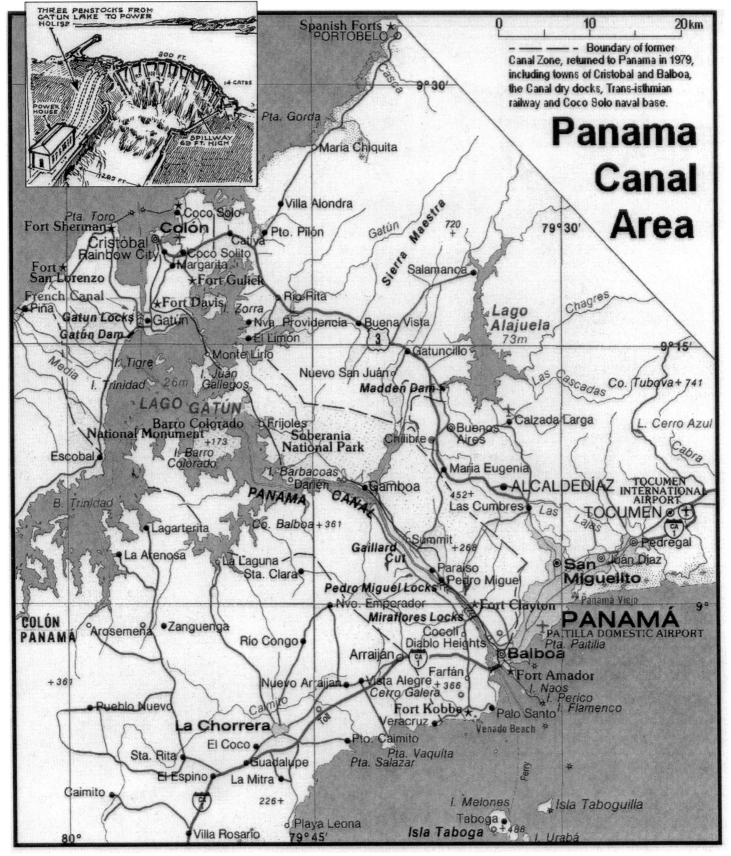

Unternehmen Elster
(Operation Magpie)

Germany was not going to give up getting first-hand intelligence information from the United States even as late as November 1944. By this time Allied forces were pushing at the gates of Germany both in the east and west. Hitler was preparing for one last offensive in the west and still promising his army and citizens that his super weapons would win the war.

In desperation the Abwehr, German Army Intelligence Service, sent two spies to America to analyze the effect of Nazi propaganda on the 1944 presidential election. This rather curious mission was conceived by Hitler's foreign minister, Joachim von Ribbentrop. In addition, the spies were told to obtain technical information on rocket developments, aircraft and ship construction and anything they could obtain on nuclear research. This information could conceivably be gotten from newspapers, magazines, technical journals, books and even radio broadcasts. They were to buy radio components in America, put them together and relay their information to Germany.

Erich Gimpel, who was in charge of Operation Pelican back in 1943, was in charge of this operation as well. He also brought along an American named William Curtis Colepaugh.

Erich Gimpel was born in Merseberg, Germany, on March 25, 1910. He became a radio engineer and while working in Berlin in March 1935 was offered a job with Telefunkan, a German firm in Lima, Peru. When World War II started in 1939, Gimpel was asked to spy on Allied shipping and report his findings by radio to a German operative in Chile.

When the United States entered the war, Gimpel was arrested, along with German Nationals and taken by ship to New Orleans and eventually to the Kenedy Internment Camp near San Antonio, Texas. Since Gimpel was a civilian he was offered the chance to remain in the U.S. and eventually become a citizen or, because his name was on an internees request list, to return to Germany. He decided on the latter and was subsequently sent to Sweden on the Swedish flag ship, *Drottningholm* in 1942.

As Gimpel relates in his book: "I was met in Stetlin. A man in civilian clothes came up to me, 'Herr Gimpel?,' he said. 'Welcome home! We've been waiting for you.' We shook hands. 'I've money for you, papers and ration cards. Go to your relatives

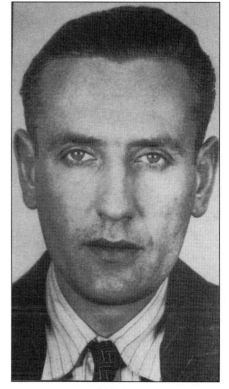

Erich Gimpel. NA

William Curtis Colepaugh. NA

and take a good rest. There's no hurry. Stay as long as you like.'

"'Many thanks. And then.'

"'Note this address: Berlin, Tripitzufer 80. Repeat!'

"'Berlin, Tripitzufer 80,' I said. I knew this was the headquarters of the German Secret Service."

Thus began Gimpel's life as Agent 146 of the Abwehr. Apparently Gimpel left a wife and two children in Peru.

Colepaugh was an American of German descent who was born in Old Black Point, Conn., on March 25, 1918. He was the son of a German mother and an American father. Billy (as Gimpel called him) stayed with his mother and she took care that he received a good education. He was an apt pupil, distinguished himself in Boy Scouts and was publicly honored for rescuing two children from drowning at the risk of his own life. He received his early education in Niantic and New London, Conn., and left high school early with very good academic reports. He graduated from Admiral Farragut Naval Academy near Toms River, N.J. and then attended the Massachusetts Institute of Technology from 1938 to 1940.

After the outbreak of war in 1939, Colepaugh became enamored of the quick German victories and met a Dr. Scholz, the German consul in Boston. He got a job as a midshipman on convoy ships from the U.S. to England and reported his experiences upon returning to Dr. Scholz. Billy was refused a commission because of his friendly attitude towards Germany.

In July 1942, Billy was arrested in Philadelphia by the FBI for not supplying proper information to the Selective Service board, but he joined the Navy after being given the opportunity to enlist rather than face prosecution. He was honorably discharged in October 1942 at the Great Lakes Naval Training Station "for the good of the service." He eventually got a job on the Swedish line *Gripsholm* that was exchanging Axis diplomats to Europe. He jumped ship at Lisbon, Portugal and presented himself to the German consul stating he wanted to help Germany win the war.

Towards the end of 1944, Erich Gimpel was summoned to the Deputy Head of Anit VI, Dr. S. of the Abwehr. He was told he was to be sent to America as soon as possible and to figure out how to get there and who to take along. The only practical way to reach America's shores was by submarine. Gimpel already knew that all eight saboteurs from *Operation Pastorious* in 1942 had been caught and that by this time Germany had lost the war, but duty bound him to fulfill his mission.

He had one request from Dr. S. as he related: "I need a proper American. The real stuff, not some seamy adventurer. You understand? He must know the latest dance steps and the latest popular songs. He must know what width one's trousers should be and how short one should have one's hair cut. He must know everything about baseball and have all the Hollywood gossip at his fingertips. This man must stay with me at least until I become assimilated."

It was not easy to find such a person in wartime Germany. All the Americans in the country were in POW camps and not one likely prospect was found among them.

However, there was a young 26-year-old American named William Curtis Colepaugh in The Hague, Holland, who was sent there by the German consul in Lisbon. No one knew what to do with him until Gimpel learned of him and decided he would make his ideal companion.

Colepaugh's hatred of America was thought to be genuine and Gimpel also noted he was one of the thirstiest and most accomplished drinkers he had ever met. He would also learn later that Billy was more interested in female companionship than being a spy.

Both men were trained at A-Schule West (Agent School West), which was located on a secluded estate named Park Zorguliet, between The Hague and suburban Schereningen. It was an SS training school which included instructors who had been on missions with the famous German commando, SS Lieutenant Colonel Otto Skorzeny.

They were instructed in the construction of radios and how to use microphotographic equipment. After their training was finished in early November 1944, they were sent to Kiel to board U-1230 commanded by First Lieut. Hans Hilbig. Gimpel went on board posing as a chief engineer. Colepaugh posed as a naval lieutenant and war reporter, but didn't fool any of the crew members. The real reason for the two spies trip was known only to Hilbig. Two kit-bags with extra strong padlocks were placed on board. They contained pistols, compasses, some radio parts, a camera, a bottle of secret ink, powder for developing invisible-ink messages and instructions for building a radio and transmitting instructions to Germany—reduced to microdot form. In addition there was American civilian clothing, $60,000 in cash and diamonds worth $100,000.

Phoney papers were provided: Gimpel would be known as Edward George Green, who was born in Bridgeport, Conn. Colepaugh used the name William Charles Caldwell, born in New Haven, Conn. They also had forged birth certificates and Selective Service cards dated in February 1946 (the Germans expected the spies to be in the United States at least two years).

U-1230 was of the 1X-C type submarines, 240 feet long with a displacement of about 1,060 tons. It left Kiel and sailed on the surface to Horton, the German submarine base in Oslo, Norway. A week was spent on submerging trials and then the last port in Norway, Christiansund was reached. From here the sub would have to sail across the Atlantic to deposit the spies on the shores of the state of Maine. By this time the Allies had control of the entire ocean and any crossing of it by sub, either above or below the sea, was extremely dangerous. U-1230 was ordered not to engage in any overt action until their mission was accomplished. They were fitted for a six-month patrol with 14 torpedoes on board.

The cross ocean trip—which started on October 6—took 46 days with many hazardous incidents along the way. Within four days of the Maine coast a message was received—"We have reason to believe the enemy may be apprised of our undertaking. Act according to your own discretion." They were to land the spies in Frenchman Bay, a body of deep water protruding 10 miles into the rugged coast of Maine.

U-1230 reached its destination off Maine on No-

vember 10 but had to lay off Mount Desert Island for more than two weeks while depth-finding equipment was repaired and to wait for the best tide and weather conditions to proceed into the bay.

They had come too far to turn back and decided to chance entering the bay and depositing the spies on shore.

Late in the afternoon of November 29, the submarine slid into the bay within a half-mile of Hancock Point. At 10:00 p.m. the sub moved to a position just over 300 yards from shore, surfaced and the two spies, who had changed into civilian clothes, got into a rubber boat and were rowed to shore by two crewmen. Before leaving the submarine several cars were noticed near the beach. So they had to wait until the area was dark again.

Each man was carrying a suitcase and a revolver in his hand. What if they met someone on the beach? Should they shoot him? This went through Gimpel's mind. The ground was soft and moist and squelched with every step, snow was falling and the branches of the trees brushed into their faces as they walked inland. They decided to make for a road for better traction, but this would be their undoing.

About this time a 28-year-old resident of Hancock Point, Mary Forni, was driving home and passed the two strangers on the West Side Road dressed in trenchcoats and carrying suitcases. At home she told her husband about sighting the men but he told her not to be so nosy. But the next morning she told her next door neighbor, Dana Hodgkins,

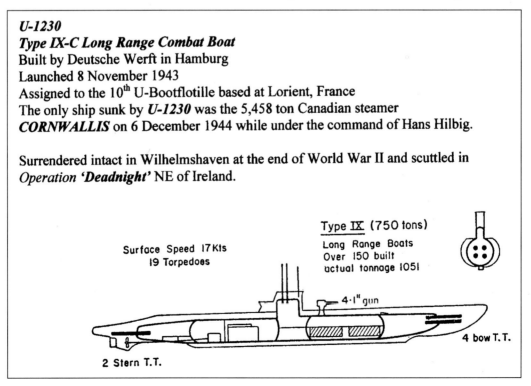

U-1230
Type IX-C Long Range Combat Boat
Built by Deutsche Werft in Hamburg
Launched 8 November 1943
Assigned to the 10th U-Bootflotille based at Lorient, France
The only ship sunk by *U-1230* was the 5,458 ton Canadian steamer
CORNWALLIS on 6 December 1944 while under the command of Hans Hilbig.

Surrendered intact in Wilhelmshaven at the end of World War II and scuttled in *Operation 'Deadnight'* NE of Ireland.

who happened to be a deputy sheriff about the incident. Hodgkins went to the area and traced footprints down to the shore. He immediately notified the FBI in Bangor.

Hodgkins' son had also spotted the two men a half an hour after they landed. Harvard M. Hodgkins, a 17-year-old Boy Scout cycled by them and thought they looked out of place. He traced their footsteps back to the shore and knew they had landed from some type of ship. That evening he reported his find to a nearby police station but was brushed off by the local sergeant at the station. Hodgkins then went to the FBI who were also skeptical.

Colepaugh related his story of the landing on November 29 to the FBI after his capture:

"On the night of Nov. 29, 1944, the captain brought the submarine to Frenchman's Bay keeping the submarine completely submerged until we were one-half mile off Crabtree Point. At this time he raised the submarine until the conning tower was above water and proceeded in this fashion to a point 300 yards from shore at Crabtree Point. Crabtree Point is just across the peninsula from Hancock Point. The submarine turned to face south at this point 300 yards from shore and Gimpel and I climbed into a rubber boat with oars to which was attached a light line to be used for the purpose of pulling the rubber boat

back to the submarine after we had landed. We had removed our naval uniforms about one-half hour before we came to this Point.

"When the rubber boat was launched, the line broke

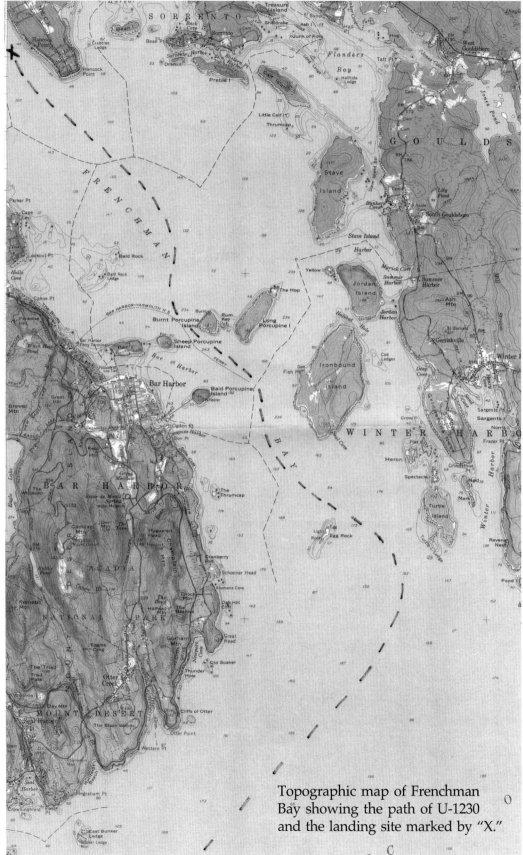

Topographic map of Frenchman Bay showing the path of U-1230 and the landing site marked by "X."

and therefore two sailors from the submarine climbed into the rubber boat with us and rowed us ashore, after which they took the boat back to the submarine. At the point where we landed there was a narrow beach of approximately six feet, then a bank over which we climbed and walked through the woods until we hit a dirt road. We had all of the items furnished us in Berlin and Kiel in our bags with the exception of those items carried on our persons. We did not bring any explosives ashore nor did we bury anything at the beach or at any other point. We did not bring the microphotographic apparatus from the submarine because as mentioned above it was excess weight in our weakened condition.

"We walked up the dirt road in a northerly direction until we came to the end of the road at which point there was a house. We then took a path in an easterly direction from the house and followed the path until it came out a macadam road. At this point the handle of the airplane luggage broke and I had to open the bag and fix the handle. At this time both GIMPEL and I took out of our pockets the .32 automatic colts which we had been carrying since we left the submarine and placed them in the bag still in the same loaded condition in which we had been carrying them. We walked in a northerly direction along the macadam road. I was carrying the bag inasmuch as GIMPEL appeared to be weaker than I was but GIMPEL was carrying the briefcase which contained the money and papers.

"About one eighth of a mile up the road after we came off the path an automobile passed us going south. It had been snowing slightly when we got off the submarine and the snow had increased so that it was snowing fairly heavily at this time. About a mile further on this road, another car passed us going in a southerly direction. At this time it was about Midnight and I would say that it was about 11:30 PM when the first car passed us. We landed at the beach from the submarine at about 11:00 PM. We continued along the macadam road in a northerly direction until we came to U.S. Route No. 1, at which time we turned left on Route No. 1 in a westerly direction.

"At about 12:30 AM a car passed us and stopped whereupon I ran up to it and indicated that we wanted a ride to Ellsworth. I ascertained that the car was a taxi and after talking to the driver he agreed to take us to Bangor for $6.00. GIMPEL got in the back seat and I rode in the front seat into Ellsworth where the driver got out to make a telephone call to his employer advising her that he was going to Bangor. We arrived in Bangor about 1:30 AM, November 30, where we went to a small restaurant to get change for a $10.00 bill after which I paid off the taxi driver and GIMPEL and I walked down to the railroad station catching a train for Portland at 2:00 AM. We arrived at Portland riding in a coach at about 6:00 AM. Here we caught another train for Boston shortly after 7:00 AM arriving in Boston at about 10:00 AM on November 30. Inasmuch as we did not have any hats we went to a hat store in Boston and purchased two hats. We made several attempts to secure hotel rooms and finally registered at the Hotel Essex shortly after Noon. We spent the night in Boston and left the hotel early the next morning taking a train for New York City. We arrived in New York City at Grand Central Station at 1:30 PM on December 1st. We checked the airplane luggage bag at Grand Central Station and went to Pennsylvania Station where we checked the brief case in one of the lockers at the station. At about three o'clock we registered at the Kenmore Hall Hotel as WILLIAM CALDWELL and EDWARD GEORGE GREEN. We did not use these two names in Germany at all nor did we use them on the submarine but saved them for use in the United States. The first time we actually used these names was in registering at the Essex Hotel in Boston although of course they had previously been placed on our identification papers in Berlin. We stayed at the Kenmore Hall Hotel from December 1 until December 9, 1944.''

This is Gimpel's story of the landing, his directives from the Abwehr and his troubles with Colepaugh:

"After landing on the shore of Maine at the Northern end of Frenchmans Bay, COLEPAUGH and myself proceeded up the road of the main highway where we walked along until we were picked up and given a ride in an automobile at a time possibly between 10:00 PM and 12:00 Midnight on November 29, 1944. This automobile took us into Ellsworth, Maine and we then arranged with the driver of the car to continue with us to Bangor, Maine, for which he charged us $6.00. After stopping in Ellsworth we arrived in Bangor about 2:00 AM. We then proceeded by train to Boston, Massachusetts where we registered into the Essex Hotel on November 30, 1944, COLEPAUGH under the name of CALDWELL and I under the name of GREEN and we were checked into this hotel to about December 9, 1944. On or about December 8th, 1944 at New York City at 39 Beekman Place, COLEPAUGH rented an apartment under the name of CALDWELL and paid two months rent at $150 per month.

"On December 22, 1944 I checked into the George Washington Hotel but I did not stay, I being registered here as EDWARD GREEN. I thereafter on the same day, December 22, 1944, checked into the Pennsylvania Hotel, New York City under the name of GEORGE COLLINS where I remained until December 30, 1944.

"While coming over on the submarine I had brought

with me a typewritten piece of paper on which appeared a mail address through which I could communicate with Germans located in Lisbon, Portugal and another address located in Madrid, Spain. I was to write to these addresses and send material back to Germany to the various officers who had sent me on this job by my agreement with them. However, I left this on the boat and do not remember the names. I gave this paper with the addresses on it to COLEPAUGH and he cut same up.

"I signed something to the following effect at Amt #6 in the Spring of 1944 which was given to me for signature by HERBERT POHLER: 'I obligate myself to exert my entire strength on behalf of Germany, otherwise I am aware that I can expect the sharpest reprisals.' At the Hague in July 1944 I signed a paper to the following effect, 'That in no event will I after entrance give information as to what I have seen here.' This paper bore a rubber stamp 'Secret' on it.

"I was to build an 80 watt radio transmitter in the United States and Germany was to start sending messages to me about one or two months after COLEPAUGH and I landed in the United States. They gave me the Leica camera in case I could not make radio contact with Germany and the officers of the SS and others with whom I was to make contact in Germany. I was to use the Leica camera to make up microdots and these were to be mailed to Germany. As to this they were not clear, however, I was to get in contact with some neutral ship to carry the letters over.

"I was to establish contact with a secret department of the American government. I was of the impression there was some government or semi-official government agency which would make contact when and if necessary with Germany in an effort to work out political problems.

"I was given no names of persons in the government with whom I should make contact but POHLER suggested the possibility of making contact with members or former members of the Klu Klux Klan who were sympathetic toward Germany. In conversation with POHLER he also brought up the name of LINDBURG but no particular reference was made to him except that he might be sympathetic toward our objectives which we believed were in favor of the United States and the termination of the war.

"On Thursday, December 21, 1944, COLEPAUGH and I went up to a clothing store where I was to get a suit of clothing which was supposedly ready for me and he said he would not go in; that he would go over and watch the ice skating. I went in to get the suit and when I came out COLEPAUGH was gone. I looked around for him and I did not find him.

"I then went home to 39 Beekman Place and the

bags were gone; that is, the two suitcases. These suitcases contained the material which was subsequently recovered in my possession on December 30, 1944 by the FBI and contained $40,000 to $50,000. COLEPAUGH, of course, knew that the money and papers we were to use were in the bags, and I was very disappointed in him. I did not believe he would do such a thing as this and I had more confidence in him. I thought possibly he might go to the station and check the bags and I then went up to the station to check to see if I could locate the bags. Fortunately the two bags were sitting in a place in the Grand Central checkroom where I could see them.

"I then waited around for three hours, 9:00 PM to 12:00 midnight, on December 21, 1944, hoping that COLEPAUGH would appear. I was afraid to ask for the bags because of my speech. COLEPAUGH did not appear so I told the man that these were my bags and described the material in the bags and made a statement claiming the bags, and they gave the two bags to me. I took these two bags to the check room of the Pennsylvania Railroad and checked them. I slept that night, December 21, 1944, at 39 Beekman Place.

"When I arrived at 39 Beekman Place, I talked to the lady who was there and asked where CALDWELL was and she indicated he left one hour ago on December 21, 1944 taking the two bags and stating he would spend Christmas with his family. I did not know where his family was located. I thought he was trying to get away with the money.

"I went to the George Washington Hotel and after thinking about the matter, having registered under the name of GREEN, believed that COLEPAUGH might be picked up by the police if he called for the bags with the checks. I therefore left the George Washington and checked into the Pennsylvania Hotel. I expected to check out of the Pennsylvania Hotel about Monday, January 1, 1945.

"I had in mind to go to South America but it was very hard to go there. I had the thought of returning to Peru where my wife and two children are located. I did not intend to go to any other city as I did not know any place other than New York.

"We had not agreed in New York because COLEPAUGH spent all of his nights out in New York and I did not know where he was. He would come in about 8:00 or 9:00 AM and I did not know what he was doing.

"It is possible I indicated to him my desire to go to a warm climate but I never mentioned Miami or New Orleans. I told him I had worked in Philadelphia for General Electric. However, I did not work there and I had not been in Philadelphia. I did not make any reserva-

tions on a Pullman at the Pennsylvania Station in New York nor at any other ticket office for a trip to Miami on January 7, 1945. If this is in the name of GREEN and CALDWELL it was intended for COLEPAUGH and he made such reservations."

After Colepaugh left the clothing store, he checked into the prestigious St. Moritz Hotel on Central Park. Hoping to pick up a woman that might be registered as Mr. and Mrs. William Caldwell. After spending two nights in the hotel Colepaugh had thoughts of giving himself up to the FBI. He went to see an old friend, Edmund F. Mulcahy, who lived in the Richmond Hill section of the borough of Queens. Mulcahy heard his story of landing by submarine in Maine and his desire to end his mission.

Mulcahy called the FBI on December 26 for Colepaugh, who was immediately picked up and taken to Foley Square in Manhattan. Colepaugh was eager to talk and told the FBI that Gimpel was using the name Edward Green, and that he bought newspapers at a newstand in the Times Building in Times Square at the corner of 42nd Street and 7th Avenue. He also described him and mentioned he liked to keep dollar bills in his breast pocket.

A surveillance was instituted on December 27 to watch for Gimpel. Three days later he entered the store and was arrested by several FBI agents. Gimpel insisted his name was Edward Green and that he was from Massachusetts. He was searched and over $10,000 and papers stating he was Edward George Green were found on him.

A search of Gimpel's room at the Hotel Pennsylvania turned up more than $44,000 cash, 99 diamonds, which were to be used for bribes, two loaded Colt pistols, a Leica camera, bottle of secret ink and blank Selective Service registration forms.

Thus ended the last known incursion on America's shores in World War II. Both spies were taken to Fort Jay on Governors Island in New York Harbor and tried by a military court. Both were found guilty of espionage and sentenced to death on Feb. 14, 1945. Fortunately for the two men, President Roosevelt died less than two months later and the new president, Harry Truman, commuted the sentences to life imprisonment.

"Topcoats and Sausages"

FBI photograph used to help back-track Gimpel and Colepaugh to the U-boat, to make positive identification at their trial. Topcoats and felt hats were not dress code in rural Maine during deer hunting season. With hunting jackets and German boots they may have gone unnoticed by either young Hodgkins or Mrs. Mary Forni. Mary, who still lives at Hancock Point, says that if they had been carrying rifles, German Mausers even, she would not have given a second glance. The pair had brought sausages from the sub's galley to quiet a dog barking on shore. Topcoats and Mausers may have worked, but topcoats and sausages was a poor choice. RG

Bangor Daily News, Jan. 3, 1945

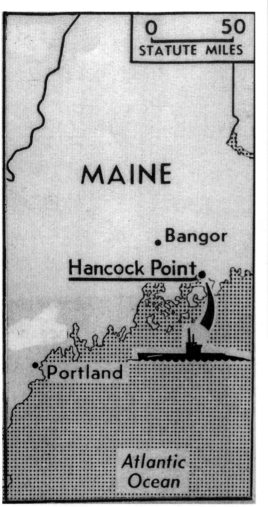

Harvard M. Hodgkins, 17, the son of Deputy Sheriff Dana Hodgkins, kneels at the site where the two spies came ashore. Harvard was greeted by a crowd at La Guardia Field in New York in December 1945. He met Coast Guardsman John C. Cullen who discovered four German saboteurs on Long Island in 1942. He also had breakfast with baseball great Babe Ruth and visited the Empire State Building and the Statue of Liberty. PHPC

Deputy Sheriff Dana Hodgkins points to a small pebbly beach by Sunset Ledge on Crabtree Neck in the Frenchman Bay area on the coast of Maine where the U-1230 dropped the two spies on the night of Nov. 29, 1944. AP/WIDE WORLD PHOTOS

Nazi Agents Landed at Hancock, Maine

excerpted from *Eastern Sea Frontier War Diary, Chapter 2*, November 1944, pp.1-2

Anticipating the possibility that an enemy submarine, estimated westbound in Canadian waters late in November, might enter the Gulf of Maine, Commander Eastern Sea Frontier ordered precautionary air sweeps in that area. Daylight air patrols were flown on several days beginning 23 November, when weather permitted. Coordinated with these flights were RCAF (Royal Canadian Air Force) flights made on 26 and 27 November, three hours before first light. No contacts were reported.

The subsequent torpedoing of (the Canadian steamship) *SS Cornwallis* [by *U-1230* on 3 Dec. 1944] confirmed earlier anticipations. Not until the FBI announcement of the capture of two Nazi agents, more than one month later, did the details come out. Interviews made by the FBI and Naval Intelligence Officers permit the piecing together of the following information concerning *U-1230*, the submarine which entered Frontier waters some time between 16 and 21 November for the purpose of landing agents.

The two agents, Eric Gimpel and William Curtis Colepaugh, boarded the *U-1230* at Kiel, Germany, on 24 September. During the next month, *U-1230* proceeded by slow stages and with several delays along the coast of Norway, put in at Horton and at Kristianson. On 6 October, *U-1230* left Kristianson and started the slow cruise across the Atlantic, reaching the Grand Banks, off the coast of New Foundland [Newfoundland, Canada] on 10 November. On the night of 16 November, *U-1230* received a radio message from Berlin advising that another German submarine bearing one or more German agents was sunk off the coast of New England and the *U-1230* should land the agents at some point other than Frenchman Bay. (This reference may have been to *U-1229*, sunk by [escort aircraft carrier *USS*] *Bogue* [CVE-9] aircraft on 20 August, for the Cominch (Commander-in-Chief, United States Fleet] Anti-Submarine Bulletin for September 1944 states that among the prisoners rescued from *U-1229* was a "self-styled English-speaking 'propaganda expert.'" Nevertheless, using his own prerogative, the Commanding Officer of *U-1230* made no change in plans. On the night of 21 November, he took radio bearings on Atlantic coast stations and fixed his position as off Mount Desert Rock, and remained in that general vicinity, making certain repairs, until 29 November. Ships sighted during this period were not attacked. At about 1700 on 29 November, *U-1230* headed in toward Frenchman Bay, took a bearing on lights at Great Duck and Baker Island; scraped the chain of a buoy in the channel on the approach to the bay, continued in successfully and surfaced partially at 2230 about one-half mile from Crabtree Neck. At approximately 2300, *U-1230* circled to the southeast with conning tower still above water and ran in until the shore was only 300 yards distant. A rubber boat was put into the water, two sailors rowed the two agents ashore and returned.

Evasion of coastal defenses had been carried out successfully by the enemy, and only after the freighter *Cornwallis* was sunk on 3 December was it possible to suspect that the submarine involved in this attack might have landed agents in the Mount Desert area. [Was the *Cornwallis* sinking a diversion action to cover the real *U-1230* mission?]RG Torpedoed southwest of Mount Desert Rock (pg. 150), in view of Acadia National Park, only five members of her crew of 49 survived. The ill-fated Canadian freighter was the only ship ever attacked by U-1230.

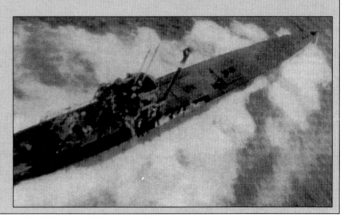

U 1229, the sister sub of U 1230, was en route to land its spy Oskar Mantel and possibly others, on the coast of Maine. It is shown under attack by U.S. Navy *Avenger* aircraft from the carrier *USS Bogue* off Newfoundland on Aug. 20, 1944. Among the survivors taken prisoner was Oskar Mantel.

5 January 1945

MEMORANDUM FOR COLONEL STIMSON:

   Subject: Note for Cabinet Meeting - Trial of 2 Spies

   There is some suggestion that the trial of the two
new men should be conducted in the same way as the earlier
trial. I think this would be a big mistake and it would not
be understood by our troops overseas. Such a trial would be
entirely too spectacular. There is no necessity for having
the Attorney General or his Office take part in it other
than to assist the military officers who would conduct it.
I believe the trial should be conducted by the Second Service
Command as a regular commission with no publicity and a mere
announcement of the result. All the fanfare over the last
trial is out of place now that thousands of our men are being
killed from week to week. It should be on a routine, purely
military basis. I think you ought to press this at Cabinet.

   Judge Patterson, General Royall and the Judge Advocate
General all strongly agree with this point of view.

                                J. J. McC.

January 7th, 1945.

The President,
The White House.

Dear Mr. President:

On Saturday the Attorney General sent me a proposed military order to be signed by the President, for appointment of a Military Commission for the trial of two alleged German spies, with prosecution to be conducted by the Attorney General and Judge Advocate General.

I am bound to say that the handling of the case in such a manner is likely to have unfortunate results. I should prefer to have the trial conducted in the way military trials are normally conducted, without any extraordinary action or notice taken of the case by officials on the highest levels.

My objections to the procedure suggested by the Attorney General are these :

1. A trial of these two men by a Military Commission formally appointed by the President, with the Attorney General of the United States and the Judge Advocate General of the Army taking part in the trial, would certainly be attended by headlines and worldwide publicity. This would almost certainly lead to charges in Germany that innocent Germans were being tried and condemned by an extraordinary legal proceeding.

2. A trial held under such conditions would be likely to lead to German maltreatment of American prisoners of war in their hands, in the opinion of high military authorities.

<u>3.</u> The effect on our fighting troops and on the public would be adverse. They would wonder why so much time and such important personnel were devoted to the trial of two obscure persons charged with an ordinary war offense, at a time when millions of Americans are daily risking their lives.

<u>4.</u> These men should be tried in the normal manner by a court martial or military commission appointed by the Army Commander in Boston or in New York. Since the Supreme Court decision in 1942, there can be no doubt as to the validity of an ordinary military trial. If the fact that the evidence against these men has been collected and prepared by the Department of Justice makes it desirable, in the opinion of The Attorney General, that members of his staff should present the case in cooperation with members of The Judge Advocate General's office, that can be easily arranged, and I should be quite willing to accept such an arrangement.

I am authorized to say that Elmer Davis of the Office of War Information concurs in these views regarding the public relation aspect and also as to the use that the Germans would make of the case.

Sincerely yours,

Secretary of War.

rpp:lm
Original taken by Lt. Col. Schieffelin, OUSW, 1-8-45.

Carbon to OCS
      AGO
      JAGO

January 10th, 1945.

The Honorable

The Attorney General.

My dear Mr. Attorney General:

Referring to our recent correspondence and conversations with respect to the trial of spies and other offenders against the law of war:

I agree that the President should be asked to promulgate a military order in the form enclosed.

I should like to assure you in this connection that I shall take steps to see to it that whenever it is proposed to convene any military commission for the trial of persons not members of the armed forces of the United States, the proceedings to be held within the continental United States or Alaska, the proposal will be reported to me in advance by the commanding general involved.

Upon the receipt of this information, I shall promptly transmit to you a concise statement indicating the basis of the commission's jurisdiction, the names of the accused, the nature of the offense, and the proposed time and place of trial. Officials of your Department, designated by you, may then confer with officials of this Department as to whether the circumstances of the case make it desirable for a military rather than a civil trial to be held, and if a military trial is decided upon whether it is desirable to appoint a representative of your office as an assistant trial judge advocate, with the privilege of participating in the proceedings.

Sincerely yours,

HENRY L. STIMSON
Secretary of War.

The duplicate originals signed by
Mr. Stimson and dispatched by
Mr. Patterson's office (lm)

REFLECTIONS OF RICHARD GAY*

1) Hard copy files at Abwehr Headquarters were carefully destroyed prior to capture in 1945, and men like Colonel Piekenbrock (Abwehr-I) and Colonel Lahousen (Abwehr-II) were disinformation pros. Not unlike the celebrated *Tagebuch* of former Abwehr chief Admiral Canaris, they all waxed innocent of harmful missions against U.S. targets. In spite of explosive hardware recovered from spies, the Abwehr brass managed to convince everyone that their U.S. sabotage missions were little more than hapless information-seeking boondoggles.

2) Information? It is common knowledge that throughout World War II Germany had more informants in the U.S. than they knew what to do with. No doubt the same is true of England, in spite of the much touted British *"Double-Cross"* catch-and-switch operations.

3) Erich Gimpel is on record that his mission was to sabotage the Manhattan Project. Would he reveal this to the FBI in 1944? Colepaugh was Gimpel's tour-guide but probably not privy to the real mission.

4) Germany had learned from British saboteurs how to halt an atom bomb project. Deuterium oxide, aka heavy-water, was the weak link. No heavy-water, no bomb. Gimpel had been on a counter-intelligence assignment in Norway against the British operations that sabotaged Germany's heavy-water supplies.

5) Was a heavy-water facility at MIT Gimpel's target? Details of a secret radar lab at MIT are now known, but Manhattan Project facilities at Cambridge and Waltham are still shrouded in mystery.

6) The fact that a Manhattan Project facility at MIT would be known to German intelligence should come as no surprise. Many scientists had German backgrounds and–as we learned later–they were not above sharing secrets!

7) In June 1944 the Abwehr had a secret meeting at the *Kaiser-Wilhelm Institute for Physics*. Aside from its "scholarly ties" with German scientists in the United States, the Institute was the site of Germany's first atomic reactor–using uranium suspended in heavy-water. It is probable that the *ELSTER* operation was conceived at this meeting.

8) Was more than one team sent on the *ELSTER* mission? *U-1230* was equipped with a snorkel allowing it to travel long distances without surfacing. A sister sub *U-1229* had the same snorkel gear but recklessly cruised on the surface and was spotted and destroyed on Aug. 20, 1944. Among the survivors taken prisoner was the spy Oskar Mantel. *U-1229's* objective was to land him in the Gulf of Maine! Was Mantel the only spy on board? Perhaps not.

9) How could the real *ELSTER* mission have gotten past World War II *intel* historians?

It was critical to protect the *ULTRA* source (*Enigma* decrypts), and probably in some part to protect the Bureau's image–at which J.E. Hoover was single-handedly adroit. The *ELSTER* mission was deep-sixed (buried) in secrecy, and the MIT lab was buried in the same crypt. Any files that were not *"deleted"* in 1945, would be classified by decades of *ULTRA* secrecy and hard to identify.

10) Prior to their departure for America, both Gimpel and Colepaugh were trained in the latest sabotage hardware and explosives.

11) Contrary to accounts that he was inept and ineffectual, Gimpel was an electronics engineer and a seasoned spy capable of accessing MIT. As a visiting scientist? Another German accent in the Manhattan Project could hardly draw attention!

12) William Colepaugh, on the other hand, was a defector and an amateur, more liability than asset, except in one area: he was the one person in Germany who could guide Gimpel into MIT, with a bookbag of explosives, in broad daylight. He had been an engineering student at MIT (twice) and on the track team!

13) In the fall of 1944, at that late stage of the war, the German high command was not likely to take a critically needed U-boat out of service for months for less than a last-ditch mission. Scarcity of U-boats was due to the Allies ability to read their coded messages. Much has been written and filmed about the exploits of Bletchley Park, the English country estate turned crypto-center–but the truth is that Bletchley Park was unable to break the *Enigma*! BP came into prominence only after receiving from Polish Intelligence a replication of the cipher machine that the Poles had cracked. In addition to this homemade Polish *Enigma*, components of an enormous computer-like apparatus nicknamed in Polish *"bomba"* (French: bombe), were exfiltrated via France from Poland to England. Abundant copies were made at Bletchley Park and used throughout the war to recover *Enigma* keys and rotor changes. *ULTRA* secret was so guarded that attacks on U-boats were restricted, in spite of losses of U.S. merchant ships, so the German High Command could

not confirm that its highest level messages were being read. (Note: There are purists who claim the term *ULTRA* is misused as a codename for the *Enigma* operation. The British equivalent of our "Top Secret" was "Ultra Secret" which became shortened in jargon to "Ultra." While the word *ULTRA* was perhaps not officially assigned as a cover name for the *Enigma* operation, it was adopted over time from routine usage. In U.S. intelligence it became double-usage, as a classification codeword, and an operation codename.)"

14) The German intelligence service (Abwehr) was not the ineffective coterie of officers that people have been led to believe. It was an enormous and well-staffed organization. A little known fact is that the Abwehr's communications intelligence **COMINT** service, B-Dienst, was breaking and reading British naval traffic, which gave them coordinates where our convoys met British escorts–and U-boat wolf packs. Winston Churchill called for daily *Enigma* decrypts to read with his morning coffee, but the image of Abwehr chief Admiral Canaris reading British Admiralty traffic with his schnapps is not so palatable.

15) *U-1230* radioman Horst Haslau, also the *Enigma* machine operator, revisited the Maine coast. Understandably he avoided mention of sinking the Canadian freighter *Cornwallis*, just off Mount Desert Island on Dec. 3, 1944, but he did disclose privately that on arrival *U-1230* was warned their "code has been penetrated" and the U.S. Navy was waiting at the designated landing site. The sub's skipper was ordered to use his own judgment for an alternate site. Frenchman Bay was probably chosen because:

a) the mountains of Acadia were a prominent landfall, and

b) their charts of Frenchman Bay dated back to cruise liners, such as Germany's *Crown Princess Cecilia* of World War I fame, and were probably better than ours. *U-1230* would have continued to receive broadcasts from Headquarters on assigned schedules while maintaining radio silence. Since they knew their presence here was comprised, sinking the *Cornwallis* may well have been an attempt to screen U.S. intelligence from the real mission.

16) The two German sailors who rowed the spies ashore stepped out of the boat and gave the Nazi salute before going back to the sub. They were possibly the first enemy dressed in a military uniform to set foot on continental U.S. soil since the Mexican War in the 1840s, and other than Poncho Villa's irregulars, the only ones in the 20th century. Since the war, one of the crewmen, Fritz Pfueger has been running a tourist hotel in Bavaria on the border with Switzerland.

* Richard Gay is a native of Bar Harbor, Maine and an ex-CIA and NSA Operations Officer (see about the authors).

Polish intelligence first broke the German *Enigma* cipher, and invented the *Bombe* to recover rotor changes and key settings. Many *Bombes* were reproduced at Bletchley Park, and later in the U.S., and were technically enhanced by the British and Americans as Germans improved their *Enigma* machines, right.. The *bombe* shown here, left, is a model to handle the four-rotor *Enigma* machine. The Poles humorously codenamed their invention *bomba* (English: bomb), an ice cream cone in Polish. When the Germans overran Poland the prototype was smuggled to England from France, hence the spelling *bombe*.

Frenchman Bay looking southwest to Bar Harbor and the mountains of Acadia National Park. Cadillac Mountain is in the middle. The broken line indicates the path of U-1230 after it entered the bay from the far left. The submarine with its 54-man crew and two spies laid on the bottom of the bay (in the middle of this scene) all day on Nov. 29, 1944. The crew could hear the sound of "lobster boats" engines coming and going above them. RG

Hancock Point looking west over Lamoine, with Blue Hill Mountain in view on upper left horizon. The broken line is the route of U-1230 as it arrived at this point nearly 14 miles inland from the mouth of Frenchman Bay. The 27-year-old captain Hans Hilbig swung the 250-foot U-boat around and backed it on the high tide into the shallow mouth of Skillings River (asterisk) with inches clearance off bottom, in order to safely land his important passengers. As the spies were put ashore, U-1230's gun crews manned all her 20mm and 37mm antiaircraft guns, with orders to open fire on anything suspicious! RG

Looking southwest across Frenchman Bay to Acadia National Park. The arrow points to Egg Rock Light. The broken line indicates the path of U-1230 entering the bay past the U.S. Navy's radio and direction-finding base at Winter Harbor on Schoodic Point in the foreground. RG

The former Winter Harbor Navy Base, surrounded by Acadia National Park on Schoodic Point, at the entrance to Frenchman Bay. During WWII it was a Radio and Direction-Finding Station. Part of it's mission was to intercept the radio signals of German U-boats, and to take fixes on their locations with its direction-finding antennas. U-1230 passed almost in shouting distance on Nov. 28, 1944. RG

Panoramic view from the Municipal Wharf at Bar Harbor. The dashed line shows the path of U-1230 coming just yards off shore! The sub entered between Schoodic Point and Egg Rock at the far right. The dashed line swings to Hancock Point in the far left. Richard Gay stands by a commemorative plaque. RG

Egg Rock Light looking east across the mouth of French-man Bay toward Schoodic Point. U-1230 entered the bay between this small island and Schoodic Point. The water tower of the U.S. Navy radio and direction-finding station can be seen in the upper left of the photo. RG

Mount Desert Rock lighthouse looking north toward Mount Desert Island and the mountains of Acadia National Park. U-1230 used this lighthouse as a guide on its way to Frenchman Bay, and on Dec. 3, 1944, it sank the Canadian ship *Cornwallis* nearby. RG

The Bar Harbor municipal pier as it may have looked in the summer of 1944 and as it looks today. U-1230 passed a few hundred yards from the end of this pier. RG

The crew of U-1230, taken on their return from the Gulf of Maine. Normally the U-boat carried a crew of 56, but there are only 54 in this photo and it is presumed that two crewmen were displaced by the two spies. The average age of the crew was 22. The skipper, Hans Hilbig, in the white cap, was 27 and a former Luftwaffe pilot. This photo belonged to Horst Haslau, who was the submarine's radioman and *Enigma* cipher machine operator. About 20 at the time, he is in the front row, extreme right, looking off to the right. One of the shortest crewmen, standing on the deck behind the second officer to the right of Hilbig, can be seen in this photograph only by the top of his service cap. RG

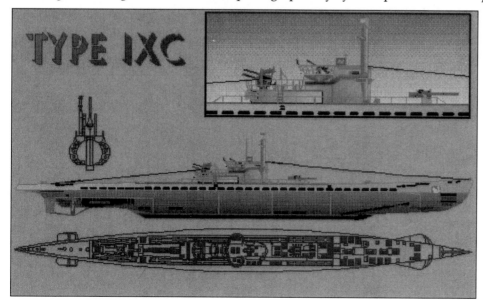

U-1230 and U-1229 were IX-C/40 type U-boats, 250 feet in length, 22.5 feet wide, 31.5 feet high, with a draft of 15.5 feet when surfaced. They were equipped with a snorkel, shown raised like a mast in this illustration, which allowed them to run great distances submerged. U-1230 came all the way across the Atlantic using its snorkel, but U-1229 ran on the surface and was spotted and sunk before reaching Maine on it's spy mission. RG

Building #1, NSGA, Winter Harbor. RG

Naval Security Group Activity, Winter Harbor began as the Otter Cliffs Radio Station, Otter Cliffs, Maine, located on Mount Desert Island, about five miles west across Frenchman Bay from the current main base location. The Otter Cliffs Radio Station was commissioned on Aug. 28, 1917, under the command of Ens. Alessandro Fabbri, USNR. Mr. Fabbri, in patriotic fervor after the declaration of war against Germany, cleared the land, built and equipped the station. He then offered it to the government as a Navy radio station to support the war effort, in exchange for a commission in the Naval Reserve and being assigned as Officer-in-Charge. He sought to make Otter Cliffs the best radio station on the East Coast. Eventually, his efforts were recognized in a promotion to Lieutenant (Junior Grade) in May 1918, and to Lieutenant in January 1919. On June 30, 1919, he was released from active duty. Lieutenant Fabbri was awarded the Navy Cross for developing the "most important and most efficient station in the world." Otter Cliffs Radio Station continued to function long after Lieutenant Fabbri left, but by 1933, the wooden buildings had become dilapidated, and due to the economic depression, Navy funds were not available for repairs. For many, it had become an eyesore on beautiful Ocean Drive on Mount Desert Island. Mr. John D. Rockefeller, Jr., was one of the influential people who desired to have it removed. While he found support for his view in several quarters in Washington, Otter Cliffs was very important to the Navy. Because of the lack of man-made noise within many miles, and the unobstructed span of ocean water between there and Europe, Otter Cliffs was among the best radio sites along the East Coast and could receive signals from Europe when no other station in the United States could. It had been invaluable in World War I when radio receivers were rather primitive. By 1930, it began to handle weather reports from Iceland and Newfoundland and emergency traffic from Europe when atmospheric conditions were so bad that Portsmouth, Boston and Washington could not copy the overseas transmissions. The Navy was willing to meet Mr. Rockefeller halfway on the removal of the radio station from Otter Cliffs. If Mr. Rockefeller would build an equally good receiving station on the coast within 50 miles of Otter Cliffs, the Navy would agree to turn over the Otter Cliffs Station to Mr. Rockefeller to include it as a donation to Acadia National Park upon the removal of the station structures. Big Moose Island, at the tip of Schoodic Peninsula about five miles across the mouth of Frenchman Bay from Otter Cliffs, seemed the ideal location. The architect's plan for the new station included a beautiful building similar to Mr. Rockefeller's residence at Seal Harbor. Artisans from all over the world contributed to the project. It has been estimated that to build the same structure today would cost $10 million. On Feb. 28, 1935, the U.S. Navy Radio and Direction Finding Station, Winter Harbor, was officially commissioned with Chief Radioman Max Gunn in charge of a complement of 11 personnel. The station's name has changed several times over the years. In 1944, it was changed to Supplementary Radio Station, U.S. Naval Radio Station, Winter Harbor. In 1950, it became known as U.S. Naval Radio Station (Receiver). The present station name, Naval Security Group Activity, Winter Harbor, became official on June 9, 1958. BY J01 SARAH URBAN, NSGA WH PUBLIC AFFAIRS

Saboteur's Documents Show Nazis Look for War to Continue Into 1946

Maine Youth Who Helped Trap Two Is Feted in City

Evidence that the German High Command expects the war to last into 1946 was furnished today when the Federal Bureau of Investigation made public the nature of documents found in the posession of Eric Gimpel and William Curtis Colepaugh, alleged Nazi saboteurs put ashore on the Maine coast from a submarine Nov. 29.

And while details of the equipment and forged papers of the two were being revealed by Earl J. Connelley, assistant director of the FBI, Harvard M. Hodgkins, 17, the Maine youth whose sharp eyes and Boy Scout training helped make their arrest possible, was enjoying a visit to New York.

One of the highlights of his trip here—a reward for his dramatic role in the capture of the alleged spies—was breakfast this morning with Babe Ruth. After his meal with the Babe young Hodgkins was scheduled to visit the Empire State Building and the Statue of Liberty.

Greeted at Airport.

Last night he was greeted by a crowd of 600 persons at La Guardia Field and met Boatswain's Mate John C. Cullen, the Coast Guardsman whose clever work led to the capture of eight German spies who landed on Long Island in 1942.

The FBI said the forged document which served notice that the German High Command is counting on at least more than another year of war was a draft board classification which read: "Local Board No. 18, Suffolk County, 419 Boylston St., Boston Mass." It carried the postal cancellation, "Boston, Mass., Feb. 6, 7 p. m., 1946."

Since draft classifications are altered or renewed periodically FBI officials pointed out, the alleged saboteur carrying the forged card would be up to date if ordered to produce his draft card after that date. Thus it was obvious that his superiors expected him to be in this country, and the war still on, after Feb. 6, 1946.

Had $60,000 in Cash.

Among the effects found in the possession of the alleged saboteurs were, according to the FBI, $60,000 in cash, forged birth certificates, naval discharge papers, radio and photographic equipment and a pistol.

...ctures on the fake birth cer-

The Colt automatics, 32 caliber, of William Curtis Colepaugh and Erich Gimpel, accused saboteurs.

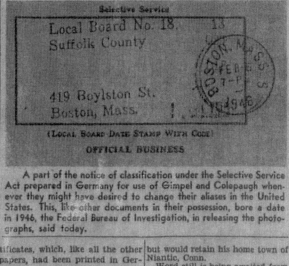

Selective Service

Local Board No. 18, 13
Suffolk County

419 Boylston St.
Boston, Mass.

BOSTON, MASS. FEB 6 7-P 1946

(LOCAL BOARD DATE STAMP WITH CODE)

OFFICIAL BUSINESS

A part of the notice of classification under the Selective Service Act prepared in Germany for use of Gimpel and Colepaugh whenever they might have desired to change their aliases in the United States. This, like other documents in their possession, bore a date in 1946, the Federal Bureau of Investigation, in releasing the photographs, said today.

tificates, which, like all the other papers, had been printed in Germany, showed that Gimpel, a native German, was to pose as Edward George Green of Connecticut, while Colepaugh was to be known as William Caldwell, but would retain his home town of Niantic, Conn.

Word still is being awaited from Washington regarding the nature of the prosecution of the two men. They may be turned over to the military authorities or tried in a civilian court.

A comparison of historic events of November 1944 and September 2001

- Our homeland security was penetrated by an underwater craft (2001: aircraft).
- Two saboteurs took the train (2001: plane) from Maine to Boston to New York City.
- An American defected to Germany (2001: Taliban), and later provided information on the Nazis (2001: Al Qaida)
- The spies were convicted by a closed secret military trial. Sound familiar?
- And a warning from the past, quoted from the spy Gimpel himself: *"America had been warned of the danger of spies and saboteurs, but after six months, then a year and then two years no one took spy warnings seriously anymore."*

William Colepaugh, background, and Erich Gimpel, foreground, are led under guard into the Fort Jay courtroom at Governors Island, New York to attend another session of their trial. Both spies are alive as of this printing (2003). Colepaugh is living quietly in the Philadelphia area in a senior care facility. Gimpel has been living in Sao Paulo, Brazil, for years, running a delicatessen selling sauerkraut. He has attended reunions of the U-1230 crew in Germany and has revisited the United States. AP/WORLD WIDE PHOTOS

The two spies sit in the courtroom at Fort Jay, Governors Island, New York. Colepaugh, third from left, sits with his counsels, left; Maj. Robert Buckley and right, Maj. Thayer Chapman. Gimpel sits at right between his counsels, Maj. Charles H. Reagin and Maj. John E. Haigney. A U.S. Army MP stands against the wall. Both spies were sentenced to die by hanging. AP/WIDE WORLD PHOTOS

Erich Gimpel was sentenced to death on Feb. 14, 1945. He was sent to several different Federal prisons, the last being in Atlanta, Georgia, before his sentence was commuted to life imprisonment after the war. In August 1955 he was pardoned and sent back to Germany. Here he talks to reporters in the Friedland Returnee Camp after his arrival in Germany. AP/WIDE WORLD PHOTOS

On July 26, 1957, Gimpel married Maria Scheidl, a model from Munich. He wrote his memoir of his spying adventures in 1957 and, in 2003, it was reissued under the title, *Agent 146: The True Story of a Nazi Spy in America*, by St. Martin's/Dunne Press. AP/WIDE WORLD PHOTOS

Nazi Spy, Once Due to Die, Deported for Illegal Entry

By the Associated Press

Erich Gimpel, one of two Nazi spies who sneaked into this country from a German submarine during World War II, was at sea today, bound for his native Germany.

The Justice Department announced yesterday that Gimpel, now 46, was deported under proceedings that began in April, 1947.

The order said Gimpel was deportable because "at the time of his entry, he was an immigrant not in possession of valid entry papers." He was taken from the Federal Prison at Atlanta, Ga., to New York City and placed aboard the S. S. Italia, which sailed yesterday.

His companion, William Cole-paugh, 37, who was born in the United States, is in Federal prison at Leavenworth, Kans.

Both Colepaugh and Gimpel were convicted of espionage after FBI agents arrested them in New York in December, 1944. That was one month after they had landed on the Maine coast by rubber boat launched from a German submarine. When caught, they had spent $3,425 of their original $60,000, some of it for materials with which to build a short-wave radio transmitter which they planned to use for sending information to Germany.

Both were given death sentences, but the White House commuted them to life imprisonment. Colepaugh's sentence later was reduced to 30 years.

Washington Star, Aug. 13, 1955.

CHARLIE HOPKINS

Charlie Hopkins spent time in Atlanta Federal Prison with Erich Gimpel in the 1950s. He said he was pleasant to talk with, spent time in the library, had class and got along with the other inmates but kept to himself quite alot. He worked in prison industries. Gimpel told Hopkins he didn't want to do the mission, but was sent under orders from Hitler because of his prior spy missions and his ability to speak English.

Hopkins related one story about Gimpel:

They were both placed in the "Hole" in Atlanta prison, Gimpel because he wouldn't give up his bottom bunk, as ordered, to another sick inmate (there were eight men to a cell with four bunk beds). He went to the prison court to ask to be sent back to his former prison, Alcatraz as he couldn't handle conditions at Atlanta anymore, but he was told to cool it as the authorities were getting ready to send him back to Germany. He was deported in August 1955.

Charlie Hopkins, a native of Jacksonville, Florida, was sent to prison in November 1952 for kidnapping. He spent three years at Alcatraz and eight years in Atlanta before being released in September 1963. Hopkins, now 71, worked in construction and as a carpet installer in Florida and now lives in Green Cove Springs, Florida.

-155-

Dick Gay, a former government agent now living in Blue Hill, and Mary Forni of Hancock Point, who spotted the two spies on the night of Nov. 29, 1944, stand on Sunset Ledge in Hancock looking across French-man Bay to Salisbury Cove in December 2001. In 2004, on the 60th anniversary of the landing, Gay's association of former intelligence officers (AFIO) hopes to commemorate the event with an historic plaque placed in view across the harbor by Acadia National Park (in the direction he is pointing). PHOTO BY MISTY EDGECOMB, ©2002 *BANGOR DAILY NEWS,* USED WITH PERMISSION

Horst Haslau was the radio operator on U-1230, the sub that landed the two spies at Hancock Point on Nov. 29, 1944. He visited the site of the landing in 1984. He stated in a newspaper interview: "I think the German navy was very familiar with the surrounding Mount Desert area, because we had sea maps accurate down to the smallest details. They were better maps than what the Park Service gives you today.

"It was November when we sent the two ashore. The weather could have been worse. We lay off Baker Island for two days, waiting for the best tides and conditions. It wasn't snowing heavily. They went ashore in a rubber boat. Two sailors from the sub dropped them off a mile up the west side of Hancock Point. We just surfaced, so the conning tower and the bridge were out of water. We had to do that because they couldn't inflate the rubber boat inside the sub.

"Our U-boat wasn't supposed to engage in any action on the way over. We stayed low and we hardly surfaced all the way from Norway to this coast here.

"I got to know them fairly well on the way over. They kept their suitcases in the radio room, where I worked. They came aboard in Kiel and were introduced as reporters. It didn't take us long to find out that they were pretty funny reporters. One was a German, and one was an American citizen." Haslau moved to the United States after the war and was a television engineer in Indiana. He attended a reunion of his sub crew in Germany in 1984, and also in 1984 and 1987, he visited Hancock Point. He died in 1991. COURTESY MS. LOIS JOHNSON, HANCOCK, MAINE

SPIES, SABOTEURS AND HOLLYWOOD

THERE WERE NUMEROUS SPY-TYPE movies made before the United States entered World War II and through the war years. One of the most important was *Confessions of a Nazi Spy*, released by Warner Bros. in 1939. It was directed by Anatole Litvak and starred Edward G. Robinson as an FBI agent, Paul Lucas as German-American Bund leader, Fritz Kuhn and George Sanders. The story line was the investigation of a vast Nazi spy ring written during a time when dozens of German spies were being picked up by the FBI. Kuhn sued Warner Bros. for five million over this and the Bund's portrayal. The suit was dropped when he was convicted of embezzling Bund funds.

A controversial 16-minute film entitled, *Inside Nazi Germany* was produced by the *March of Time* as a single-subject newsreel for its January 1938 monthly release. It has been called "the first commercially released anti-Nazi American motion picture." It began with raw footage shot by Julien Bryan in Germany. However, the content of the film was bland and disappointing. Jack Glenn, the director, filmed re-enactments, using anti-Nazi German-Americans living in Hoboken, NJ. These fake scenes included military training, propaganda, censoring mail, listening to Hitler on the radio, collecting money, political prisoners, and concentration camps. Tom Orchard arranged for some charwomen working in *March of Time*'s New York office building to pose as Catholic nuns in jail, filmed through makeshift jail bars cut out of cardboard in front of the camera lens. Glenn persuaded American pro-Nazi Fritz Kuhn to stage some scenes in his German-American Bund office. When Kuhn discovered he had been tricked, Walter Winchell reported that he was recorded screaming "I will be ruint, ruint!" at a screening in the *March of Time* building.

The mixture of real and fake images was accompanied by an anti-Nazi narration, ending with the following: "Nazi Germany faces her destiny with one of the great war machines in history. And the inevitable destiny of the great war machines of the past has been to destroy the peace of the world, its people, and the governments of their time."

The Hollywood film most directly related to the two Nazi saboteur landings was *They Came to Blow Up America* released in August 1943 by 20th Century Fox. The film was originally entitled, *School for Saboteurs*, then *School for Sabotage* and at some point during production became, *They Came to Blow Up America*.

Film Statistics:
Screen play by Aubrey Wisbert
Original story by Michel Jacoby
Director of Photography: Lucien Andriot A.S.C.
Directed by: Edward Ludwig
Cast:
Carl Steelman – George Sanders
Frau Reiker – Anna Sten
Mr. Craig – Ward Bond
Colonel Manheim – Dennis Hoey
Dr. Baumer – Sig Ruman
Mrs. Steelman – Elsa Janssen
Kirschner - Egon Brechers
Eichner – Rex Williams
Zellerbach – Charles McGraw
Hauser – Sven-Hugo Borg
    Schonzeit – Kurt Katch
    Fritz – Otto Reichow
    Manheim's Aide – Walter O. Stahl
    Zugholtz – Andre Charlot
    Kranz's Aide - Arno Frey

Scene from *They Came to Blow Up America.*

Scenes from *They Came to Blow Up America*

Article from *Variety*,
Wed., April 21, 1943.

They Came To Blow Up America
(Melodrama)

20th-Fox production. Stars George Sanders. Features Anna Sten. Supporting cast: Ward Bond, Dennis Hoey, Sig Ruman, Ludwig Stossel, Robert Barrat, Poldy Dur, Ralph Byrd, Elsa Janssen, Rex Williams, Charles McGraw, Sven Hugo Borg, Kurt Katch, Otto Reichow, Andre Charlot, Arno Frey, Sam Wren, Etta McDaniel, Peter Michael, Dick Hogan, Lisa Golm, Wolfgang Zilzer. Director, Edward Ludwig. Producer, Lee Marcus. Screenplay, Aubrey Wisberg. Original story, Michael Jacoby. Photography, Lucien Andriot. Art direction, James Basevi, John Ewing. Sets, Thomas Little, Al Orenbach. Editor, Nick De Maggio. Costumes, N'Was McKenzie. Special photographic effects, Fred Sersen. Music, Hugo W. Friedhofer. Musical direction, Emil Newman. Tradeshown at studio, April 20, 1943. Running time: 73 MINS.

This is a story created to show America what it faces at the hands of Nazi saboteurs, landed from submarines at night and who take their places in the American manner of living. The idea was drawn patently from the case of the Nazis who figured in headlines about a year ago, and who were executed after a speedy trial. Instead of following such saboteurs after they enter the country, however, picture, interesting throughout in every department, takes its theme in the events and substance leading up to their landing here, most of the action unfolding in Germany. Film originally was titled, 'School for Sabotage,' and should score at box office as supporting feature.

George Sanders plays the role of an FBI man of German parentage, who is ordered to take the place of a Bund member and go back to Germany, to attend the Nazi school of sabotage, regarded the most complete in the world. Everything is planned for his successful masquerade, and he goes through with his assignment, despite appearance of the other man's wife. Well known Nazi methods take care of this circumstance, to relieve him of immediate danger, which later crops up as he is about to disembark from the sub landing him on American soil. Story carries him through suggestion of a romance, through sabotage school which shows interesting developments of the fiendish art, to ultimate conclusion with arrest and execution of Nazis who accompany him to America.

Star is well-cast in his role, delivering capital performance in a fast-moving screenplay by Aubrey Wisberg, equally fast-paced by Edward Ludwig's direction. Ludwig does not permit a single moment to drag, and Lee Marcus, as producer, has given picture fine mantling. Individual scenes embody high degree of interest, to which entire cast contributes with outstanding effect. Standouts here are Poldy Dur, the Austrian girl whom Sanders helps escape; Ludwig Stossel, as father brokenhearted when he believes his son a traitor to America, and, in lesser degree, Anna Sten, Ward Bond, Elsa Janssen, Dennis Hoey.

Lucien Andriot's photography is entirely up to par, Fred Sersen being responsible for special camera effects. Film, which Michael Jacoby authored originally, generally provides excellent fare.

Synopsis of *The House on 92nd Street*

This is a story of the FBI in wartime.

For years before Pearl Harbor, Federal agents were probing the activities of Nazi Bunds, propagandists and spies whose orders emanated from the German Embassy in Washington.

In Hamburg, at a school for spies, is a young German-American, Bill Dietrich (William Eythe). He was approached by Nazi agents in America, and after conferring with the FBI, accepts the Nazi offer to work for Germany. It's through his help that the FBI hopes to break up the spy ring.

On May 13th, 1941, Franz Von Wirt is struck down and killed by a taxi while crossing a street. At the morgue, a policeman, suspicious of the dead man's identification, calls the FBI. Inspector George Briggs (Lloyd Nolan) examines a letter for secret writing and discovers a message: "Mr. Christopher will concentrate on Process 97."

Back in New York, Bill delivers his credentials which had been "doctored" to Elsa Gebhardt (Signe Hasso), the proprietress of a gown shop located in a house on 92nd Street. She introduces him to Johanna, Max and Conrad, other Nazi agents. They help Bill rent an office on Columbus Circle where he is visited by Colonel Hammersohn. In the next office, FBI men are taking pictures of the conversation through specially treated mirrors. Plans are made to set up a secret Nazi radio station with Bill in charge. Bill takes the messages and then beams them to an FBI transmitter where harmless information is substituted, then rebroadcast to Germany.

Elsa sends for Bill and gives him the papers of the scientific formula, Process 97, to be radioed to Germany immediately. Bill learns that an Appleton laboratory scientist, Charles Roper (Gene Lockhart) is also a Nazi agent who got the plans out of the closely guarded plant through memorization of the formula. Upon Roper's confession, the FBI proceeds to a bookshop to get the final report he has secreted in a book for Mr. Christopher, but it has already been picked up. Later, however, it falls into Bill's hands to transmit to Germany, rushed through by Elsa.

Colonel Hammersohn meanwhile has found out who Bill really is and has him brought back to Elsa's apartment for questioning and disposal. Tipped off, the FBI agents close in on the house on 92nd Street. Elsa changes into men's attire and tries to escape, but Conrad, mistaking her for the FBI, shoots. "Mr. Christopher" drops to the floor as Federal agents break into the house.

Scene from *The House on 92nd Street*, released in 1945.

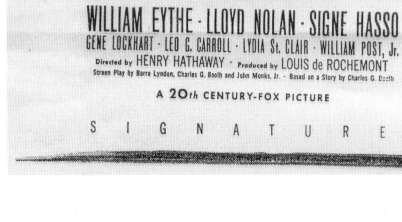

Screen Play by Barre Lyndon, Charles G. Booth and John Monks, Jr. Based on a story by Charles G. Booth.

Director of Photography: Norbert Brodine, A.S.C.
Directed by: Henry Hathaway

Cast:

Bill Dietrich - William Eythe
Briggs (Inspector) - Lloyd Nolan
Elsa Gebhardt - Signe Hasso
Charles Ogden Roper - Gene Lockhart
Hammersohn - Leo G. Carroll
Johanna Schwartz - Lydia St. Clair
Walker - William Post, Jr.
Max Coburg - Harry Bellaver
Adolphe Lange - Bruno Wick
Conrad Arnulf - Harro Meller
Gus Huzmann - Charles Wagenheim
Emil Kline - Alfred Lindar
Luise Vadja - Renee Carson
Dr. Appleton - John McKee
Major General - Edwin Jerome
Freda Kassel - Elisabeth Neumann
Jackson - George Shelton
Colonel Strassen - Alfred Zeisler
Narrator - Reed Hadley

Bit Players:

Admiral - Rusty Lane
Von Wirt - Salo Douday
Sergeant - Paul Ford
Customs Officer - William Adams
Policeman - Lew Eckles
Interne - Tom Brown
F.B.I. Man - Bruce Fernald
Aide - Benjamin Burroughs
Colonel - Douglas Rutherford
F.B.I. Agent - Jay Wesley

Saboteurs:
    Frieda Altman
    William Beach
    Hamilton Benz
    Henry Cordy
    Mita Cordy
    James J. Coyle
    Hans Hansen
    Kenneth Konopka
    Scott Moore
    Delmar Nuetzman
    John Zak
    Gertrude Wottitz

Bit German - George Brandt
German Saboteur - Bernard Lenrow
Jap - Yoshita Tagawa
Customer - Sheila Bromley

Scientists:
    Elmer Brown
    Jack Cherry

Toll Guard - Victor Sutherland

Scenes from *The House on 92nd Street.*

Instructor - Stanley Tackney

Trainees:
    Robert Culler
    Vincent Gardenia
    Carl Benson
    Frank Richards
    Ellsworth Glath
    Edward Michaels
    Harrison Scott
    Anna Marie Hornemann
    Sara Strengell
    Eugene Stuckmann
    Marriott Wilson
    Harold Dyrenforth

Travel Agent - Frank Kreig
Watchmaker - Antonio J. Pires
Deliver Boy - Danny Leone
Policeman - Fred Hillebrand
Attendant at Morgue - Edward Marshall

FBI Secrets Filmed

by Eugene Schrott (FBI Enforcement Bulletin, November, 1945)

"The House on 92nd Street," a motion picture released by Twentieth Century-Fox Film Corporation, tells the epic story of how American Law Enforcement outwitted the best brains of the German Intelligence Service in their attempts to steal our military secrets.

The movie is a bold and exciting experiment in motion picture making, and it took all the experience and skill that Twentieth Century-Fox had at its command to film this story of the FBI in wartime. The picture is unique, because it's a story constructed from the files of the Federal Bureau of Investigation, and re-enacted for the camera, at the locations the original events took place where possible.

To film it, many obstacles had to be overcome. The first of these was to get the Bureau's permission to allow Producer Louis DeRochemont to use the material gathered on the case. DeRochemont visited J. Edgar Hoover and convinced him that what he had in mind coincided with Hoover's ideas of what a motion picture about the Bureau should be. Once convinced, he not only offered the necessary data, but the entire facilities of the Bureau as well. He gave permission to use the laboratory, offices and file rooms as settings, scientists and agents of the Bureau to play minor parts, and one of his assistants to supervise the production.

Reams of records and thousands of photographs were placed at the disposal of John Monks, Jr., as a basis for his screenplay. He used them shrewdly and well, to make a story that is filled with adventure and thrills. To direct the picture, DeRochemont hoped for the services of Henry Hathaway, so he set about interesting him in what he had. Hathaway needed little coaxing for this was right up his alley. Always a stickler for realism, as evidenced by his "Wing and a Prayer," he saw a chance to really show what he could do in this line.

Before Hathaway started shooting, he insisted that the principal players, cameramen and sound engineer, watch the thousands of feet of secret motion pictures, and hear hundreds of phonograph recordings FBI Agents had made of the enemy agents, whose story was to be re-enacted. When shooting actually started, everyone connected with the picture knew exactly what to strive for.

The FBI communication system, one of the finest in the world, is depicted in action, and fascinating shots in the Laboratory explain several methods of bringing out secret writing. Gun identification, fingerprint and lipstick files are also shown in operation. The biggest filing room in the world, where almost 100,000,000 sets of fingerprints are neatly tucked away so that any one of them can be brought out in less than three minutes, is also shown in a short scene. Several FBI systems of surveillance, ingenious methods never suspected by the ordinary layman, are shown on the screen for the first time, along with the men and women of the Bureau who perform these near miracles.

To reproduce all this, before the actual backgrounds where the events originally occurred, was a problem of major proportions. The case which "The House on 92nd Street" duplicates is based on what happened in New York, so the task was taken there, and the picture filmed right on the spot. Offices, beauty parlors, book stores, hotel lobbies, and portions of war plants were used as settings. Although the owners of these places felt it was their patriotic duty to help, many were a little worried about having their places used as part of a picture dealing with spies and saboteurs. In order to placate their fears, Twentieth Century-Fox did everything possible to protect them, even going as far as to pay for a brochure which was sent to all of one shops clients, explaining what was being done.

Since some of the action took place on the streets, in parks and public buildings, a means had to be devised whereby these sequences could be filmed without causing crowds to gather. The problem was solved by the FBI when they loaned the company one of their special surveillance vehicles which they used for secret photography. Inside, the camera crew could point their lenses in any direction without being seen by people passing by, and they were able to get naturalness never before seen in a motion picture which was made from a script.

Star and famous supporting actors plated scenes right in the heart of New York without anyone paying the slightest attention to them. Although it was a nerve racking business for Director Hathaway, the actors, and the crew, it was really surprising how seldom they were discovered at their picture snatching.

Another problem confronting the company was sound equipment light enough to be carried wherever their sets happened to be. The lightest unit capable of recording sound of feature picture quality weighed a ton. Twentieth Century-Fox engineers ingeniously built it into 14 metal suitcases which could be taken anywhere.

The movie had to be peopled by the most untheatrical actors obtainable, in order to sustain the feeling of realism, and because many of the bits and small parts are played by FBI men who make no attempt at acting.

William Eythe, whose smooth, easy way of working is fast making him a top star, plays an FBI undercover man, and his performance never for a moment sinks into the obviously dramatic. Although he worked on New York streets in half a dozen scenes, pedestrians never once stopped to listen to what he was saying, which is certainly a recommendation for his acting. Bill was in New York when the picture started shooting, and enjoyed his stay in the big city because he was financially able to do all the things he dreamed about during the lean years when he tried to break into the theatre. Living in a penthouse only a few blocks from his former dingy furnished room, he got a real thrill from frequenting expensive restaurants, sitting in the best seats at the hit shows, and going everywhere in cabs and limousines.

The feminine lead is played by Signe Hasso, a young Scandinavian actress. Signe began her career as an actress at the age of 11, when she played one of the children in the Swedish Royal Theater production of "Imaginary Invalid" by Moliere. She later won a scholarship to the National Academy of Dramatic Arts, and at 18 toured Europe, playing the title role in Schiller's "Mary Stuart." In her native Sweden she won the All-Scandinavian acting award, and the Adersdervahl Award, the two highest honors any Scandinavian actress can achieve. Unlike the "Oscars" given by the Academy of Motion Picture Arts and Sciences, these are not just honors. They carry with them a considerable cash prize. Since coming to America in 1941 she has mastered English, and now speaks with only a slight accent, which is one of the chief reasons she was cast in the movie. She's playing the part of a Nazi agent, a woman smart enough to run a fashionable gown shop, and clandestinely rule over a gang of saboteurs.

Among the male supporting players Leo G. Carroll heads the list. He plays a German who has made a career of espionage. Smooth, suave and sophisticated, he impersonates the original, who was an attaché of the German Embassy for 20 years. Carroll was starring on Broadway in "The Late George Apley," while he worked on "The House on 92nd Street," so his working hours had to be arranged to take care of matinees and play rehearsals. Born in England, Carroll went on stage just before the First World War. He came to America with his second show, and has been a well known New York actor ever since. He would like to come to Hollywood, but is afraid he couldn't stand the quiet life. He thinks the absence of the floodlights would make him unhappy.

The second feminine lead is played by Lydia St. Clair, a French woman, making her American debut in pictures. She left Paris in 1940, and sailed for America on the last boat to leave Bordeaux. This was the *SS Washington*, which was torpedoed on her way to America. Since coming to this country she has taught French, and acted in the theatre. Her greatest hit since arriving in New York was the second lead in "Trio," in which her performance received high praises from the critics.

There's also a newcomer to Twentieth Century-Fox's contract list, who is seen in a most effective role. She's Renee Carson, portraying a hairdresser sent over by the Nazis, who lays the groundwork for the experts who come later. Renee was born in Paris, the daughter of an American father and a French mother. She began her theatrical career at 16, playing sketches at the Follies Bergere in Paris. In French motion pictures she was known as "the typical American girl," but since coming to the United States, the only American girl she has played was a native of Brooklyn. She's an excellent actress, expert at dialects. She was discovered by a Twentieth Century-Fox talent scout while playing in a little theatre production of "Doughgirls."

There are a half dozen other fine actors making their motion picture debuts in "The House on 92nd Street." Most of them play a nasty assortment of German spies and saboteurs. Bruno Wich, a feature actor in the New York production of "I Remember Mama," portrays a weasly little man, whose bookshop is a collecting station for the Nazi information service. Alfred Linder, former German revue star, has the role of a spy who specializes in information about ship movements. In 1932 Linder was playing Goebbels in a satire on the Nazis. A year later, when Hitler came into power, he was put behind barbed wire. He was released six months later and skipped to France, and worked his way to the United States. Harry Bellaver, cast as a strong-arm man working for German agents, has a tough face but a gentle voice. He started life as a coal miner, but was persuaded by Jasper Deeters to play a part in "The Harry Ape," and then gradually drifted away from mining coal to acting. Most nervous of these motion picture newcomers was John McKee, who is making his first trip before the cameras, after 52 years in the theatre. Tall, slender and dignified, he plays the owner of a war plant.

One of the few regular Hollywood actors appearing in the movie is Gene Lockhart. He portrays a quiet mousy little man who sells the plans for a secret weapon to the enemy. He's quiet, and smooth, but despicable. His performance is excellent. Gene was in New York resting up from a USO camp tour, when the Twentieth Century-Fox troupe arrived.

"The House on 92nd Street" is a picture in which the cameraman deserves more praise than is usually bestowed upon him, and Norbert Brodine did a remarkable job. He shot hundreds of scenes which would ordinarily have been considered impossible. His photography has the feeling of reality usually seen only in newsreels, combined with the high quality of a feature. The sound crew had the difficult job of recording dialogue with an entirely new type of equipment, and Sound Engineer W.D. Flick delivered a first-class job.

The movie started as an experiment which turned out so successfully it will undoubtedly cause a small revolution in the technique of motion picture making. It is unique in that the story is predicated on the truth, and it has been told right where it originally happened. Twentieth Century-Fox has given the screen a new kind of realism.

SELECTED BIBLIOGRAPHY

Abella, Alex & Scott Gordon, *Shadow Enemies, Hitler's Secret Terrorist Plot Against the United States*, The Lyons Press, Guilford, CT., 2002.

Bishop, Eleanor, *Prints in the Sand, The U.S. Coast Guard Beach Patrol During World War II*, Pictorial Histories Publ. Co., Inc., Missoula, MT., 1989.

Breuer, William, *Nazi Spies in America, Hitler's Undercover War*, St. Martin Paperbacks, New York, 1990.

Canedy, Susan, *America's Nazis, A Democratic Dilemma: A History of the German American Bund*, Markgaf, Menlo Park, CA., 1990.

Carlson, John Roy, *Under Cover, My Four Years in the Nazi Underworld of America*, E.P. Dutton & Co., Inc., New York, 1943.

Dasch, George J., *Eight Spies Against America*, Robert M. McBride Co., New York, 1959.

Farago, Ladislas, *The Game of the Foxes, The Untold Story of German Espionage in the United States and Great Britain During World War II*, David McKay Company, Inc., New York, 1971.

Gimpel, Erich, *Agent 146: The True Story of a Nazi Spy in America*, St. Martin's/Dunne, New York, 2003.

Hadley, Michael L., *U-Boats against Canada*, McGill-Queen's University Press, Montreal, 1985.

Hynd, Alan, *Passport to Treason, The Inside Story of Spies in America*, Robert M. McBride & Co., New York, 1943.

Kahn, David, *Hitler's Spies, German Military Intelligence in World War II*, MacMillan Publishing Co., Inc., New York, 1978.

Morison, Samuel Eliot, *The Atlantic Battle Won*, Little, Brown and Company, Boston, 1962.

Rachlis, Eugene, *They Came to Kill, The Story of Eight Nazi Saboteurs in America*, Random House, New York, 1961.

Sayers, Michael & Albert E. Kahn, *Sabotage! The Secret War Against America*, Harper & Bros., 1942.

Tully, Andrew, *The FBI's Most Famous Cases*, William Morrow & Co., New York, 1965.

Witcover, Jules, *Sabotage at Black Tom, Imperial Germany's Secret War in America, 1914-1917*, Algonquin Books of Chapel Hill, Chapel Hill, NC, 1989.

Organizations which have information pertaining to the subjects of this book.

Sharkhunters International

Sharkhunters International Inc., founded by Harry Cooper in 1983, is the main organization in the world dedicated to submarine history of all wars and all countries. It publishes *KTB* Magazine 10 times a year, which is the official publication of U-boat history in the world.

For information or membership contact:
Sharkhunters International
P.O. Box 1539
Hernando, FL 34442
Phone: (352) 637-2917 FAX: (352) 637-6289
sharkhunters@earthlink.net
www.sharkhunters.com

International Spy Museum

The International Spy Museum, a new museum exploring the craft, practice, history and contemporary of espionage, opened in Washington, D.C., in July 2002. It is the first public museum in the United States solely dedicated to espionage and the only one in the world to provide a global perspective on an all but invisible profession that has shaped history and continues to have a significant impact on world events.

The museum features the largest collection of international artifacts ever placed on public display. Many of the objects are on display for the first time outside of the intelligence community. These artifacts are used to illustrate the work of famous spies and pivotal espionage actions as well as to help bring to life the strategies and techniques of the men and women behind some of the most secretive missions in world history.

In development for more than seven years, the museum drew upon the knowledge of leading experts and practitioners in the intelligence community.

The museum is located at 800 F Street N.W. in Washington D.C. There is a gift shop and restaurant on the premises. They are open daily except for Thanksgiving, Christmas and New Years Day. Hours of operation are: 10 A.M. to 8 P.M., April-October and 10 A.M. to 6 P.M. November-March.

INFORMATION AND LOGO COURTESY INTERNATIONAL SPY MUSEUM.

AFIO

The Association of Former Intelligence Officers is a non-profit, non-political, educational association of former intelligence professionals and supporters. Its educational focus is on fostering understanding of the vital importance and role of U.S. intelligence in historic, contemporary and future contexts. It has chapters throughout the United States. For information contact:

AFIO Central Office
6723 Whittier Ave. Suite 303A
McLean, VA 22101-4533
Phone: (703) 790-0320 FAX: (703) 790-0264
afio@afio.com

ABOUT THE AUTHORS

Stan Cohen is a native of West Virginia and a 1961 graduate of West Virginia University with a degree in geology. He has been a resident of Missoula, Montana since 1961 and has been a consulting geologist, engaged in the ski business and involved with various local museums through the years. Since 1976, he has owned Pictorial Histories Publishing Company. He has authored or co-authored 71 books and published 300 including *East Wind Rain, A Pictorial History of the Pearl Harbor Attack; Destination Tokyo, A Pictorial History of Doolittle's Tokyo Raid; Enemy on Island: Issue in Doubt, A Pictorial History of the Battle of Wake Island;* The *Forgotten War* series, Vols. 1-4, *A Pictorial History of Alaska and Northwestern Canada in World War II; The Trail of '42, A Pictorial History of the Alaska Highway;* and *The Games of '36, A Pictorial History of the 1936 Olympic Games in Germany.*

A retired professor from the Criminal Justice Department at San Francisco State University, Don DeNevi is now employed by the California Department of Corrections at San Quentin State Prison. He not only teaches and counsels the condemned on death row, but also supervises the recreation and fitness programs for 7,500 inmates. He has authored, edited and co-written 31 books, including his latest *Mob Nemesis–How the FBI Crippled Organized Crime; Tennis Past 50; Inside the Minds of Madness–The Story of the FBI's Legendary Behavioral Science Unit* (Prometheus, Fall, 2003), and the forthcoming, *Who Murdered King Tut–How Two Detectives Using Modern Day Forensics Solved a 3,400 Year Old Mystery.* In addition to playing tennis on a daily basis, he paints watercolors of imaginary landscapes. He lives in Menlo Park with his two cats.

Richard Gay is a native of Maine, born in Bar Harbor and currently living in Blue Hill. He is an alumnus of Lafayette College, Université Laval (Quebec), University of Maine, and University of Maryland. He speaks a number of European and Asian languages, and since returning to Maine has taught languages at Husson College, the Maine Maritime Academy, and College of the Atlantic (Bar Harbor). He is a pilot and member of the Bar Harbor squadron of the Civil Air Patrol. He is a former CIA and NSA operations officer, and special assistant to the president of AFIO (see page 165). He is a member of the *Phoenix Society* of ex-NSA officers, and is vice president of the New England chapter of ex-CIA officers. He served in that agency under Allen Dulles, John McCone, William Raborn, Richard Helms and William Colby. He is writing an espionage novel and has two autobiographic short stories being published in a book, *Spies Lives,* to be out soon. Gay, left, is pictured here at ex-CIA director Richard Helms, right, home in Georgetown, DC in October 2000.